San Francisco
GIANTS
ALMANAC

FROM MAYS & MCCOVEY THROUGH 1987 DIVISION CHAMPIONSHIP

30 YEARS OF BASEBALL BY THE BAY

BY NICK PETERS

NORTH ATLANTIC BOOKS, BERKELEY, CALIFORNIA

Editor's note: The editor, author and co-publishers wish to thank official Giants' photographer Dennis Desprois for his generosity and help in providing many of the photographs for this publication. We also thank Duffy Jennings, Dave Aust and Robin Carr of the Giants' publicity department for their assistance and cooperation.

San Francisco Giants Almanac

ISBN 1-55643-040-X

Published by North Atlantic Books
        2320 Blake Street
        Berkeley, California 94704

Cover photographs by Dennis Desprois
Cover design by Paula Morrison

San Francisco Giants Almanac is sponsored by the Society for the Study of Native Arts and Sciences, a nonprofit educational corporation whose goals are to develop an ecological and crosscultural perspective linking various scientific, social, and artistic fields; to nurture a holistic view of arts, sciences, humanities, and healing; and to publish and distribute literature on the relationship of mind, body, and nature.

Library of Congress Cataloging-in-Publication Data

Peters, Nick.
        San Francisco Giants almanac.

        Rev. ed. of: Giants diary / Fred Stein and Nick Peters. c1987.
        1. San Francisco Giants (Baseball team)—History.
I. Stein, Fred. Giants diary. II. Title.
GV875.S34P48 1988   796.357′64′0979461   88-19534
ISBN 1-55643-041-8
ISBN 1-55643-040-X (pbk.)

CONTENTS

1

DAY BY DAY HIGHLIGHTS

1958

April 15—A capacity crowd of 23,449 jammed Seals Stadium for the Giants' historic West Coast opener. Ruben Gomez responded with a six-hit, 8-0 victory over the Los Angeles Dodgers. Daryl Spencer hit the first major league home run at Seals Stadium, and rookie Orlando Cepeda homered in an eleven-hit attack.

April 16—The first night game at the Giants' park found the Dodgers spoiling the party with a 13-1 romp behind Johnny Podres. Duke Snider hit one of the longest home runs in Seals Stadium history, a 425-foot shot over the right-field wall.

April 18—Hank Sauer hit two home runs, including the first at the L.A. Coliseum, but the Giants' first road game was a 6-5 loss to the Dodgers before 78,682. Rookie Jim Davenport collected three hits, but failed to tag third base in the ninth, costing San Francisco a run.

April 20—Two home runs by Danny O'Connell powered a 12-2 victory at Los Angeles. Willie Mays had three hits, including a home run, in three at bats, scoring thrice and collecting three RBI.

April 23—The Giants began their first of a series of comeback victories, scoring four times in the bottom of the ninth for an 8-7 triumph over the Cardinals. Davenport singled, Mays was safe on an error, Cepeda hit a two-run triple with two outs, and Spencer hit a game-winning homer.

April 24—Sauer's two homers, including a two-run shot in the ninth, downed the Cardinals, 6-5. Hank became the first National League slugger to homer in twelve parks.

April 26—Mays hit his first home run in a San Francisco uniform, a solo shot off the Cubs' Glen Hobbie. It was his 188th career homer and it helped Johnny Antonelli down Chicago 3-1 for his first victory.

April 30—The Giants vaunted power erupted for five home runs in a 10-1 rout of the Phillies behind Antonelli's six-hitter. Davenport belted two homers and Cepeda, Spencer, and Bob Schmidt hit one apiece.

May 4—Unheralded Roman Mejias hit three homers to lead the Pirates to a 6-2 victory in the opener, but the Giants gained a split of the doubleheader when Eddie Bressoud's run-scoring single in the tenth won the nightcap, 4-3. Cepeda had two homers and a double in the twin bill.

May 5—This was the greatest comeback in S.F. history, even though it fell short by one run. The Pirates entered the bottom of the ninth leading 11-1, but had to survive a nine-run Giants rally before emerging 11-10 winners. The eruption featured two-run pinch doubles by Jim King and Antonelli, a three-run homer by Ray Jablonski, and a solo homer by Cepeda for the final run. The game ended when pinch hitter Don Taussig popped to second with the bases loaded.

May 6—Left-hander Mike McCormick, 19 years old, scattered three infield singles in a three-hit, 7-0 victory at Pittsburgh. Schmidt cracked a three-run double in the five-run first and Cepeda homered.

May 12—Mays hit two home runs, including a grand slam off Ed Roebuck, pacing a 12-3 victory at L.A. Mays finished with five RBI.

May 13—Mays hit two more homers in a 16-9 crunching of the Dodgers, the Giants setting a major league record with fifty total bases. Mays totaled fifteen total bases, also belting two triples among his five hits. Spencer was overshadowed, but he had two homers, a triple, a double, six RBI, and thirteen total bases in the offensive orgy.

May 21—Mays hit a home run in the tenth at Cincinnati, handing Hal Jeffcoat a 5-4 defeat.

May 25—The "new" Giants were embroiled in their first brawl during a 5-2, 6-1 sweep before 35,797 partisan Pittsburghers. The fight broke out in the opener and was triggered by a beanball battle between Gomez and Vernon Law. Mays tackled Cepeda to prevent The Baby Bull from possibly striking someone with a bat.

June 5—The Giants beat Milwaukee 5-4 in the twelfth. Mays led off the final inning with a single and Jim Finigan doubled, but Hank

Aaron threw Mays out at the plate. Cepeda then hit Gene Conley's first pitch for a game-winning homer. Cepeda had four hits.

June 22—Willie Kirkland's fourteenth-inning homer edged the Phillies 5-4 in the opener of a doubleheader, Antonelli firing six shutout innings for the win. Gomez had a 1-0 lead in the sixth inning of the second game, but a curfew rule halted the game at Philadelphia. When it was resumed on July 23, the Phillies won, 3-2.

July 4—The Giants trailed the Cubs 5-1 entering the bottom of the ninth in the opener of a doubleheader, but scored five runs to win, 6-5. Pinch hitter Spencer's bases-loaded walk opened the scoring and Kirkland followed with a two-run pinch single. With two away,, Mays belted a two-run, game-winning single off Dick Drott. The Cubs won the second game, 6-1.

July 6—Lightning struck twice for Larry Jackson and the Cardinals. On July 5, Jackson walked Willie Kirkland with the bases full in the bottom of the ninth for a 5-4 Giant victory; the next day, there were two outs and the bases loaded in the ninth again. This time, Jackson hit Jim Davenport with a pitch for another 5-4 triumph.

July 11—Cepeda's three-run homer off Jeffcoat in the twelfth produced a 7-4 victory. The Giants were ahead 4-0 when a two-run homer by Frank Robinson helped create a 4-4 tie.

July 12—Cepeda's 420-foot, three-run homer beat Warren Spahn and the Braves 5-3, pulling the Giants to within one-half game of Milwaukee.

July 13—Felipe Alou's run-scoring single in the bottom of the ninth edged the Braves 6-5 and gave the Giants the league lead. Cepeda hit his third homer in three days.

July 28—The blazing Giants swept a doubleheader at Philadelphia 3-2 and 2-1 to tie for first. Alou's two-run homer won the opener for McCormick, and Kirkland had the game-winning RBI in Gomez' four-hitter in the nightcap.

July 29—Robinson's homer in the eighth gave the host Reds a 3-2 lead, but Mays' single and Jablonski's two-run homer lifted the Giants to a 4-3 victory in the ninth. It was San Francisco's eighteenth win on its last at bats.

August 10—Davenport walloped two of the Giants' five home runs in a 12-8 victory at L.A. Pinch-hitter Bob Speake, O'Connell, and Spencer hit the other homers. Davenport belted five hits and scored four runs, giving him eight hits and three homers in two games.

August 19—Antonelli hit the first home run by a pitcher at Seals Stadium and pitched a ten-inning five-hitter in a 4-3 victory. Kirkland belted a run-scoring triple.

August 27—Cepeda's bases-loaded walk off Bob Trowbridge in the twelfth shaded Milwaukee 4-3 and snapped the Braves' eight-game win string over the Giants. Spencer stroked a two-run homer.

August 30—The Giants swept a day-night doubleheader over the Dodgers, 3-2 and 3-1. Davenport hit two homers in support of Gomez in the first game and Mays had a two-run homer and three RBI behind McCormick's five-hitter in the finale. The crowd was cleared from the stadium after 16,905 attended the day game; then 9,865 watched the night game.

August 31—Bob Schmidt's grand slam off Sandy Koufax in the first inning started a 14-2 drubbing of the Dodgers. Schmidt finished with six RBI and Mays had three of the Giants' fifteen hits, including a two-run homer.

Sept. 1—A crowd of 19,800 attended the memorable second game of a morning-afternoon doubleheader with the Dodgers. The Giants won the four-hour, 35-minute contest with two runs in the sixteenth, taking five of the six games in the Labor Day weekend series. Schmidt's homer in the ninth forced extra innings. S.F. Police Chief Frank Ahern died of a heart attack in the fifteenth inning. Carl Furillo's RBI gave L.A. a 5-4 lead in the sixteenth, but Whitey Lockman's homer tied it in the bottom of the inning. Then Jablonski beat out a bunt single and scored on errors by John Roseboro and Furillo following a bunt by Gomez. Mays went 5-for-5 with two doubles and a homer as the Giants won the opener 3-2, and was 11-for-20 in the series with four homers.

Sept. 4—The Giants clobbered the Dodgers 13-3 at the Coliseum to take a final 16-6 edge in the season series. Podres was routed in an eight-run first, Stu Miller pitched a five hitter, Mays and Cepeda homered, and Alou and Bressoud each totaled three RBI.

Sept. 12—The host Phillies were swamped 5-2 and 19-2 in a twin bill, Mays raising his average to .333 with six hits. Davenport homered to lead the opening win for Gomez. He added a three-run, inside-the-park homer in an eight-run first inning of the second game, finishing the day with seven hits and seven runs scored.

Sept. 20—Ruben Gomez fired a three-hitter, all by Bobby Gene Smith, in a 5-1 victory at St. Louis. Mays' three hits give him the batting lead at .340. He also stole his thirtieth base, becoming the first man to do it three times since Kiki Cuyler in 1930.

Sept. 28—The Giants concluded their first S.F. season with a 7-2 victory over the Cardinals. Mays belted three hits, including a homer, to finish with a .347 average (highest of his career), but Richie Ashburn won the batting title at .349.

Oct. 8—Ernie Broglio and Marv Grissom were traded to St. Louis for Billy Muffett, Hobie Landrith, and Ben Valenzuela, a costly move because Broglio blossomed into a Cardinals star.

Dec. 3—Gomez and catcher Valmy Thomas were swapped to the Phillies for Jack Sanford, who eventually pitched S.F. to its only pennant in 1962.

1959

March 25—The Giants acquired pitcher Sam Jones from St. Louis in exchange for first baseman Bill White and third baseman Ray Jablonski.

April 10—The Giants opened the season at St. Louis with a 6-5 victory on Jackie Brandt's RBI double in the ninth. Johnny Antonelli was the winner, backed by home runs from Bob Schmidt and Willie Kirkland.

April 11—Jones made his San Francisco debut against his former teammates at St. Louis, striking out seven in a 5-2 victory. Orlando Cepeda belted two doubles and had four RBI. White, for whom Jones was traded, was hitless in four trips, striking out thrice.

April 12—The Giants swept the Cardinals when Cepeda's two-out, 400-foot, ninth-inning triple cracked a 3-3 tie in a 6-3 victory. Felipe Alou added a two-run homer.

April 18—Jack Sanford pitched a one-hitter against the Cardinals at Seals Stadium and Cepeda belted his fifth homer in four games. Sanford had a no-hitter until pinch hitter Stan Musial led off the seventh with a bloop single. St. Louis scored in the first inning when Sanford issued three walks, hit a batter, and uncorked a wild pitch.

May 2—The Giants took the league lead with a seventeen-hit attack and an 8-5 victory at Milwaukee. Willie Mays had four singles and scored four runs, and Willie Kirkland supplied the power with two home runs. Catcher Hobie Landrith also homered, while Sanford raised his record to 4-1.

May 11—A twenty-hit splurge buried the Pirates, 14-4. Sanford, Kirkland, Brandt, and Schmidt each had three hits, including two doubles and four RBI by Schmidt. A six-run sixth broke open the game.

May 13—Jones pitched a two-hitter and struck out a league-high twelve Phillies in a 6-0 victory. Jones had a no-hitter until Willie "Puddinhead" Jones singled with two down in the seventh. Mays hit a three-run homer in a five-run first; outfielder Leon Wagner also homered.

May 14—The Giants got a well-pitched gem for the second straight day when Mike McCormick fired a three-hitter and struck out nine in an 8-0 romp over the Phillies. McCormick had a no-hitter until Granny Hamner hit a pinch double in the eighth. Mays hit a three-run homer for the second day in a row; Daryl Spencer and Wagner also homered.

May 26—Sandy Koufax had a 4-2 lead entering the ninth inning at Los Angeles, but the Giants rallied for a 6-4 victory on a dramatic, pinch-hit grand-slam by Wagner. Brandt walked, Alou singled, and Spencer walked, loading the bases. Wags then smacked Art Fowler's second pitch for the game-winning homer.

June 4—Lew Burdette, who had beaten the Giants thirteen straight times since 1954, had a 5-1 lead entering the fourth inning at Milwaukee. But two home runs and a double by Cepeda drove in seven runs and powered an 11-5 victory. Cepeda started his splurge with a two-run homer in the fourth. One inning later, he ripped a 500-foot, three-run homer, the first blast to clear the left field bleachers at County Stadium. He added a two-run double in the eighth.

June 12—Mike McCormick pitched an abbreviated five-inning no-hitter while downing the Phillies 3-0 at Philadelphia. Richie Ashburn singled in the sixth, but the game was rained out and the final outcome was based on the last completed inning. Hobie Landrith hit a two-run homer and National League President Warren Giles ruled that it wasn't an official no-hitter.

June 19—Brandt's two-run single in the bottom of the tenth gave the Giants a 4-3 victory over Milwaukee before 22,934 at Seals Stadium and lifted them into first place over the Braves. It was 2-2 after nine innings, but Billy Bruton's homer off Jones pushed the Braves ahead. In the bottom of the inning, Mays walked and raced to third on Cepeda's single off Bob Buhl. Don McMahon walked Spencer and Brandt struck the game-winning blow.

June 21—Hank Aaron belted two-run homers off Antonelli, Miller, and Gordon Jones to power the Braves to victory at Seals Stadium. "It's a good park for right-handed hitters," Aaron said following the only three-homer game of his career.

June 26—McCormick three-hit the Phillies 8-0, with Brandt belting a grand slam in the five-run seventh and Mays cracking a

420-foot homer.

June 29—Davenport and Mays hit back-to-back home runs off Stan Williams in the thirteenth, giving the Giants a 6-4 victory at Los Angeles and snapping the Dodgers' seven-game win string. It was Davvy's second homer of the game.

June 30—Official scorer Charlie Park of the L.A. *Mirror* deprived Sam Jones of a no-hitter against the Dodgers. Jim Gilliam grounded to Andre Rodgers with two down in the eighth and the Giants shortstop had difficulty picking the ball up. It was ruled a controversial hit and Sad Sam finished with a one-hitter and ten strikeouts. Mays' two-run homer off Don Drysdale in the third produced a 2-0 victory.

July 30—Willie McCovey, batting .372 with twenty-nine homers and ninety-two RBI at Phoenix, made a sensational major league debut against Robin Roberts in a 7-2 victory over the Phillies at Seals Stadium. McCovey had four hits in as many trips, including two triples, to begin a brilliant career. Willie became the first player to collect four hits in his first major league game since Casey Stengel of the Dodgers, September 17, 1912.

August 2—McCovey hit his first of 521 major league homers, a two-run shot off the Pirates' Ron Kline, in a 5-3 victory. McCovey boosted his average to .500 (9-18) and Antonelli won his fifteenth game.

August 5—McCovey continued to tear the cover off the ball, blasting two homers off Bob Buhl in a 4-1 victory over the Braves. Mays added a home run and Sanford was the winner as San Francisco climbed into first place.

August 7—Mays' two-out, ninth-inning single beat the Reds 3-2, giving him two singles and a double in support of Antonelli's sixteenth victory.

August 9—Don Newcombe was 4-0 against the Giants in '59 until Cepeda's tenth-inning home run produced a 4-3 victory over the Reds for Sanford.

August 10—The Giants trailed 2-0 entering the ninth at St. Louis, but rallied off Larry Jackson to post a 3-2 victory. Wagner started the surge with a one-out pinch single, and singles by Davenport and Mays ruined the shutout bid. McCovey's infield single made it 2-2 and, after Cepeda struck out, Kirkland cracked a run-scoring double.

August 11—Willie Kirkland was the hero again with four RBI, including a game-winning single in the tenth for a 5-4 victory at St.

Louis. Kirkland belted a three-run homer in the first and scored a run in the fourth, but it was 4-4 after nine. Mays doubled and scored on Kirkland's hit in the tenth.

August 13—The Cubs and the Giants set a National League record when their regulation game consumed 3 hours and 50 minutes. Chicago hit five home runs and belted nineteen hits at Wrigley Field, winning 20-9. Mays and Kirkland homered for the Giants. George Altman hit two for the winners.

August 25—Antonelli became the league's first eighteen-game winner and hit a two-run homer in a 12-5 runaway at Pittsburgh. Spencer also homered for the Giants.

August 31—Sandy Koufax struck out eighteen Giants for a new National League record, erasing Dizzy Dean's seventeen, but needed Wally Moon's three-run homer in the ninth to win 5-2 before a crowd of 82,974.

Sept. 11—The Giants lost to the Phillies 1-0 on a three-hitter by Robin Roberts, who gained revenge for McCovey's blockbuster debut. The Phillies ace held the rookie first baseman hitless this time, snapping his twenty-two-game hitting streak which fell one short of the National League record for a rookie held by Richie Ashburn.

Sept. 12—Jones became a twenty-game winner by downing the Phillies 9-1 and vaulting the Giants into the league lead by one game. Cepeda backed the four-hitter with a home run.

Sept. 17—The Giants enjoyed their final moment of glory for the season when Mays' four hits and five RBIs pounded Warren Spahn and the Braves 13-6 for a two-game lead with eight games to go. Sanford was the winner and Eddie Bressoud and Davenport hit homers to neutralize a pair by third baseman Eddie Mathews.

Sept. 20—The final game at Seals Stadium attracted 22,923, but wasn't a joyous occasion. The Dodgers won 8-2 behind Johnny Podres, sweeping the series and knocking S.F. from first to third.

Sept. 22—Outfielder George Altman landed a telling blow to the Giants' pennant hopes with a two-run, ninth-inning homer for a 5-4 Cubs victory at Wrigley. The Giants had taken the lead with two runs in the eighth, but ex-Giant Alvin Dark triggered the winning rally off Jones and Altman came through with two away.

Sept. 23—Mays belted two homers and Cepeda one, and Antonelli had a 3-0 lead while bidding for victory number twenty, but Cal Neeman's homer in the tenth off Eddie Fisher gave the Giant-killing Cubs a 9-8 decision.

Sept. 26—Hard-luck Sam Jones pitched a seven-inning no-hitter at St. Louis, but League President Giles ruled it unofficial. Rain wiped the last two innings out, but Jones won his twenty-first game 4-0 on home runs by Mays and McCovey. It was the first no-hitter, official or not, against the Cardinals since 1919.

Oct. 5—Demolition began at Seals Stadium, a sad day for Bay Area baseball lovers.

Nov. 30—The Giants traded outfielder Jackie Brandt and pitcher Gordon Jones to the Orioles for pitchers Billy O'Dell and Billy Loes.

Dec. 15—Don Blasingame, who batted .289 for the Cardinals, was acquired by the Giants in exchange for Spencer and Wagner. The deal was made because the Giants desperately needed a leadoff batter, but it was a bust because The Blazer fizzled.

1960

April 12—The historic opener at Candlestick Park attracted 42,269 and a host of dignitaries, including Vice President Richard Nixon. Sam Jones fired a three-hitter for a 3-1 victory and Mays started a sixteen-game batting streak. The distinction of hitting the first home run at Candlestick went to ex-Giant Leon Wagner.

April 16—Jones retired seventeen straight batters and had a no-hitter until pinch hitter Walt Moryn homered with two outs in the eighth. Sad Sam settled for a one-hitter and a 6-1 victory.

April 30—Willie McCovey clouted two home runs off "cousin" Don Drysdale and the Giants posted a 6-3 victory at Los Angeles.

May 7—The Giants trailed the Pirates 5-0 entering the seventh before erupting for six runs in a 6-5 victory. The six-run seventh featured a 397-foot, inside-the-park grand slam by shortstop Eddie Bressoud off Harvey Haddix.

May 13—Mike McCormick fired a six-hit, 3-0 victory over the Dodgers to give the Giants their seventh straight victory and an 18-7 record. It also was the club's third consecutive shutout, following successive 1-0 two-hitters over the Phillies by Jones and Sanford. A bases-loaded walk won for Jones and Landrith hit an RBI single in behalf of Sanford.

May 15—Johnny Antonelli blanked the Dodgers 2-0, and Orlando Cepeda blasted a 420-foot triple to center. L.A. manager Walter Alston said it was the hardest-hit ball into the teeth of a wind he had ever seen.

June 12—As a pinch hitter, McCovey blasted his first major league grand slam, and Cepeda bashed a three-run double in a

16-7 romp over the Braves. The game consumed three hours and fifty-two minutes, equaling the major league record for nine innings.

June 18—Manager Bill Rigney was fired by Horace Stoneham despite three straight wins over the Phillies and a 33-25 record. Tom "Clancy" Sheehan took over and the Giants beat the Phillies 7-4 before losing five in a row. Sheehan finished the season with a 46-50 record.

June 24—Mays enjoyed one of his finest all-around performances in a 5-3 victory at Cincinnati. Wondrous Willie belted two home runs, singled, stole home, scored thrice, knocked in three runs, and made ten putouts.

June 30—Jack Sanford needed only ninety-one pitches to dispatch the Pirates 11-0 in the first game of a doubleheader. Mays was the hitting hero with two doubles and a home run. In the second game, Dick Stuart slugged the Bucs to an 11-6 victory with three home runs and a two-run single.

July 15—This was the famous fog game against the Dodgers. Shortly after McCovey's triple was lost in a thick mist, umpire Frank Dascoli halted the game for 24 minutes in the third inning. Three balls were dropped in the eerie conditions and the Giants were beaten, 5-3.

July 17—McCovey, batting .214 and fielding poorly, was optioned to Tacoma.

July 19—Juan Marichal's debut was as sensational as McCovey's the previous season. The Dominican right-hander hurled a no-hitter until the Phillies' Clay Dalrymple hit a pinch single with two outs in the seventh. Marichal struck out twelve and won 2-0. Two days later, Robin Roberts returned the favor, allowing the Giants only one hit, by Felipe Alou.

August 25—Mays hit an inside-the-park grand slam in a seven-run rally against the Reds, giving the Giants an 8-5 victory.

August 27—Felipe Alou ended Lew Burdette's scoreless innings streak at 32 2/3 innings with a fourth-inning homer in a 3-1 victory over the Braves. Alou's hit protected the National League record of 46 1/3 scoreless frames by the Giants' Carl Hubbell in 1933.

August 28—A 15-2 Giants victory capped a three-game series with the Braves that drew 94,047 to Candlestick Park. That raised the season total to 1,605,871, an all-time Giants record. The previous high was 1,600,793 by the 1947 New York club.

Sept. 3—McCormick won a 1-0 pitchers' battle from Koufax at Los Angeles. Felipe Alou provided the offense with a home run.

Sept. 7—During a 6-5 loss at Milwaukee, manager Tom Sheehan emerged from the dugout to yank Jack Sanford, but the veteran right-hander beat him to the punch. Before Clancy could get to the infield, Sanford stalked past him. Sanford was fined $200 for showing up the skipper.

Sept. 15—Mays walloped three triples and a double, including a 420-foot three bagger off Turk Farrell in the eleventh inning for an 8-6 victory over the Phillies.

Sept. 19—The Giants registered their first doubleheader sweep of the year, 11-4 and 4-1 over the Cubs. Willie Kirkland cracked two homers in the opener and Bob Schmidt hit a grand slam in the nightcap.

Oct. 20—The Giants landed in Japan for the start of a sixteen-game goodwill tour headed by President Horace Stoneham and Lefty O'Doul. McCovey hit eight home runs and Mays added seven to dazzle the Japanese fans and power the Giants to an 11-4-1 record.

Oct. 31—Andre Rodgers was swapped to the Braves for Alvin Dark, who was named manager while the Giants were in Japan.

Dec. 14—Johnny Antonelli, who frequently complained about the San Francisco wind currents, and Willie Kirkland were traded to Cleveland for Harvey Kuenn during the winter meetings at St. Louis.

1961

April 12—Catcher Tom Haller's first major league hit, a seventh-inning homer, cracked a 1-1 tie and lifted the Giants to a 2-1 victory over the Pirates' Vern Law. Haller, a $50,000 bonus baby, had a second chance after right fielder Roberto Clemente dropped his foul fly. Billy Loes, making his first start since 1958, was the winner.

April 25—Willie Mays made what many regard as his finest fielding play as a San Francisco Giant in a 3-1 victory over the Dodgers. With the fleet Maury Wills on third base, Wally Moon hit a sinking liner to left center. Mays made a one-handed catch and rifled a 300-foot throw to the plate to double up Wills, who tagged at third after the catch.

April 27—The Giants swapped Don Blasingame, Bob Schmidt, and Sheldon Jones to Cincinnati for slugging catcher Ed Bailey.

April 28—Warren Spahn fired a no-hitter against the Giants in the opener of a remarkable three-game series at County Stadium in Milwaukee. Sam Jones was a 1-0 loser, yielding an unearned run in the first and pitching a five-hitter.

April 30—The incomparable Mays belted four home runs and drove in eight runs to power a 14-4 victory at Milwaukee. Jose Pagan added two homers, and Felipe Alou and Orlando Cepeda contributed one apiece as the club tied a major league record with eight home runs. The Giants also hit five homers in a 7-3 victory April 29, equaling the major league mark of thirteen homers in two games.

May 7—Cepeda's tape-measure home run helped to clobber the Phillies 7-0 at Connie Mack Stadium. The three-run homer off Robin Roberts cleared the roof of the second deck, a drive of more than 500 feet.

June 22—Mays hammered two home runs off Bob Buhl in an 8-6 loss at Milwaukee. It marked the second time in six weeks that Mays had belted a pair off Buhl, having turned the trick at Candlestick Park on May 13 with a grand slam and a two-run shot in an 8-5 victory.

June 28—The Giants and the Phillies played the longest night game in major league history. They went at it for five hours and 11 minutes before a curfew halted the proceedings with the game tied at 7-7 after fifteen innings at Philadelphia.

June 29—Mays blasted three home runs in the first game of a doubleheader at Philadelphia, the Giants winning, 8-7. He hit a pair of two-run shots off Dallas Green and a solo off Frank Sullivan.

July 4— Orlando Cepeda accumulated eight RBI in a 19-3 debacle against the Cubs at Wrigley Field in Chicago.

July 11—San Francisco hosted the All-Star Game and 44,115 showed up on a blustery day at Candlestick. Mays doubled home the tying run in the tenth and scored the winner on Roberto Clemente's single for a 5-4 National League victory. Stu Miller gained lasting fame by being blown off the mound in the ninth and being charged with a balk.

July 29—Phillies manager Gene Mauch ordered Mays to be intentionally walked in the first inning and Cepeda followed with his first major league grand slam, giving the Giants a 4-3 victory.

August 2—Juan Marichal pitched a one-hitter against the Dodgers, winning 6-0. Tommy Davis' single in the fifth inning ruined the no-hit bid.

August 23—The Giants erupted for five home runs in the ninth inning at Cincinnati, demolishing the Reds, 14-0. The outburst tied the major league record for homers in an inning. The Giants who took part in the outburst were Cepeda, Felipe Alou, John Orsino, Mays, and Davenport. Davvy's was an inside-the-park job. The ninth inning included eleven hits by the Giants. Cepeda homered and singled in the prodigious rally, while McCovey doubled and singled.

Sept. 25—Cepeda had four RBI and catcher John Orsino had two homers in a 10-2 rout at Philadelphia. Cepeda's binge gave him 140 RBI, the most ever for a Giant first baseman. Johnny Mize had the previous high mark with 138 in 1947.

Oct. 10—The Giants lost four players to the expansion draft, stocking the New York and Houston franchises. Sam Jones and Joe Amalfitano were selected by the Colt .45s, and Hobie Landrith and Ray Daviault went to the Mets.

Nov. 30—In a trade that was to pay huge dividends for the Giants in 1962, pitchers Billy Pierce and Don Larsen joined the club in exchange for Ed Fisher, Dom Zanni, Bob Farley, and Verle Tiefenthaler. The foursome went to the White Sox in two separate deals on the same day at the winter meetings in Miami.

1962

April 10—Juan Marichal hurled a three-hitter and Willie Mays hit the first pitch Warren Spahn threw to him for a home run in a 6-0, Opening Day victory over the Braves. A crowd of 39,811 watched Juan strike out Hank Aaron three times.

April 14—Orlando Cepeda and Felipe Alou each hit two home runs in a 13-6 blasting of the Reds. The Giants were off to a 5-0 start, outscoring opponents, 37-13.

April 16—Giants showed the Dodgers what kind of a year it was going to be by clobbering L.A. 19-8 in their first Candlestick Park meeting as Mays, Alou, and Jim Davenport homered.

April 21—The Comeback Kids were at it again. Behind Cincinnati 6-1, the Giants rallied on home runs by Alou and Ed Bailey for an 8-6 victory.

April 29—The finest pitching of a championship season found Jack Sanford and Billy Pierce each firing three-hit shutouts in a 7-0, 6-0 sweep of the Cubs before 40,398. Mays' two-run homer provided the punch in the opener and Bailey homered in the nightcap.

April 30—Right-hander Gaylord Perry, a $90,000 bonus baby, made his first major league complete game a four-hit, 4-1 victory over Pittsburgh. It was his third start and it placed the Giants in first place with their sixth straight win.

May 4—Plane trouble forced a landing at Salt Lake City and the Giants did not arrive at Chicago until 6 A.M., yet they mustered enough energy for an 11-6 pounding of the Cubs. The victory was the club's tenth in a row, increasing its league lead to 2 1/2 games.

May 10—Billy O'Dell blanked Bob Gibson and the Cardinals, 6-0. Willie McCovey, substituting in left field, cracked a three-run homer to support the four-hitter.

May 26—Mays was the slugging hero with two homers, a triple, and four RBI in a 7-6 conquest of the Mets. Willie's homer in the eighth tied the game, and he won it with a two-run homer off Jay Hook in the tenth.

May 27—Manager Casey Stengel made his first Candlestick Park visit with the Mets, but a brawl and the Giants' 7-1, 6-5 sweep spoiled the show for the venerable skipper. Cepeda and pitcher Roger Craig went at it, as did Mays and Mets' infielder Elio Chacon.

June 1—Giants made their first regular-season return to New York since 1957 and thrilled many of their old fans among the 43,742 in attendance with a 9-6 victory over the Mets. McCovey hammered two homers off Craig, Mays added number seventeen, and Davenport notched his first major league grand slam.

June 12—Billy O'Dell struck out twelve batters at Philadelphia and went the distance for a 4-3 victory as Ed Bailey belted a home run in the top of the twelfth to break a tie.

July 4—The Giants treated their fans to plenty of fireworks in an 11-4, 10-3 sweep of the Mets. McCovey drove in seven runs in the opener with a pair of homers and two sacrifice flies. Mays registered five RBI with a pair of homers in the second game. It still was a "costly" day for the home team, though, because the Giants gave $150,000 to sign Santa Clara pitcher Bob Garibaldi.

July 6—Marichal struck out thirteen Dodgers, a season high for the Giants, in a 12-3 romp over L.A. The victory squared the series and S.F. won it 10-3 the next day on homers by Mays and Davenport.

August 6—Mays belted five hits in as many trips, blasting two home runs and registering five RBI in a 9-2 rout of the Phillies. Lefty Billy Pierce won his tenth game of the season.

August 10—Mays' first-inning homer and four RBI powered the

Giants to an 11-2 rout of the Dodgers in the opener of a three-game series with the Dodgers, pulling S.F. to within 4 1/2 games of first-place L.A.

August 11—Willie McCovey's three-run, pinch homer off Don Drysdale with two outs in the sixth inning produced a 5-4 victory over the Dodgers. The blow snapped Drysdale's eleven-game win string, gave Billy Pierce his two-hundredth major league victory, and slashed the L.A. lead to 3 1/2 games.

August 12—The Dodgers were furious because excessive water between first and second in the first two games of the series at Candlestick Park hampered their running game. Umpire Bill Jackowski ordered sand to be placed in the area prior to the final game of the series, but it didn't matter. Marichal's four-hitter and Jose Pagan's hitting produced a 5-1 victory, cutting the lead to 2 1/2 games.

August 23—Reserve infielder Ernie Bowman almost single-handedly beat the Mets 2-1 at New York, ending a tailspin that had the Giants drop six out of seven. Bowman homered in the fifth and added the game-winning single in the tenth.

August 24—Orlando Cepeda belted five hits, including two homers, and totaled four RBI in a 6-0 romp at Philadelphia. Billy O'Dell pitched the shutout.

Sept. 3—The opener of a crucial, four-game series found the Giants winning their first game ever at Dodger Stadium, 7-3, after losing ten in a row at Los Angeles. Jack Sanford registered his twentieth victory of the season and his fourteenth in a row, and Mays and Haller homered.

Sept. 5—After the Dodgers squared the series with a 5-4 victory the previous day, Marichal and Bob Bolin collaborated on a 3-0 shutout. Juan suffered a leg injury in the sixth while beating fleet Willie Davis to first base, and Bolin mopped up.

Sept. 6—The Giants rallied with four runs in the ninth to down the Dodgers 9-6 and climb within 1 1/2 games of the lead. Drysdale was behind 4-0 after three, but Frank Howard's two-run homer off O'Dell created a 4-4 tie in the fourth. Harvey Kuenn's RBI-hit in the eighth was neutralized by Tommy Davis' homer, and it was 5-5 entering the ninth. Cepeda's bases-loaded walk cracked the tie and Harvey Kuenn followed with a three-run double off Ron Perranoski.

Sept. 11—Jack Sanford blanked the Pirates 2-0 for his sixteenth consecutive victory and a 22-6 record. Felipe Alou belted a home run. Sanford, unbeaten since June 17, had his string snapped on September 15 in a 5-1 loss at Pittsburgh.

Sept. 12—Mays collapsed in the dugout at Cincinnati, suffering from fatigue, during a 4-1 loss to the Reds. The Giants went on to drop six in a row, seemingly dropping out of the race.

Sept. 19—Haller's two home runs helped to snap the losing streak in a 7-4 victory at St. Louis.

Sept. 21—Gaylord Perry, recalled from Tacoma, gave the Giants a lift with an 11-5 victory at Houston. Mays collected four hits.

Sept. 26—Billy Pierce raised his record at Candlestick to 11-0 and Haller knocked in four runs with a home run and a double to defeat St. Louis 6-3 and keep Giant flag hopes alive.

Sept. 29—The Giants had a chance to tie for the lead with a makeup doubleheader against Houston. Spirits were high when Sanford's twenty-fourth victory downed the Colt .45s in the opener, 12-5. But Bob Bruce defeated the Giants 4-2 in the second game, keeping them one game behind with one game remaining.

Sept. 30—One of the most tension-filled days in San Francisco baseball history found Mays' eighth-inning homer off right-hander Turk Farrell edging the Astros, 2-1. The Giants then huddled around clubhouse radios and reacted deliriously when Gene Oliver of the Cardinals hit a home run to down the Dodgers 1-0 and force a playoff.

Oct. 1—Pierce's three-hit pitching and two home runs by Mays guided the Giants to a decisive 8-0 victory in the opening playoff game before 32,660 at Candlestick. Mays's forty-eighth and forty-ninth homers gave him the major league lead and Pierce completed a 12-0 season at home. Cepeda and Davenport also homered for the Giants, but the issue was decided in the first inning when Felipe Alou doubled with two away and Mays bashed a home run to right center off Sandy Koufax.

Oct. 2—The playoffs shifted to Los Angeles and the Giants jumped to a 5-0 lead. But the Dodgers, shut out for 35 innings, erupted for seven runs in the sixth and won it in the ninth, 8-7 on Maury Wills's running and poor fielding by Gaylord Perry.

Oct. 3—The Giants won their only San Francisco pennant in dramatic fashion at Dodger Stadium, rallying with four runs in an improbable ninth for a 6-4 victory. The Dodgers went ahead, 3-2 in the sixth on Duke Snider's single and Tommy Davis' homer, and made it 4-2 in the seventh with the help of Wills' record 103d and 104th stolen bases. With Ed Roebuck pitching, Matty Alou triggered the winning rally in the ninth with a pinch single. Kuenn forced him, but McCovey and Felipe Alou walked, loading the bases. Mays singled off Roebuck's glove for 4-3, leaving the bases loaded. Stan Williams took over and Cepeda's sacrifice fly produced a tie. A wild pitch sent Mays to second and Ed Bailey was walked intentionally, again filling the sacks. Davenport then walked, forcing home the go-ahead run. Pierce, in relief, retired the Dodgers in order in the bottom of the ninth and the jubilant Giants headed for the World Series.

Oct. 4—The World Series seemed anticlimactic as Whitey Ford downed the Giants 6-2 in Game 1 before 43,852 gloomy fans at Candlestick. Clete Boyer's seventh-inning homer cracked a 2-2 tie.

Oct. 5—Sanford pitched a three-hitter and McCovey blasted a home run to give the Giants a Series-squaring, 2-0 victory in Game 2. A crowd of 43,910 watched at Candlestick.

Oct. 7—The Series shifted to New York and 71,434 saw Yankee right-hander Bill Stafford prevail over Pierce, 3-2. Stafford had the Giants blanked until Bailey hit a two-run homer in the ninth.

Oct. 8—Second baseman Chuck Hiller became the first National Leaguer to hit a grand-slam homer in the World Series, powering a 7-3 Giants victory in Game 4. Hiller's blow off Marshall Bridges snapped a 2-2 tie in the seventh. Ex-Yankee Don Larsen was the winner in relief; Haller also homered for the Giants.

Oct. 10—The Yankees took a 3-2 edge in the Series when Tom Tresh's three-run homer in the eighth inning erased a 2-2 tie and gave New York a 5-2 victory. Jose Pagan homered for the Giants.

Oct. 15—After three days of rain, the Giants once again tied the Series when Pierce's 5-2 victory shackled the Yankees before 43,948 at Candlestick. Cepeda, hitless in twelve previous Series at bats, had three hits and two RBI.

Oct. 16—The moment of truth, with 43,948 at the edge of their seats, came with two on and two out in the bottom of the ninth. McCovey lined sharply to second baseman Bobby Richardson and the Yankees won the Series, 1-0. Ralph Terry pitched a four-hitter and had a perfect game until Sanford's two-out single in the sixth. The Yankees scored on Tony Kubek's double-play grounder in the fifth.

Nov. 30—Pitcher Dick LeMay and utility outfielder Manny Mota were traded to Houston for Joe Amalfitano, a former Giants bonus baby. It wasn't a good move because Mota went on to become the National League's career pinch-hit leader.

Dec. 15—Another questionable deal sent pitchers Mike McCormick and Stu Miller and catcher John Orsino to the Orioles in exchange for pitchers Jack Fisher and Billy Hoeft and catcher Jim Coker.

1963

April 9—The defending National League champions opened the season with a 9-2 romp at Houston. Home runs by Willie Mays, Willie McCovey, Orlando Cepeda, and Felipe Alou powered a seventeen-hit attack. It was the first time four homers were smacked against the Colt .45s.

April 10—Giant catcher Ed Bailey's pinch-hit grand slam off Don McMahon defeated the Colt .45s, 8-7.

April 16—Opening Day at Candlestick resulted in Juan Marichal's six-hit, 7-0 victory over the Dodgers. It was the great right-hander's fourteenth consecutive victory at home.

May 3—It was Willie Mays Day at the Polo Grounds and 49,431 paid to honor the Giants superstar. He received a telegram from President John Kennedy. Wondrous Willie doubled and knocked in a run in a 5-3 victory. Duke Snider hit two homers for the Mets and, as usual, was overshadowed by Mays.

May 11—Sandy Koufax pitched a no-hitter and downed the Giants 8-0 at Los Angeles. The Dodgers lefty had a perfect game until Bailey walked with one out in the eighth.

June 2—Mays belted three home runs in a 6-4 victory at St. Louis. The victims were Ernie Broglio, Bob Humphreys, and Bobby Shantz. Mays was hitless in eighteen trips before connecting off Broglio in the first. The blast off Humphreys carried an estimated 480 feet.

June 11—Juan Marichal scattered seven hits and Willie McCovey took care of the offense with a three-run homer in the sixth for a 3-0 victory at Dodger Stadium.

June 12—Right-hander Bobby Bolin set a San Francisco Giants record with fourteen strikeouts in a 3-1 victory over the Cubs. McCovey supplied the pop by belting two home runs off Bob Buhl for the third time in his career.

June 15—Juan Marichal pitched the first Giants no-hitter in thirty-four years, a 1-0 victory over Houston before a crowd of 18,869 at Candlestick. The Giants collected only three hits off Dick Drott, scoring in the eighth on a leadoff double by Davenport and a two-out two-bagger by Chuck Hiller. The no-hitter was the first for the franchise since Carl Hubbell smothered the Pirates 11-0 on May 8, 1929.

June 22—Billy O'Dell, an avid golfer, said he wanted to work quickly so he could get home to watch the U.S. Open on television. He took only one hour and 58 minutes in a two-hit, 3-0 triumph at Milwaukee. But this wasn't the Giants' fastest game. Jack Sanford won in one hour and 36 minutes on June 14.

July 2—Marichal defeated Warren Spahn 1-0 on Mays' one-out homer in the sixteenth inning in what is regarded as the finest game in S.F. history. It was a classic pitching duel because Spahn, forty-two years old, was 11-3 with five straight victories and Marichal was 12-3 with eight in a row entering the game. A crowd of 15,921 witnessed the gem, which concluded at 12:31 A.M. in Candlestick.

July 7—The Giants' top regular-season crowd (42,787) watched Jim Ray Hart make a sensational major league debut in the opener of a doubleheader with the Cardinals. Hart doubled, walked with the bases loaded, singled, and scored the tying run on Bailey's double in the thirteenth. He was intentionally walked in the fifteenth as S.F. pulled out a 4-3 victory. In the second game, Bob Gibson hit Hart with a pitch in the first inning, cracking the rookie's shoulder blade.

July 12—Willie McCovey hit a pair of two-run homers off Art Mahaffey in a 7-5 loss at Philadelphia. The blasts made Stretch the number one home-run hitter among Giants left fielders with twenty-five. Monte Irvin held the record with twenty-four in 1951.

July 19—McCovey extended his hitting streak to twenty-four games in a 5-2 loss at Cincinnati. The streak was the best in the bigs in 1963 and tied the Giants' modern record, shared by Freddie Lindstrom in 1930 and Don Mueller in 1955. Joe Nuxhall of the Reds snapped the string the next day.

August 22—Mays flashed his all-around excellence in an 8-6 victory over the Braves. In addition to a game-winning single, he scored on a passed ball only four or five feet behind catcher Del Crandall, walked and scored another run, robbed Lee Maye of extra bases with a diving catch in the third, and broke up a double play to keep the winning rally alive and set the stage for Felipe Alou's three-run homer.

August 27—Mays hit his four-hundredth career homer, a shot off the Cardinals' Curt Simmons, to power a 7-2 victory.

Sept. 3—Juan Marichal defeated the Cubs 16-3 for his first twenty-win season.

Sept. 7—Home runs by McCovey, Mays and Cepeda defeated Don Drysdale and the Dodgers, 5-3. The round-tripper was McCovey's tenth among his twenty-four lifetime hits off Drysdale.

Sept. 10—The Giants lost 4-2 at New York, but Jesus and Matty Alou were pinch hitters and Felipe started, marking the first time three brothers appeared in the same batting order in major league history.

Sept. 15—The Giants had an all-Alou outfield for one inning during a 13-5 romp at Pittsburgh. The eighteen-hit attack featured four apiece by Cepeda and Hiller. Mays scored three runs and knocked in four.

Sept. 22—McCovey rapped three home runs off the Mets in the first four innings during a 13-4 runaway. The blasts accounted for five RBI and included two-run pokes off Jay Hook and Galen Cisco. The outburst hiked his total to forty-three homers, tops in the league. He finished with 44.

Dec. 3—One of the biggest trades in Giants history sent Felipe Alou and Ed Bailey to Milwaukee in exchange for pitchers Bob Shaw and Bob Hendley and catcher Del Crandall.

1964

April 14—Opening Day at Candlestick Park produced a surprise when the Giants purchased Duke Snider and his 403 lifetime homers from the Mets. Mays hit two home runs off Warren Spahn and Haller and Orlando Cepeda and Jim Ray Hart homered in an 8-4 victory over the Braves.

April 15 — Mays' three-run homer in the tenth inning lifted the Giants to a 10-8 victory over the Braves, who had taken the lead in the top of the inning.

April 22—McCovey walloped three home runs in an 8-6 victory at Milwaukee. Stretch connected off Denny LeMaster in the second, Tony Cloninger in the third, and Phil Niekro in the fifth.

May 16—The Giants rallied with two outs in the fifteenth to edge the Mets, 6-4. Tom Haller started things with a single and Jim Davenport followed with a game-ending homer off Galen Cisco.

May 17—The Giants registered their second double shutout in their San Francisco history when Bob Hendley and Ron Herbel pitched a 6-0, 1-0 sweep of the Mets. Hendley fired a three-hitter in the opener and Herbel, making his first major league start, hurled a seven-hitter and struck out eight in the nightcap.

May 31—The Mets had won the first two games of the series, so

57,037 jammed Shea Stadium for a doubleheader with the Giants. S.F. won the opener 5-3, but blew a 6-1 lead in the second game, and the game was tied 6-6 in the seventh. The score remained tied until the Giants scored twice in the twenty-third for an 8-6 victory, ending the longest game (7 hours and 23 minutes) in history. The twin bill took thirty-two innings and lasted 9 hours and 52 minutes. The Giants won it on Davenport's triple, Cap Peterson's intentional walk, Del Crandall's ground-rule double, and Jesus Alou's run-scoring infield single. Haller and Alou each had four of the seventeen S.F. hits, and Gaylord Perry struck out nine in ten shutout innings of relief. Several years later, Perry admitted this was the game in which he began experimenting with a spitter.

June 17—McCovey's pinch-hit home run with one on in the ninth downed Joe Nuxhall and the Reds, 3-2.

June 20—Harvey Kuenn belted three singles, a double, and a home run to crush the Cardinals 14-3 at St. Louis.

June 21—Hal Lanier, playing in his fourth major league game, ripped two singles, a double, and a home run to help the Giants overcome the Cardinals 7-3 at St. Louis.

June 22—McCovey slugged a grand slam off John Tsitouris in the sixth inning at Cincinnati to lift the Giants from a 0-2 deficit to a 6-2 victory.

June 24—Ron Herbel struck out fourteen batters and outdueled Jim O'Toole for a 2-1 victory at Cincinnati.

June 27—Tom Haller belted two homers, including a three-run shot, to fuel a 9-1 romp at Los Angeles.

June 28—Herbel shaded Don Drysdale and the Dodgers 1-0 at L.A., with ninth-inning relief from Billy O'Dell.

July 10—Rookie Jesus Alou slashed five singles and a home run during a 10-3 romp over the Cubs at Wrigley Field. Alou connected off six different pitchers in the only six-hit performance in S.F. history. It was the first six-hit effort in the National League in four years.

July 26—Sandy Koufax had a 2-1 lead at Dodger Stadium until the Giants erupted for four runs in the ninth for a 5-4 victory, their first ever over the great lefty at L.A. Mays doubled for a 3-2 lead in the dramatic ninth, and Jim Ray Hart followed with a 400-foot homer off Koufax.

August 14—Former teammate Ed Bailey had the only hit as Bob Bolin fired a one-hit, 3-0 victory over the Braves in his finest major league performance.

August 24—A crowd of 36,034 at Los Angeles gave Willie Mays a standing ovation after his two spectacular catches paced a 4-2 Giants victory. Each catch was regarded better than his fabled 1954 World Series grab of Vic Wertz's long drive. Mays robbed Ron Fairly of extra bases when he made a catch on his knees in left center. Then he took at least a double away from Tommy Davis with a superb catch in right center.

Sept. 1—Masonari Murakami, the first Japanese to play in the majors, made his debut in a 4-1 loss at New York. Murakami went on to pitch eleven scoreless innings in his first five games.

Sept. 12—Orlando Cepeda hit a grand slam and a two-run homer for six RBI in a 9-1 trampling of the Phillies.

Oct. 3—Mays hit home runs off the Cubs' Bob Buhl and Lindy McDaniel, but the Giants were eliminated from pennant contention after a 10-7 loss to the Cubs.

1965

Feb. 1—The Giants reacquired catcher Ed Bailey by sending pitcher Billy O'Dell to the Braves.

April 12—Juan Marichal pitched nine scoreless innings on Opening Day at Pittsburgh but the Pirates and Bob Veale ruined the Giants' day with a 1-0 victory on Bob Bailey's tenth-inning homer off the Dominican Dandy.

May 2—Willie McCovey hit two home runs, including the game-winner in the tenth off Bob Miller, for a 4-2 victory at Dodger Stadium.

May 4—Dissatisfied with their roster, the Giants began a series of May swaps by sending pitcher Jim Duffalo to the Reds for reliever Bill Henry. On May 22, Jose Pagan went to Pittsburgh for Dick Schofield in a trade of infielders. Finally, on May 30, Bailey, Harvey Kuenn, and Bob Hendley were dealt to the Cubs for young slugger Len Gabrielson and catcher Dick Bertell.

June 20—Jim Ray Hart was the hitting hero in a 4-3, 7-3 sweep of the Pirates at Candlestick. In the opener, he hit an RBI double in the seventh inning for a 2-2 tie and cracked a 420-foot, game-winning homer off Alvin McBean leading off the fifteenth. Hart added a two-run triple in the second game.

June 28—Juan Marichal blanked the Dodgers 5-0 for his tenth straight victory over them at Candlestick.

July 10—Marichal was heading for his third career one-hitter with two down in the ninth, but settled for a two-hit, 7-0 victory over the Phillies. Juan posted his seventh shutout among fourteen wins and Jim Davenport stroked a home run.

July 19—The Giants signed left-hander Warren Spahn following his release by the Mets. Spahn, forty-four years old, came to the Giants with a 360-241 lifetime record.

July 27—Spahn pitched a four-hitter in his second start for S.F., picking Lou Brock off base twice, but was a 3-0 loser to the Cardinals' Bob Purkey.

August 8—Spahn hurled his 361st victory, and his first with the Giants, when he won at St. Louis, 6-4. Baseball's number six all-time winner received home run support from Mays, McCovey, and Jesus Alou.

August 15—Murakami made his first major league start and Hart hammered his first grand slam, the Giants overcoming a 4-1 Philadelphia lead to win, 15-9.

August 22—Bloody Sunday at Candlestick and 42,807 watched in amazement as Marichal struck the Dodgers' John Roseboro on the head with a bat. Marichal, who was suspended for nine days and fined $1,750, scuffled with the L.A. catcher in the third inning and there was a 14-minute delay while order was restored. Then, Mays's 450-foot, three-run homer beat Sandy Koufax 4-3 before the largest Giants crowd of the season.

August 26—The Giants were short of pitchers during an 8-0 loss to the Pirates, so outfielder Matty Alou went to the mound and fired two scoreless innings, striking out three.

August 27—The largest crowd of the season, 56,167 at New York, saw McCovey smash two home runs and Mays one in a 9-2 victory over the Mets. Mays' fortieth homer was his sixteenth of the month, equaling the National League record set by Ralph Kiner in 1949.

August 29—Mays hit his record seventeenth home run of the month, a three-run blow off Jack Fisher in the third, to power an 8-3 victory at New York. The homer was Mays' 494th, passing Lou Gehrig and making Willie fifth on the all-time list. Mays was the unanimous National League Player of the Month for his seventeen homers and twenty-nine RBI.

Sept. 7—Hart knocked in all three S.F. runs and Bob Shaw shackled the Dodgers 3-1 at L.A. to give the Giants the league lead.

Sept. 9—Marichal four-hit the Astros 4-0 for his tenth home win, Tom Haller accounting for two RBI with a home run and a sacrifice fly. The victory maintained the Giants' half-game lead over the Reds and the Dodgers, who downed the Cubs 1-0 on Koufax's perfect no-hitter over Bob Hendley's one hitter.

Sept. 10—The score was tied and the bases were loaded when McCovey strode to the plate as a pinch hitter against the Reds' Ted Abernathy. Stretch hit a grand slam and the Giants went on to a 5-3 victory.

Sept. 13—Mays hit his five-hundredth career homer and his forty-seventh of the season in the fourth inning at Houston against Don Nottebart, and Juan Marichal pitched his twenty-second victory, 5-1. The win was the Giants' eleventh straight and gave them a 2 1/2-game league lead.

Sept. 14—The Giants were behind 5-2 entering the ninth inning at Houston. They scored a run, and Jesus Alou was on base with two outs and Mays at the plate. Everyone knew Willie was going for the fences, and he was embroiled in a battle with reliever Claude Raymond. Mays fouled off four 3-2 pitches before sending one soaring for a 450-foot home run and a 5-5 tie. Davenport's pinch single in the tenth produced a 7-5 victory, the club's twelfth straight.

Sept. 16—Bob Bolin was a 5-1 winner at Houston, extending the winning streak to fourteen games.

Sept. 28—Mays hit his fifty-first home run in the first inning off Larry Jaster, tying Johnny Mize's all-time Giants record, in an 8-6 loss to the Cardinals at Candlestick. It also was Willie's two-thousandth career game.

Oct. 3—Mays's fifty-second home run, coming against the Reds' Billy McCool on the final day of the season, established a new Giants single-season record and powered a 6-3 victory.

Dec. 1—Reserve outfielder Matty Alou was traded to Pittsburgh for pitcher Joe Gibbon and catcher Ozzie Virgil. Mateo went on to win a batting championship for the Bucs.

1966

April 12—Juan Marichal pitched a perfect game for six innings and finished with a three-hit, 9-1 rout of the Cubs on Opening Day. Willie Mays contributed a two-run homer.

April 24—Mays hit his 511th home run, a 415-foot, two-run shot off Jim Owens at Houston, to tie Giant great Mel Ott's National League record. The Giants won, 4-2.

May 4—Mays, in a 3-for-23 slump after his 511th homer, belted Claude Osteen's first pitch in the fifth inning for number 512, becoming the all-time National League record-holder. Osteen had gone 96 2/3 innings without yielding a gopher ball prior to the historic blast. Joe Gibbon pitched a four-hit, 6-1 victory over the Dodgers at Candlestick.

May 7—The Giants erupted for thirteen runs in the third inning at St. Louis and crushed the Cardinals 15-2 behind Juan Marichal.

May 8—Apparently feeling they had more than enough offense following the outburst, and unable to convince Orlando Cepeda to shift from first base, the Giants swapped The Baby Bull to the Cardinals for left-hander Ray Sadecki. It was a controversial swap because of Cepeda's popularity. Sadecki felt the heat and went 3-7 the rest of the season, whereas Cepeda kept hitting and went on to become the league's MVP in 1967.

May 13—Jim Davenport's home run in the seventeenth inning beat the Mets 5-4 at New York. Bob Priddy pitched three scoreless innings for the victory, the Giants' twelfth in a row.

May 17—Mays recorded three throwing gems in a 2-1 loss at Los Angeles. Playing right field because of an injury, Mays nailed Willie Davis at third in the fourth; robbed Maury Wills and doubled Don Drysdale off first in the sixth; and threw to Willie McCovey, whose relay nipped Wills at the plate in the eleventh.

May 26—Marichal went the distance in a six-hit, fourteen-inning victory over the Phillies. Jim Bunning was taken out in the eleventh after hooking up with Juan in a scoreless duel, and the Giants scored the only run of the game in the fourteenth on Davenport's triple and Bob Barton's sacrifice fly.

May 31—Marichal defeated the Reds 5-3 at Cincinnati for a 10-0 record, best in the majors.

June 27—Mays' homer produced a 2-1 victory over Bob Gibson at St. Louis. It was his 522d homer, passing Ted Williams and into the number three spot on the all-time list. Ron Herbel was the winner.

July 9—The Giants staged two great comebacks to edge the Reds 8-7 in twelve innings. McCovey drove in the club's first six runs, belting two homers among four hits. Stretch hit a two-run shot in the first, but the Reds were ahead entering the bottom of the ninth. Mays singled and McCovey's 420-foot homer to center made it 6-6. After the Reds scored an unearned run in the twelfth,

Tito Fuentes doubled with two outs and Tom Haller hit a homer for the win.

July 8—Davenport hit a pinch-hit grand slam and infielder Bob Schroder hit a game-tying single in his major league debut. Marichal downed the Cardinals 7-2 for his fourteenth victory.

July 22—Gaylord Perry struck out fifteen Phillies, the most by a Giants pitcher since Christy Mathewson's sixteen in 1903, in a two-hit, 4-1 victory. Perry, who fanned Richie Allen four times, had a no-hitter until Clay Dalrymple singled with one out in the eighth.

August 12—Perry registered a three-hit, 1-0 victory over the Astros on Mays' 400-foot homer off Mike Cuellar in the ninth.

August 16—Mays hit a solo homer off the Cardinals' Al Jackson in the third inning of Perry's 3-1 victory. It was Willie's 534th, tying Jimmy Foxx for number two on the all-time chart.

August 17—Mays waited only one day to pass Foxx, hitting 535 off the Cardinals' Ray Washburn in the fourth inning, triggering a 4-3 victory. Plate umpire Chris Pelekoudas was so excited over the record smash, he was the first to shake Willie's hand, later apologizing to National League President Warren Giles for the instinctive gesture.

August 20—Gaylord Perry defeated the Braves 6-1 for a 20-2 record, becoming the majors' first twenty-game winner. He then proceeded to lose six straight.

August 31—Marichal mastered the Mets 2-1 at New York and the victory marked the first time the club had two twenty-game winners the same season since Sal Maglie and Larry Jansen in 1951.

Sept. 6—Sadecki pitched his finest game with the Giants, firing a three-hit, 6-0 victory at Dodger Stadium.

Sept. 7—Mays had a sore leg, so he was playing right field instead of center. He singled in the twelfth and took off on Frank Johnson's single to right center, scoring the winning run by knocking the ball out of catcher John Roseboro's glove for a 3-2 victory at L.A.

Sept. 16—Willie McCovey hit what is regarded as the longest home run in Candlestick Park history, a 500-foot bolt to right, in a 5-4 loss to the Mets.

Sept. 17—McCovey hit three home runs against the Mets, the first two off Dennis Ribant and a two-run shot in the tenth off Larry Miller for a 6-4 victory.

Oct. 1—The Giants swept a doubleheader at Pittsburgh, 5-4 and 2-0, to leapfrog over the Bucs into second place, two games behind the Dodgers. Outfielder Ollie Brown drove in three runs with a homer and a double in the opener, but the best was yet to come. Bob Bolin fired a one-hitter and belted a run-scoring double in the second game, Bill Mazeroski spoiling the no-hit bid in the second inning.

Oct. 2—There was an outside chance for a San Francisco pennant if the Giants won and the Dodgers lost a doubleheader at Philadelphia, a situation that would have forced a makeup of an S.F. rainout. The Giants did their part; McCovey's two-run pinch homer in a four-run eleventh downed the Bucs, 7-4. But L.A. split at Philly and won by 1 1/2 games.

Dec. 13—One of the Giants' greatest trades sent Bob Priddy and Cap Peterson to the Senators for left-hander Mike McCormick, who was the Cy Young Award winner in 1967.

1967

April 13—Mays and McCovey homered, and Gaylord Perry pitched a four-hitter in a 2-0 victory at Atlanta.

April 29—Juan Marichal struck out eleven and fired a five-hit shutout in a 5-0 victory at Los Angeles. It was the middle game of the Giants' first-ever, three-game sweep at Dodger Stadium.

May 3—Marichal hurled a four-hitter at New York, winning 8-0 and boosting his career record against the Mets to 18-0, including eight shutouts.

May 4—Mike McCormick posted his first victory for the Giants since 1962 and launched his Cy Young Award campaign with a 3-1 decision at New York.

May 14—Ollie Brown, two days after being struck on the jaw by a Claude Raymond pitch, gained revenge against the Houston reliever with a two-run, 400-foot homer off him for a 4-3 victory over the Astros. Brown also doubled and scored in the two-run eighth off Don Wilson before connecting in the ninth with two outs.

May 26—Marichal six-hit the Dodgers 4-1 for his eighth straight win following an 0-3 start. Juan extended his mastery over L.A. to 14-0 at Candlestick, raised his career record to 138-61 and upped his won-lost percentage to .693, surpassing Whitey Ford's major league record of .690.

June 1—Gaylord Perry two-hit the Pirates 7-1, and catcher Dick Dietz belted his first major league home run, a three-run shot off Pete Mikkelsen.

June 4—The Giants recorded the third double shutout in their San Francisco history, 7-0 and 5-0 against the Mets. Joe Gibbon pitched a four-hitter in the opener and McCormick fired an eight-hitter in the second game.

June 13—Mays' grand slam off Barry Latman in the tenth inning at Houston earned a 6-2 victory. Mays, who failed as a pinch hitter with the bases full in the sixth, connected for his first slam since 1962. The game-winning blow also was his career home run number 550. Shortstop Hal Lanier made his first error in seventy-two games.

June 29—An eleven-run first inning chased Bob Gibson and the Giants rolled to a 12-4 victory at St. Louis. The outburst came on the heels of a nineteen-hit attack in Ray Sadecki's 9-1 romp over the Cardinals on June 28.

July 4—The Mets posted an historic, 8-7 victory over the Giants at Shea Stadium. They defeated Marichal for the first time in twenty decisions, belting fourteen hits and scoring eight runs (five earned) off the flashy right-hander in 5 1/3 innings.

July 8—Marichal upped his record to 15-0 against the Dodgers at Candlestick, but Jim Ray Hart was the hero of the 8-4 victory. Hart belted two homers, including the one-hundredth of his career, and pulled the Giants from a 4-2 deficit to a 5-4 lead with a three-run wallop off Don Drysdale in the fifth.

July 9—Mike McCormick, who entered the starting rotation on June 19, went ten innings to beat Claude Osteen and the Dodgers 1-0 on a five-hitter.

July 15—McCormick defeated the Astros 9-1 for his eighth consecutive victory and a 12-3 record.

July 23—Jim Ray Hart went wild in a doubleheader at Chicago. His two homers off Ferguson Jenkins won the opener 5-2, and he added a home run and a double in a 6-3 loss to Joe Niekro in the nightcap.

July 31—Jack Hiatt's pinch-hit grand slam off Elroy Face cracked a 4-4 tie and downed the Pirates 8-4 at Candlestick.

August 6—Jesus Alou belted seven hits in eleven trips, lifting his average to .303, in a 9-7, 4-1 doubleheader sweep of the Mets.

August 27—McCormick fired a 2-0 victory over the Braves for his second straight five-hit shutout. He previously had downed the Cardinals 6-0 on August 23.

Sept. 1—In one of the greatest wasted efforts in S.F. history, Gaylord Perry pitched sixteen shutout innings at Cincinnati and didn't get a decision in the Giants' 1-0, twenty-one-inning victory. Perry, who scattered ten hits and struck out twelve, was 15-17 with nine one-run losses during the season. Frank Linzy fired five shutout innings for the win in the longest night game (5 hours and 41 minutes and twenty-one innings) in National League history.

Sept. 15—McCovey belted two home runs off Steve Blass, including a two-run game winner in the sixth, to power Perry's 6-3 triumph at Pittsburgh.

Sept. 22—Tom Haller's ninth-inning homer off Alvin McBean edged the Pirates 1-0 for Ray Sadecki, who pitched a four-hitter and struck out seven.

Sept. 23—The Giants were behind 4-3 in the eighth, but Willie McCovey's grand-slam homer off Juan Pizarro produced an 8-4 victory over the Pirates.

Sept. 26—Mays hit two home runs in an 8-3 rout of the Mets, increasing his National League record to fifty-six two-homer games.

Sept. 27—McCovey hit his third grand slam of the season, and his second in four days, handing Tug McGraw and the Mets a 7-2 defeat.

Sept. 30—McCovey's run-scoring single in the sixth inning gave the Giants a 3-2 victory over the Phillies in the opener of a doubleheader and clinched second place for the club.

Oct. 1—McCormick pitched a five-hit, 2-1 victory over the Phillies to finish his Cy Young Award season with a 22-10 record and a 2.84 ERA. His victory total tied Jim Lonborg of Boston and Earl Wilson of Detroit for the major league lead.

1968

Feb. 13—Catcher Tom Haller was traded to the Dodgers for infielders Ron Hunt and Nate Oliver, marking the first deal between the clubs since Jackie Robinson was acquired by the Giants in 1956 and did not report.

April 11—Mike McCormick pitched thirteen innings against the Pirates, yielding only six hits and one run, but was not involved in the decision in Pittsburgh's 3-1 victory.

April 14—Jim Ray Hart hammered three home runs in a 13-2, 3-1 doubleheader sweep of the Phillies. His two-run shot in the fourth inning broke a 1-1 tie in the second game.

April 23—Jim Davenport's third career grand slam downed Chris Short and Philadelphia 7-1 for Juan Marichal.

May 4—Willie McCovey set a Giants record with his eighth career grand slam in an 11-6 loss to the Cardinals' Larry Jaster. Stretch had been tied with Mel Ott, George Kelly, and Willie Mays.

May 31—Dick Dietz apparently walked with the bases loaded and no outs in the ninth inning at L.A., but plate umpire Harry Wendelstedt ruled he didn't make a sufficient effort to get out of the way of the pitch. Don Drysdale worked out of the jam, posted a 3-0 victory for a record-tying fifth straight shutout, and went on to a record for scoreless innings.

June 6—Hart belted three-run homers off Rick Wise and Turk Farrell in a 7-2 victory over the Phillies.

June 15—Marichal scattered sixteen hits in a 9-5 victory over the Mets for his sixth straight complete game and eighth win in a row. McCovey's single kayoed Tom Seaver in the first and Stretch homered on his next at bat.

June 23—McCovey clouted home runs in the first and third innings off Jim Bunning, powering Marichal's tenth straight victory, a 2-1 decision at Pittsburgh.

June 25—Bobby Bonds hit a grand slam off John Purdin in the sixth inning for a smashing major league debut in a 9-0 rout of the Dodgers. It was the first grand slam by a rookie in his first major league game since Willie Duggleby hit one for the Philadelphia Nationals in 1898! Bonds' blast stole the thunder from Ray Sadecki, who pitched a two-hitter and struck out ten.

June 26—Dave Marshall's two-out, eighth-inning pinch single broke up Don Drysdale's no-hit bid in a 2-1 loss to the Dodgers right-hander.

June 27—Willie McCovey hit two homers for four RBI off Bill Singer, but the Dodgers defeated Juan Marichal 6-5 for their first victory in sixteen decisions against him at Candlestick.

July 14—Hank Aaron's five hundredth home run, a three-run shot off Mike McCormick, paced the Braves to a 4-2 victory at Atlanta.

July 20—Sadecki fired another two-hitter and struck out eleven in a 1-0 victory over Houston. Mays scored from first on a single by Hart.

July 23—McCovey's tenth-inning homer off right-hander Jack Lamabe downed the Cubs 4-3 for Marichal's eighteenth victory.

July 28—Marichal's run-scoring single in the eleventh defeated the Astros 4-2 at Houston for his fifteenth straight complete game and a 19-4 record.

August 1—Marichal three-hit the Dodgers 2-0 for a 20-4 record. It was his sixteenth consecutive complete game and his seventh career shutout against Drysdale.

August 4—Bobby Bolin continued his mastery of the Pirates with a five-hit, ten-strikeout, 2-0 victory. In his previous start against them, at Pittsburgh on June 21, he hurled a four-hit shutout.

August 7—Willie McCovey hit two home runs against the Phillies, including a game-winning shot in the eighth off Dick Hall, for a 4-3 victory.

August 11—Sadecki fired a four-hitter, struck out thirteen, and walked none in a 2-1 victory over the Mets.

August 14—McCovey's tenth-inning single at Pittsburgh produced a 2-1 victory and snapped Ron Kline's streak of ten straight relief wins. Gaylord Perry pitched a three-hitter and the run off him was unearned.

August 19—Bobby Bolin pitched an eleven-inning, 1-0 victory at New York, striking out ten Mets.

August 24—Ty Cline hit his first home run in four years, a three-run blast in the fifth inning off Don Drysdale, to boost the Giants from a 3-2 deficit to a 9-7 victory over the Dodgers.

August 26—Gaylord Perry pitched a one-hit, 3-0 victory over the Cubs, losing a no-hitter on Glenn Beckert's seventh-inning single.

Sept. 14—Mays hit a pair of homers off the Reds' Gerry Arrigo, including a three-runner in the fifth, during Bolin's 9-1 victory. It was Willie's fifty-eighth two-homer performance.

Sept. 17—Perry fired a no-hitter in a 1-0 victory over the Cardinals before 9,546 under the lights at Candlestick. Perry struck out nine and walked two in the one-hour, 40-minute gem. Ron Hunt's one-out homer in the first provided all the scoring off Bob Gibson, who pitched a four-hitter and fanned ten Giants.

Sept. 18—Ray Washburn returned the favor the next afternoon, hurling the first St. Louis Cardinal no-hitter since Lon Warneke in 1941. Washburn was embroiled in a scoreless duel with Bolin until the Cardinals scored in the seventh and eighth for a 2-0 victory.

Sept. 20—Marichal defeated the Braves 9-1 on a five-hitter, lifting his record to 26-8. It was the most victories for a Giants pitcher since Carl Hubbell's twenty-six in 1936. Nobody had won more since Christy Mathewson notched twenty-seven in 1910.

Sept. 27—Mays' home run in the fifteenth inning off Ted Abernathy gave the Giants a 3-2 victory at Cincinnati.

Oct. 11—Clyde King, forty-three years old, was named manager of the Giants. Herman Franks stepped down after four consecutive second-place finishes.

Oct. 14—In the expansion draft to stock the new San Diego and Montreal franchises, Giants Jesus Alou, Ty Cline, and Don Hahn went to the Expos, and Ollie Brown, Mike Corkins, and Rafael Robles were taken by the Padres.

1969

April 12—Juan Marichal did it all in a 5-1 victory over the Padres, belting two doubles and a home run against the expansion club.

April 25—Jack Hiatt's greatest day as a Giant produced seven RBI in a 12-8 victory over Houston. The catcher started things with a two-run homer in the first and capped his performance with a game-winning grand slam in the thirteenth.

April 27—Willie McCovey's three-run homers in each game powered an 8-5, 4-3 doubleheader sweep of the Astros. His three-run shot off Dan Schneider cracked a 5-5 tie in the seventh inning of the opener, and it was 2-1 Houston when he connected in the second game off Jack Billingham. Mac's eight home runs tied the National League record for April.

April 29—Bobby Bonds belted a home run off George Culver in the thirteenth inning for a 4-3 victory over the Reds. Bonds finished with three RBI.

June 6—McCovey hit two home runs off Rick Wise to support Gaylord Perry's five-hit, 4-0 victory orver the Phillies. Willie, with nineteen homers, moved five games ahead of Roger Maris' record 1961 pace. The power show came in the midst of a sixteen-game batting streak in which Stretch socked eleven homers and batted .453.

June 24—Willie Mays and Giant Manager Clyde King had an angry exchange in the Houston dugout over Mays' exclusion from the starting lineup. Each played down the incident, which insiders say was the beginning of King's demise as the S.F. skipper.

June 28—McCovey blasted two homers, including a first-inning grand slam off Jack Fisher, and finished with five RBI to power a 12-5 rout at Cincinnati.

July 4—The Giants erupted with some holiday fireworks in a 7-6, 7-3 sweep at Atlanta. Bob Burda's two-run pinch homer tied the opener in the ninth inning, and he delivered a game-winning two-run double in the eleventh. Bonds hit three homers in the twin bill, two in the first game.

July 20—Gaylord Perry hit his first major league homer off the Dodgers' Claude Osteen, 25 minutes after Neil Armstrong and Buzz Aldrin walked on the moon. The Giants won, 7-3.

July 23—McCovey's home runs off Blue Moon Odom and Denny McLain led the National League to a 7-3 victory in the All-Star Game at Washington. Stretch was named the game's MVP.

August 5—Marichal, Ron Hunt, and Bonds hit home runs on successive at bats off John Boozer for a 6-2 victory in the opener of a doubleheader at Philadelphia. The Giants also won the second game 5-3 for a half-game lead in the National League West.

August 9—The Giants purchased reliever Don McMahon from Detroit. The veteran stabilized the bullpen and went on to become the club's pitching coach.

August 26—Willie McCovey drove in six runs, four with his tenth career grand slam, in a 13-4 romp over the Phillies.

Sept. 12—Marichal fired a one-hitter for a 1-0 victory over the Reds. "It was my best game ever," remarked Juan, who posted his eighteenth victory and lost a no-hitter on Tommy Helms's single in the third.

Sept. 13—The Reds shaded the Giants 6-4 but Bobby Bonds' thirtieth homer made him only the fourth player in history to join the thirty-homer, thirty-steals club. On August 13, Bonds stole his thirty-second base, erasing Mays' S.F. record of thirty-one, set in 1958.

Sept. 16—Juan Marichal pitched a five-hitter for a 2-0 victory over the Braves, his nineteenth. Coupled with the one-hitter over the hard-hitting Reds in his last start, Juan regarded the games his best back-to-back career victories.

Sept. 22—Mays' six-hundredth career homer, coming with one on and the game tied in the seventh inning at San Diego, gave the Giants a 4-2 victory. The blast came in a pinch-hit role (for George Foster) and was belted off Mike Corkins. In the same game, Bonds struck out for the 176th time, breaking Dave Nicholson's major league mark. Five days later, Foster collected his first major league hit in a 2-1 loss at L.A.

Sept. 28—McCovey homered off Pete Mikkelsen at L.A. for his forty-fifth, and final, home run of the season, a career high.

Dec. 9—McCovey was named National League MVP, edging Tom Seaver 263-243, in the baseball writers' voting. Each collected eleven first-place votes.

Dec. 12—The Giants swapped pitcher Ray Sadecki and outfielder Dave Marshall to the Mets for outfielder Jim Gosger and infielder Bob Heise. They also sent pitcher Bob Bolin to Seattle for outfielders Steve Whitaker and Dick Simpson.

1970

Jan. 17—Willie Mays was named Player of the Decade by *The Sporting News.*

April 17—Second baseman Ron Hunt and infielder Bob Heise were unlikely heroes in a 16-9 victory at Cincinnati. Hunt hit his first major league grand slam as a pinch hitter, tagging Ray Washburn, and finished with six RBI. Heise added five RBI as S.F. overcame an 8-3 deficit.

May 8—Willie Mays hit his 605th and 606th career homers, both off Gary Gentry, in a 7-1 victory at New York. Miguel Puente was the winner.

May 10—Willie McCovey walloped two homers, including his twelfth grand slam, to hammer the Mets, 11-7. Stretch slugged a two-run shot off Nolan Ryan in the third and the four-run job off Tug McGraw in the fourth to finish with six RBI. It was his second grand slam of the season, the first having come off Bill Stoneman of the Expos on April 26.

May 13—Tito Fuentes' three-run homer and two-run triple accounted for all the scoring in Rich Robertson's 5-1 triumph at San Diego.

May 19—Right-hander Frank Linzy was traded to St. Louis for Jerry Johnson in a swap of relievers.

May 23—The Giants pounded out twenty-three hits, but San Diego scored a team-record seventeen runs in a 17-16, 15-inning donnybrook at Candlestick. Following the wild one, Clyde King was replaced as manager by Charlie Fox, who guided the club to a 67-53 record. Willie Mays had four hits, four RBI, and two homers. McCovey added a double, a home run, and four RBI. Nate Colbert, who had five hits, smashed a two-run homer in the eleventh for a 6-4 Padres lead, but Ron Hunt's two-run single made it 6-6 in the bottom of the inning. The 5-hour, 29-minute contest and King's S.F. managerial career ended shortly after Steve Huntz hammered a leadoff homer in the fifteenth off Miguel Puente.

May 24—Charlie Fox's first day as Giant manager produced two McCovey home runs off ex-teammate Ron Herbel in a 6-1, 7-6 doubleheader sweep of the Padres.

June 26—Gaylord Perry pitched a three-hit, 4-1 victory over the Braves for his fifth straight win. It was his second three-hitter in ten days, following a 3-2 decision over the Cubs on June 16.

July 8—Jim Ray Hart, in his second game after returning from an injury, hit for the cycle within five innings in a 13-0 victory at Atlanta. He capped his performance with a three-run homer off Phil Niekro and a bases-loaded triple off Aubrey Gatewood in the Giants' eleven-run fifth. The six RBI in an inning were the most for a National Leaguer since Fred Merkle turned the trick in 1911.

July 18—Willie Mays collected his three-thousandth hit in the second inning of a 10-1 drubbing of the Expos at Candlestick. Ron Hunt was hit by a pitch for the 119th time in his career, breaking Frank Robinson's previous National League record of 118.

August 8—The Giants entered the bottom of the ninth trailing 5-1, but scored six times for a 6-5 victory over the Astros. Tito Fuentes' bases-loaded walk made it 5-4, and Mays followed with a two-run single. Pitcher Skip Pitlock homered for S.F.

August 22—Hal Lanier's one-out single in the eighth spoiled Chicago lefty Ken Holtzman's no-hit attempt during the Cubs' 15-0 rout.

August 28—Juan Marichal posted his two-hundredth major league victory by stopping the Pirates, 5-1. The Dominican Dandy, off to a slow start following a negative reaction to penicillin, won his sixth straight for a 9-9 record and became the only post-World War II pitcher to win two-hundred games within eleven years.

August 29—Bobby Bonds struck out three times as the Giants fell behind the Astros 9-2, but his three-run homer was the big blow in a seven-run eighth for 9-9. Bonds' run-scoring single won it in the tenth, 10-9.

August 30—Giants left-hander Ron Bryant hurled his first major league complete game, smothering the Pirates on two hits, both by Roberto Clemente, in a 2-1 victory.

Sept. 6—Gaylord Perry began a string of three consecutive four-hit shutouts by baffling the Braves 1-0 at Atlanta. Four days later, Houston succumbed to him 11-0, and on September 15, the Braves were thumped 8-0 at Candlestick, giving Gaylord a 21-13 record.

Sept. 9—Mays walloped two homers off Larry Dierker, notching five RBI in a 9-5 victory over the Astros. Willie's fifth two-homer game of the season raised his career total to 626.

Sept. 19—Perry fired a three-hit shutout at San Diego, 3-0, the fourth straight whitewash equaling Sal Maglie's club record set in 1950. Perry's scoreless-innings streak was snapped at thirty-nine in his next start.

Sept. 23—The host Dodgers bolted to an 8-0 lead after six innings, but Dick Dietz's grand slam off Jim Brewer was the telling blow in the Giants' nine-run seventh. L.A. tied the game, but S.F. won it 14-10 on Ken Henderson's three-run homer in the tenth.

Sept. 25—Willie McCovey hit two homers off Pat Dobson, including a 450-footer, and George Foster hit his first major league homer, but the Giants were beaten by the Padres, 7-4.

Oct. 1—Bobby Bonds tripled on his final at bat of a season-ending, 5-4 loss at Houston for his two-hundredth hit, the first S.F. player to reach that total since Mays bashed 208 in 1958. Bonds also scored his 134th run, a new S.F. mark. Russ Hodges retired after twenty-two years as the Giants announcer. Hodges, who made "Bye, Bye Baby" his trademark and had seen all of Mays' 628 homers to that point, died the following April.

Oct. 19—One of the greatest swaps in S.F. history seemed insignificant at that time. Former bonus baby pitcher Bob Garibaldi was traded to Kansas City for catcher Fran Healy. It was Healy who eventually was swapped back to the Royals for Greg Minton, who became the greatest right-handed reliever in modern Giants history.

Dec. 30—Ron Hunt, not one of manager Charlie Fox's favorites, was traded to the Expos for first baseman Dave McDonald. It was a giveaway because McDonald never played for the Giants.

1971

April 6—It was a good omen when the Giants opened their championship season at San Diego with a 4-0 victory. Juan Marichal pitched the shutout and Willie Mays hit the first pitch he saw for a first-inning homer off Tom Phoebus.

April 7—Giant shortstop Chris Speier made his major league debut a smash with a double, single, and two RBI in Gaylord Perry's 7-3 victory over the Padres. Mays homered again, added a grand slam in a 7-6 loss the next day, and made it four in four games during a 6-4 victory at St. Louis on April 10.

April 12—A crowd of 29,847 turned out for the home opener and Perry responded with a three-hitter and eleven strikeouts to stump the Padres, 5-0. Alan Gallagher hit a two-run homer in the five-run second off Clay Kirby. It was Perry's eighth straight win.

April 14—Tito Fuentes' two-out single in the eleventh edged the Astros 2-1, giving the Giants sole possession of first place, a lead they never relinquished.

April 16—Marichal had a no-hitter until Ken Rudolph of the Cubs led off the ninth with a single to left. Juan finished with a two-hit, 9-0 victory, retiring twenty-four of the first twenty-five batters despite a 32-minute rain delay. Dick Dietz, George Foster, and Healy homered, the latter going 4-for-4.

April 23—Right-hander Steve Stone registered his first major league complete game, pitching a five-hit, 2-0 victory at Pittsburgh. For an encore, left-hander Ron Bryant blanked the Bucs 2-0 on three hits the next day.

April 28—Rookie George Foster, playing because Mays was injured, went 4-for-4 with a double, homer, and three RBI in a 5-3 victory at Atlanta.

May 2— Willie McCovey hit two home runs, including the game-winner off Tony Cloninger in the thirteenth inning for a 4-3 victory at Cincinnati.

May 6—The Bay Area baseball writers threw a fortieth birthday party for Mays at a downtown hotel. Commissioner Bowie Kuhn was among the guests and manager Charlie Fox, an Irish tenor, sang "Willie Boy" to the music of "Danny Boy."

May 15—Marichal blanked the Dodgers on a six-hitter, 1-0. The Giants collected only two hits off Bill Singer, but they came in the seventh when Mays doubled and scored on Dietz's single. S.F. increased its division lead to nine games.

May 20—Fran Healy continued to exhibit his Midas touch, belting a three-run, eighth-inning double to trigger a comeback at Wrigley Field. McCovey's three-run homer in the ninth downed the Cubs, 8-7.

May 29—A day that will remain infamous for Giants fans. The club, bulging with young outfielders, traded George Foster to Cincinnati for shortstop Frank Duffy and pitcher Vern Geishert, who never played for San Francisco.

May 30—Mays' two-run, eighth-inning homer lifted the Giants to a 5-4 victory over the Expos. Mays's 1,950th run broke Stan Musial's National League record.

June 6—Mays' double triggered a two-run ninth for a 3-3 tie against the Phillies in the nightcap of a doubleheader. Mays' one-out homer off Joe Hoerner in the twelfth earned a 4-3 victory, snapping a five-game losing streak.

June 18—The Giants began a five-game sweep of San Diego by winning a doubleheader, but it wasn't easy. The Padres scored five runs in the ninth inning of the second game to lead 9-5, but S.F. erupted for five in the bottom of the inning for a 10-9 thriller. Dietz's two-run pinch double did the big damage, the winning run scoring on an error following the blow.

June 20—Another doubleheader sweep in the series. McCovey's three-run pinch homer capped a five-run eighth for a 6-2 victory over the Padres in the opener and Steve Stone fired a three-hit, 2-0 gem in the second game.

June 23—Juan Marichal and Milt Pappas were hooked up in a 2-2 battle until Ken Henderson homered to start the three-run eighth. After Dietz walked, Marichal belted a two-run homer for a 5-2 victory over the Cubs.

July 3—Left-hander John Cumberland, acquired by the Giants the previous year from the Yankees in a trade for Mike McCormick, pitched a four-hitter for his first major league complete game, a 10-1 conquest of the Cardinals.

July 9—The Giants erupted for six runs in the ninth inning to jolt the Dodgers 7-4 at L.A. Chris Speier and Tito Fuentes triggered the rally with singles, but the crushing blows were a two-run triple by outfielder Jimmy Rosario and a two-run single by Dick Dietz.

July 21—McCovey's ninth-inning grand slam off Pittsburgh right-hander Dave Giusti downed the Pirates 8-4 at Three Rivers Stadium.

July 31—Dave Kingman, playing his second major league game, put on a power display in a 15-11 thumping of the Pirates. Kingman replaced McCovey early in the game and belted a run-scoring double in the fourth, setting the stage for his grand slam off Giusti in the seven-run seventh. Willie Stargell homered twice for the Bucs.

August 1—The Giants power crushed the Pirates 11-7 and 8-3 in a homer-filled doubleheader. Mays' two-run double and McCovey's three-run homer in a five-run eighth won the opener. Then Kingman clouted a pair of two-run homers off Dock Ellis in the second game. Stargell hit two homers again.

August 4—Bob Gibson posted his two-hundredth victory and his tenth in a row over the Giants since Gaylord Perry's no-hitter in 1968. The Cardinals' right-hander won 7-2 at St. Louis and Ted Kubiak hit a three-run homer.

August 8—Perry's home run in the fifth created a 2-2 tie, and he went the distance in a 4-2, 11-inning victory at Chicago. Speier's two-run single won the game, snapping a six-game Giants losing streak.

Sept. 1—Left-hander John Cumberland pitched a four-hit, 4-0 victory over the Braves. Dave Kingman was hospitalized following an emergency appendectomy.

Sept. 3—The Giants exploded for a 16-6 destruction of the Astros behind Mays' four hits, including two of them in the seven-run eighth. Willie belted two doubles and a triple; his three-run double and Dick Dietz's three-run homer were the big hits in the eighth. Fuentes also had four hits among the Giants' season-high twenty.

Sept. 4—Right-hander Don Carrithers pitched a three-hitter and Bobby Bonds' first-inning homer off Ken Forsch held up for a 1-0 victory over the Astros. Carrithers struck out eight and did not allow a hit after the third inning.

Sept. 5—Houston right-handers Jack Billingham and J.R. Richard stifled the Giants in a 1-0, 5-3 doubleheader sweep by the Astros, beginning a seven-game slide by the Giants. The second game was significant because Richard struck out a record fifteen batters in his major league debut.

Sept. 13—Losing for the eighth time in nine games, the Giants had their lead slashed to two games in a wild, 5-4 loss to the Dodgers. Marichal was ejected by umpire Shag Crawford for giving the choke sign. Jerry Johnson, Maury Wills, and Bill Buckner also were booted during a beanball duel. On a positive note for S.F., Dave Kingman returned to the lineup with a single, a double, and a triple.

Sept. 14—The Giants trailed the Dodgers 3-1 entering the bottom of the seventh, but Chris Speier's homer and a three-run shot by Bobby Bonds gave S.F. the lead until Manny Mota's three-run double in the ninth earned a 6-5 L.A. victory, cutting the Giants' league lead to one game.

Sept. 30—Marichal won at San Diego on the final day, 5-1, giving the Giants the division crown by one game over the Dodgers. Kingman's two-run homer in the fourth off Dave Roberts was the key blow. S.F. won only eight of its final twenty-four games, but Marichal was responsible for four of those victories and the team finished 90-72.

Oct. 2—The Giants hosted the playoff opener against the Pirates and were confident following their season dominance of Pittsburgh. A crowd of 40,977 watched McCovey and Fuentes rip two-run homers in the four-run fifth as the Giants posted a 5-4 victory.

Oct. 3—Pirate first baseman Bob Robertson hit three home runs, a National League Championship Series record, to give the Bucs a 9-4 victory before 42,562 at Candlestick, and snapping a six-game losing streak on the Giants' field.

Oct. 5—Marichal pitched a four-hitter when the playoffs shifted to Three Rivers Stadium, but home runs by Robertson and Richie Hebner gave the Pirates a 2-1 victory behind Bob Johnson and Giusti.

Oct. 6—Pittsburgh earned a World Series trip by blasting the Giants 9-5 for a third consecutive playoff victory. Hebner belted a three-run homer off Perry in the second, and Al Oliver homered in a four-run sixth that snapped a 5-5 tie. McCovey had a three-run homer and four RBI in a losing cause.

Nov. 29—Compounding the felony following the earlier Foster trade, the Giants sent Duffy and Perry to the Indians for left-hander Sam McDowell, who went from "Sudden Sam" to "Seldom Sam" in a horrible 1972 effort.

1972

April 2—The Giants traded reserve catcher Fran Healy to Kansas City for minor league pitcher Greg Minton, who ten years later would blossom into the greatest reliever in San Francisco Giant history.

April 15—The baseball season began following a ten-day strike. Juan Marichal wasn't hindered by the layoff, firing a 5-0 shutout of the Astros on Opening Day.

May 11—The end of an era for the Giants. Willie Mays was traded to the Mets for pitcher Charlie Williams and $150,000. Mays was batting .184 in nineteen games and had not homered since September 26, 1971, when he belted his 646th against the Reds. This was the beginning of a housecleaning that helped Horace Stoneham financially, but stripped the club of its fading superstars.

May 22—The Giants were trailing 8-0 at Dodger Stadium, but Dave Kingman clouted a pair of home runs, including a grand slam, to pace a 9-8 comeback. His slam was hit in the third inning off Tommy John.

May 27—Rookie Ed Goodson belted four hits, including his second major league homer and a double in an 11-9 victory at Atlanta.

June 11—Ron Bryant pitched a five-hit, 3-1 victory over the Cubs in the second game of a doubleheader. The win snapped an eight-game losing streak, longest in S.F. history. Ex-Giant Bill Hands pitched a 4-0 victory for Chicago in the opener.

June 27—Bobby Bonds smashed a 3-2 curve for a home run off Atlanta's Cecil Upshaw in the tenth inning, giving the Giants a 3-2 triumph.

July 4—Rookie Jim Barr joined the Giants' rotation, and celebrated the occasion with a three-hit, 3-1 victory over the Phillies.

July 2—Willie McCovey's fourteenth career grand slam tied Hank Aaron and Gil Hodges for the National League record and guided the Giants to a 9-3 rout of the Dodgers. Reliever Randy Moffitt posted his first major league victory and received a congratulatory telegram from his tennis-star sister, Billie Jean King, who was playing at Wimbledon.

August 15—Garry Maddox slugged a two-run homer in the fifth inning and a grand slam in the sixth, each off Hands, in a 7-5 victory over the Cubs.

August 16—Ken Henderson belted four hits, scored four runs, and knocked in five to power a twenty-hit, 14-9 romp over the Cubs. Tito Fuentes added a pair of two-run singles.

August 22—Marichal was the victim of a one-hitter for the second time in the season. Pittsburgh's Nelson Briles retired twenty in a row before losing a perfect game on Henderson's searing liner off the top of first baseman Willie Stargell's glove with two outs in the seventh. Stargell's double in the first drove home the Pirates' unearned run.

August 23—Jim Barr fired a two-hit, 8-0 victory over the Pirates, retiring the last twenty-one batters after Bob Moose led off the third with a walk.

August 29—Barr retired the first twenty batters at St. Louis, setting a major league record of forty-one in a row over two games, in a 3-0 victory. (Harvey Haddix held the former mark of thirty-eight straight outs in 1959.) Bernie Carbo's two-out double in the seventh snapped the string, and Barr settled for a three-hitter. Kingman chased home all the runs with a three-run double in the ninth.

Sept. 9—Jim Willoughby edged Don Gullett 2-1 in a pitching gem that found each youngster firing a three-hitter. The Reds led 1-0 until Jim Ray Hart walked with one away in the ninth and Kingman followed with a home run on an 0-2 pitch.

Sept. 16—McCovey, who missed two months of the season with a broken arm, and rookie Gary Matthews each slammed a pair of homers in an 8-5 victory at Atlanta. Matty's homers were the first two of his major league career.

Nov. 29—Steve Stone, who would become a Cy Young Award winner in 1980, and Henderson were swapped to the White Sox for right-hander Tom Bradley.

1973

April 9—Chris Speier's one-out homer in the fifth off Mike Caldwell cracked a 1-1 tie and gave the Giants a 2-1 Opening Day victory at Candlestick. Ron Bryant didn't allow a hit over the final five innings and finished with a four-hitter over the Padres.

April 11—Jim Wynn's two homers had the Astros ahead by one entering the ninth, but Chris Speier led off with a walk and Willie McCovey belted a game-winning, two-run homer for a 5-4 victory.

April 12—McCovey became the eighth National Leaguer to wallop a pair of homers in one inning, connecting off Ken Forsch and Jim Crawford in the eight-run fourth during a 9-3 crunching of the Astros. The first two-homer inning in the National League since Sid Gordon did it for the 1949 Giants included a three-run blast and a solo shot. Gary Thomasson added a two-run homer in the fourth.

April 25—Juan Marichal required only eighty-nine pitches to shackle the Cubs 5-0 at Wrigley Field. Juan's fifty-first career shutout gave him a 4-1 record.

April 27—Jim Barr fired a two-hit, 5-0 victory at St. Louis, defeating Bob Gibson.

April 28—For an encore, Jim Willoughby pitched a four-hit, 1-0 victory at St. Louis, getting the run on Bobby Bonds' leadoff homer in the first.

May 1—One of the greatest comebacks in Giants history occurred after the Pirates held a 7-1 lead with two outs in the bottom of the ninth and Speier on first. The club scored seven times to win 8-7, with Chris Arnold providing a pinch-hit grand slam and Bonds a three-run double.

May 8—Bonds hit a leadoff homer in the first, a two-run shot in the fifth, and a two-run single in the eighth to pace a 9-7 victory over the Cardinals. McCovey and Dave Kingman stroked back-to-back homers in the fourth off Gibson, Mac's smash going some 500 feet.

May 26—Garry Maddox cracked a double and four singles, collecting five hits off four different Montreal pitchers in a 10-3 runaway. The splurge raised Maddox' average to .377.

June 3—The Giants rallied for four runs in the ninth to shade the Phillies, 5-4. Kingman started the comeback with a single and Dave Rader homered. Tito Fuentes singled with two outs and Maddox hit a 1-2 pitch for the game-winning homer.

June 15—McCovey's three-run homer in the top of the tenth outlasted Greg Luzinski's two-run shot in the bottom of the inning, hoisting the Giants to a 4-3 victory at Philadelphia, Bryant's eighth in a row.

June 20—The Giants were beaten by the Reds 7-5, but Bonds' leadoff homer in the first was his twenty-second as the first batter, erasing Lou Brock's National League record of twenty-one.

June 22—Jim Barr retired the last fifteen batters in a six-hit, 5-1 victory over Houston. Ed Goodson did the damage with a three-run homer in the first off Don Wilson and a two-run blast in the seventh off Jim Crawford.

July 15—McCovey became the fifteenth player to hit four-hundred home runs when he belted a pair of solos to back Marichal's four-hit pitching in a 12-0 drubbing of the Pirates in the opener of a doubleheader. Pittsburgh won the second game, 7-2. The shutout was Marichal's fifty-second and last.

July 24—Bobby Bonds, climaxing his finest season, was the All-Star Game MVP at Kansas City, belting a home run and a double and collecting two RBI in the Nationals' 7-1 victory.

July 26—Picking up where he left off in the dream game, Bonds slapped a three-run homer in the first game and a two-run shot in the nightcap to power a 10-2, 6-5 sweep at San Diego.

August 12—Bonds, who earlier tripled and homered, hit a run-scoring single in the thirteenth to down the Mets, 8-7. The victory gave the Giants a 10-0 record in extra innings.

August 17—McCovey hit his twenty-second and twenty-third homers off Bob Moose and Bryant hurled six perfect innings in a 5-3 victory at Pittsburgh.

August 25—Tom Bradley hurled a four-hitter and defeated Tom Seaver 1-0 at New York. The performance reversed the Mets' 1-0 decision August 24, when Jerry Koosman prevailed over Marichal in ten innings.

Sept. 3—The Dodgers were ahead 8-1 entering the seventh inning, but the Giants came out on top, 11-8, on Bonds's grand slam in the ninth inning. Kingman hit his seventh homer in ten games.

Sept. 30 — Ron Bryant beat the Reds 4-3 on the final day for his twenty-fourth victory, the last Giants pitcher in 13 years to win twenty. Elias Sosa registered his eighteenth save and appeared in his seventy-first game, equaling Hoyt Wilhelm's club record. Bonds hit his thirty-ninth homer, just missing becoming the first forty-home-run, forty-stolen-base man in history. Second baseman Fuentes made only six errors in 160 games.

Oct. 25—McCovey and outfielder Bernie Williams were traded to the San Diego Padres for left-hander Mike Caldwell, interrupting McCovey's career with the club after fifteen years.

Nov. 17—Bonds was named Player of the Year and Bryant was selected Pitcher of the Year by *The Sporting News,* the first time both awards went to players from the same team.

Dec. 7—Marichal, with 238 victories and a 2.78 ERA in his illustrious Giants career, was sold to the Red Sox. Within a span of nineteen months, the club had disposed of the three greatest players in San Francisco's major league history: Mays, McCovey, and Marichal.

1974

March 15—Ron Bryant was injured in a swimming pool accident at Yuma, requiring thirty stitches in his side. His record dipped from 24-12 to 3-15 and he never regained his winning form.

April 8—On the day Henry Aaron hit home run number 715 at Atlanta, Garry Maddox belted a run-scoring single in the first and a three-run homer in the fifth for a 4-3 victory over the Reds at Candlestick. John D'Acquisto, Elias Sosa, and Randy Moffitt collaborated on the shutout, giving the Giants first place with a 4-0 record.

May 1—Maddox belted two doubles and had three RBI in the fifth inning, the Giants chasing Steve Carlton with nine runs in a 13-8 rout of the Phillies. Gary Matthews led off and ripped four hits, including a homer, scored four times, and knocked in three runs.

June 28—Charlie Fox resigned as manager after the Giants lost fourteen of their last seventeen games for a 33-42 record and dropped 16 1/2 games out of first place. Wes Westrum was promoted from the coaching ranks and took over the club.

July 3—Matthews' home run off Vicente Romo in the tenth gave the Giants a 3-2 victory over the Padres.

July 13—Matthews and Dave Rader each belted four hits in an eighteen-hit, 13-3 romp over the Phillies. Steve Ontiveros added three hits and four RBI, and Dave Kingman walloped a two-run homer.

July 21—The fourth doubleheader shutout in the club's S.F. history found the Expos falling, 4-0, 2-0. Jim Barr pitched a six-hitter in the opener and D'Aquisto had a no-hitter for six innings of the second game, finishing with Sosa's help in the ninth and a combined two-hitter.

August 4—The Giants dropped the opener of a doubleheader 4-2 to the Braves, but Mike Caldwell fired a no-hitter in the second game until Aaron rapped a one-out double in the eighth. Caldwell finished with a four-hit, 5-2 victory, raising his record to 7-0 at Candlestick.

August 31—D'Aquisto downed the Cardinals 3-2 for his tenth victory, becoming the first Giants rookie to win that many since Ruben Gomez in 1953.

Sept. 3—John Montefusco made an auspicius major league debut, replacing Bryant while the Giants trailed 3-2 at Dodger Stadium. He worked out of a bases-loaded, first-inning jam, blasted a two-run homer, and went the rest of the way on a six-hitter to win, 9-5. Matthews hit a grand-slam homer.

Sept. 6—D'Aquisto pitched a four-hit, 2-0 victory at Atlanta. The hard-throwing right-hander struck out five for a total of 148, most by a Giants rookie since 1900.

Sept. 16—Jim Barr needed only one hour and 38 minutes to stop the Braves on seven hits, 4-2. Bobby Bonds and Gary Thomasson homered, but the big news was that only 748 attended, representing the smallest crowd in Candlestick history.

Sept. 22—Montefusco beat the Reds 6-0 on a seven-hitter and hammered a home run in the eighth. Kingman and Chris Speier socked back-to-back homers off Don Gullett in the second.

Oct. 1—Fuentes doubled for his one thousandth career hit as the Giants pounded the Padres, 7-2. A little more than two months later, on December 6, the popular second baseman and minor league pitcher Butch Metzger were traded to San Diego for infielder Derrel Thomas.

Oct. 22—Bonds, only one year after he was regarded the best player in the National League, was traded to the Yankees for outfielder Bobby Murcer. It was the first swap ever involving ballplayers with six-figure salaries.

1975

Feb. 28— Dave Kingman was sold to the Mets.

April 13—John Montefusco pitched a four-hit, 5-0 victory over the Braves in the opener of a doublheader. Gary Matthews had a homer, a double, and a single to power a 3-1 second-game triumph for a sweep.

May 4—Continuing to trade away promising young talent, the Giants swapped Garry Maddox to the Phillies for Willie Montanez. Maddox blossomed into a Gold Glove center fielder, whereas Montanez was unhappy with his S.F. surroundings and didn't last long with the club.

May 9—Bryant was traded to St. Louis for outfielders Larry Herndon and Tony Gonzalez, a good move for the Giants because Bryant was finished as a winning pitcher.

May 18—Jim Barr fired a two-hitter to down his "cousin" Cardinals 2-0. Gentleman Jim had a no-hitter until Lou Brock led off the seventh with a single. Von Joshua's double and a sacrifice fly by Murcer accounted for the first S.F. run. Montanez tripled and scored on Chris Speier's single for the other.

May 24—Bobby Murcer's most productive day with the Giants included a three-run homer and a bases-loaded triple for six RBI in a 10-3 demolition of the Cubs behind Barr.

May 27—Montefusco fired a 1-0 shutout at Philadelphia, the Giants winning in the tenth on a run-scoring double by Glenn Adams.

June 4—Adams blasted a pair of homers at Chicago, including a three-run shot off Rick Reuschel, to lead the Giants' 10-8 victory.

June 1—Murcer connected for a pair of two-run homers in the eighth and ninth innings at Montreal to lead a 13-5 victory.

August 1—Montanez and Chris Speier opened the ninth with back-to-back home runs off J.R. Richard in a 3-2 win over the Astros.

August 24—Right-hander Ed Halicki fired a no-hitter and struck out ten, smothering the Mets 6-0 before 24,132 in the second game of a Candlestick Park twin bill. Montanez' two-run single in the first gave Halicki all the support he needed. Kingman's grand slam off Barr powered New York to a 9-5 decision in the opener.

August 27—Montefusco struck out a career-high fourteen Expos in a 9-1 victory.

August 31—The Count followed with thirteen strikeouts in 8 1/3 innings while defeating Steve Carlton and the Phillies, 5-4. Montefusco surpassed D'Acquisto's club rookie strikeout record in the process.

Sept. 2—Johnnie LeMaster became the forty-third player to hit a home run on his first major league at bat, connecting for an inside-the-park blast off Don Sutton in a 7-3 victory over the Dodgers.

Sept. 21—Montefusco concluded the Giants' home schedule with a 4-1 victory over the Padres. It was his fourteenth victory, most by a Giants' rookie since Larry Jansen in 1947.

Nov. 7—Montefusco was named National League Rookie Pitcher of the Year by *The Sporting News.* The Count, whose 215 strikeouts approached Grover Cleveland Alexander's rookie record of 227, was accorded a similar honor by the baseball writers.

1976

Jan. 9 — Charles Ruppert, vice-president of the Giants and Horace Stoneham's son-in-law, announced the sale of the Giants to Toronto interests for $13.35 million, provoking outrage in the Bay Area.

Feb. 11 — A preliminary injunction, instigated by new San Francisco Mayor George Moscone, prevented an immediate move to Toronto.

March 2 — Bob Lurie and Bud Herseth, introduced by Moscone, came up with a last-ditch deal to purchase the Giants for $8 million and keep them in the Bay Area.

April 9 — Bill Rigney returned to manage the Giants after an eighteen-year absence. Opening Day attracted 37,261, the largest home crowd in ten years, to Candlestick. Montefusco responded with a 4-2 victory over the Dodgers behind home runs by Bobby Murcer and Gary Matthews.

May 23 — Montefusco pitched a no-hitter until the sixth and settled for a three-hit, 1-0 victory over Phil Niekro and the Braves in ten innings. Derrel Thomas triggered the winning rally with a one-out single and advanced on Glenn Adams' grounder. Pinch hitter Dave Rader was walked intentionally and Larry Herndon was hit by a pitch, loading the bases. Chris Speier then hit a game-ending, fielder's-choice grounder.

May 25 — Murcer belted a grand slam in the fifth, but the Giants needed two runs in the eighth to edge the Astros, 7-6. Murcer's one-out single and Willie Montanez' two-out homer did the damage. Monty slashed four hits.

June 11 — Montefusco fired a three-hitter against the Mets, winning 5-0 on a three-run homer by Murcer in the first and a two-run shot by Marc Hill in the second.

June 13 — Montanez, batting .309 and wishing to be traded, had his wish granted when he was dealt to the Braves for Darrell Evans and Marty Perez.

June 23 — Evans made an impressive Candlestick Park debut with the Giants, powering a 7-6, 8-7 sweep of San Diego. His two-run homer in the eighth off Butch Metzger won the opener and he added a grand slam in the third inning of the nightcap off Rich Folkers.

July 15 — Ed Halicki defeated the Phillies, 1-0 in a tidy one-hour, 32-minute game.

August 15—Evans belted two homers, including a three-run blow in the ninth, during a 9-5 victory at Philadelphia.

Sept. 11—Jack Clark, promoted from Phoenix, hit his first major league homer off Jack Billingham in an 8-5 loss to the Reds.

Sept. 25—Matthews smashed three home runs in support of Jim Barr's 10-0 blanking of the Astros. Matty became the first Giant to hit three in one game since Willie McCovey in 1966, the outburst raising his season total to nineteen. Barr pitched a six-hitter and helped himself with a two-run triple.

Sept. 29—Montefusco pitched the first away no-hitter in the Giants' San Francisco history, tripping the Braves 9-0 at Atlanta. The brash right-hander threw only ninety-seven pitches, ninety-two of which were fastballs in a four-strikeout performance. Johnnie LeMaster was the offensive star with a triple, a double, and three RBI.

Oct. 7—In a surprise move, Joe Altobelli was named manager for 1977, succeeding Bill Rigney, who announced his retirement on Sept. 21.

Oct. 30—Larry Herndon was named National League Rookie of the Year by *The Sporting News*.

Dec. 10—Ken Reitz, eager to return to the Cardinals following a lackluster year with the Giants, was swapped to St. Louis for pitcher Lynn McGlothen. The trade was the second between the clubs in two months. Dave Rader, John D'Acquisto, and Mike Caldwell were shipped to St. Louis on October 4 in exchange for Willie Crawford, Vic Harris, and John Curtis.

1977

Feb. 11—Bobby Murcer and Steve Ontiveros were traded to the Cubs for two-time National League batting champion Bill Madlock.

April 19—Jack Clark became a regular at age twenty-one and slapped three hits in a 7-4 victory at Houston.

April 26—A contract hassle, similar to the one that cost the Giants Gary Matthews between seasons, prefaced the swapping of three-time All-Star Game shortstop Chris Speier to the Expos for shortstop Tim Foli.

May 8—Left-hander John Curtis pitched a two-hitter and belted a triple among his three hits in a 10-0 domination of the Mets.

June 18—Clark cracked a pinch homer off Goose Gossage in the eleventh inning for a 7-5 victory over the Pirates.

June 27—Willie McCovey, who returned to the Giants after a three-year exodus, became the only player in major league history to connect for a pair of home runs in the same inning twice in his career when he came through in a ten-run sixth at Cincinnati, powering a 14-9 thriller. Mac began with a one-out blast off Jack Billingham and capped the uprising with a grand slam off Joe Hoerner. The slam was his seventeenth, earning a tie with Henry Aaron for the National League record.

July 22—A pair of unexpected heroes combined talents to beat Steve Carlton and the Phillies, 6-2. Tim Foli ripped a solo homer in the sixth and a two-run shot in the seventh. Randy Elliott added a two-run homer in the sixth.

August 1—McCovey walloped two home runs, including his eighteenth grand slam, off Wayne Twitchell in a 9-2 victory at Montreal. The slam gave Stretch the all-time National League record, leaving only Lou Gehrig ahead of him with twenty-three.

Sept. 3—Bill Madlock hit two solo homers, but it took Foli, snapping a 0-for-26 slump, to belt a pinch single in the fourteenth inning for a 6-5 victory over the Cardinals.

Sept. 7—McCovey doubled off Mario Soto for his two-thousandth hit and belted his 489th home run in a 6-3 victory over Cincinnati.

Sept. 18—It was Willie McCovey Day at Candlestick Park, honoring the great slugger's comeback season. He didn't disappoint, exhibiting his flair for the dramatic with a two-out, run-scoring single in the bottom of the ninth, beating the Reds, 3-2.

Oct. 2—Gary Alexander belted a pinch homer in a 3-1 loss to the Padres, setting a club record of 11 such home runs. The previous Giants high was ten, by the championship 1954 aggregation.

1978

Feb. 28—The Giants sent Derrel Thomas to the Padres for first baseman Mike Ivie, a good move until off-the-field problems compelled the Giants to trade Ivie in 1981.

March 15—The biggest swap in San Francisco history: the Giants obtained left-hander Vida Blue from the A's after Commissioner Bowie Kuhn disallowed his shift to the Reds over the winter. To get the Oakland ace, the Giants gave up seven players: Gary Alexander, Dave Heaverlo, Jerry Johnson, Gary Thomasson, Alan Wirth, Mario Guerrero, and Phil Huffman.

April 28—Willie McCovey's bases-loaded double in the eighth inning at Pittsburgh gave John Montefusco a 5-4 victory over John Candelaria.

May 14—The Giants, who went into first place on May 12, padded their lead with a 5-4, 4-3 doubleheader sweep of the Cardinals, each victory attained in extra innings. Terry Whitfield's two-out homer in the twelfth won the opener, and he triggered the winning rally with a leadoff double in the tenth inning of the nightcap. After Mike Sadek sacrificed and Bill Madlock was walked intentionally, Marc Hill belted a two-out pinch single.

May 19—Rick Monday hit a pair of three-run homers off Montefusco before 53,846 at Dodger Stadium, but the Giants parlayed sixteen hits into a 10-7 victory. Darrell Evans hit a pair of solo homers and Madlock mashed a three-run blow.

May 23—The Giants erupted for three runs in the bottom of the ninth to edge the Astros, 3-2. Hill, pinch hitter Tom Heintzelman, and Madlock each hit run-scoring singles.

May 26—A crowd of 44,688, largest ever to see a night game at Candlestick, watched Knepper and McCovey baffle the Dodgers, 6-1. Knepper fired a six-hitter and McCovey took care of the offense with a two-run single in the first and a three-run, 497-foot homer in the fifth.

May 28—Mike Ivie's pinch-hit grand slam capped an electrifying, 6-5 victory over the Dodgers before 57,475. Los Angeles had a 3-0 lead erased in the five-run sixth, an inning featuring Ivie's smash off Don Sutton.

June 12—Ed Halicki pitched a one-hitter and Clark cracked a run-scoring double in the sixth for a 1-0 victory over the Expos. Ellis Valentine's leadoff single in the second was the only hit off Halicki. Steve Rogers lost on a three-hitter.

June 21—Halicki came through again, pitching a three-hit, 3-0 victory over the Reds. The Giants collected only five hits off Tom Seaver and scored all three of their runs in the fourth. Roger Metzger's two-run double did the big damage.

June 30—The Giants wasted a lot of slugging in a 10-9, 10-5 doubleheader loss at Atlanta. McCovey belted home run number five-hundred, off Jamie Easterly, and Ivie added a pinch-hit grand slam in the opener, becoming the only player ever to achieve the feat twice in the same season. Clark also got into the act, blasting three home runs in the twin bill.

July 11—Vida Blue became the first pitcher to start for both leagues in the All-Star Game when he went to the mound for the Nationals at San Diego. The lefty was roughed up for three runs, but his team rallied for a 7-3 victory.

July 17—The Giants registered a rarity in a 9-7 victory at St. Louis when Evans and Whitfield each belted five hits.

July 23—Jim Barr defeated the Pirates 3-1, but the big news was Clark's first-inning single. It extended his batting streak to twenty-five games, erasing the modern Giants mark of twenty-four by Freddie Lindstrom, Don Mueller and McCovey. Clark's closest call came on July 16, when he doubled as a pinch hitter against the Cardinals to make it seventeen in a row. The streak ended at twenty-six, a span of games in which Clark batted .368 with twenty-nine RBI.

July 25—St. Louis scored twice in the ninth for a 2-1 lead over Blue, but the Giants roared back with a pair in the bottom of the ninth for a 3-2 victory. Larry Herndon hit a one-out single, and Ivie followed with his specialty, a pinch homer.

August 4—Blue pitched a two-hitter to edge the Dodgers 2-1 before 49,317. Vida retired twelve straight before Ron Cey hit a leadoff homer in the fifth. Madlock cracked a 1-1 tie with a leadoff homer off Doug Rau in the eighth, helping Blue to his tenth straight victory.

August 12—History repeated for Madlock, whose eighth-inning homer off Tommy John broke a tie and gave the Giants and Bob Knepper a 3-2 triumph at Dodger Stadium.

Sept. 1—Clark's eighth-inning home run downed Steve Carlton and the Phillies, 4-3.

Sept. 27—Bob Knepper edged the Padres 1-0 for his sixth shutout, most for the Giants in one season since 1969.

1979

March 9—The Giants signed outfielder Billy North as a free agent. He went on to set a San Francisco record with fifty-eight stolen bases, four shy of the club's all-time mark.

April 10—Vida Blue defeated the Padres 4-2 before 57,484, the largest Opening Day crowd in the Giants' history. It was 2-2 entering the last of the ninth. Willie McCovey hit a two-out pinch single off John D'Acquisto and John Tamargo followed with a game-winning pinch homer.

May 12—Del Unser stood between a second no-hitter for Ed Halicki, who pitched a two-hit, 4-1 victory over the Phillies. A pair of singles by Unser were the only hits off the rangy right-hander. Johnnie LeMaster had three hits and Darrell Evans had two RBI.

May 17—Halicki recorded his second straight two-hitter, stopping the Astros 3-0 at Houston. Halicki was at the peak of his game with the back-to-back gems, but a bacterial infection struck him shortly thereafter and he seldom pitched effectively again.

May 25—The Giants won a battle of homers over the Braves, 6-4. The clubs tied a major league record with five home runs in one inning. After Jeff Burroughs and Bob Horner connected in the top of the fourth to give Atlanta a 4-1 lead, the Giants blasted three homers in the bottom of the inning to lead, 5-4. McCovey, Mike Sadek, and Bob Knepper did the damage. Jack Clark added a homer in the eighth.

June 9—McCovey came off the bench at Pittsburgh and powered a three-run homer off Grant Jackson in a 6-2 victory for Blue. The blast was his 512th, lifting him over Mel Ott as the number one left-handed home run hitter in National League history. It also was Stretch's sixteenth pinch homer, second on the all-time list.

June 15—McCovey's three-run homer in the thirteenth off Darold Knowles beat the Cardinals, 9-6. It was his second of the game for a career total of 515. Big Mac would never hit two in a game again.

June 26—Darrell Evans, batting as a pinch hitter, led off the ninth with a home run for a 6-5 victory over the Braves. Billy North's homer triggered a five-run first for the Giants.

June 28—Satisfied that they would not be able to keep Bill Madlock in San Francisco, the Giants swapped him and pitcher Dave Roberts to Pittsburgh for pitchers Ed Whitson, Al Holland, and Fred Breining. It seemed like a poor move at the time, Mad Dog leading the Bucs to a pennant, but the Giants needed pitching help and they got it for years to come. They also indirectly landed Mike Krukow, Al Oliver, and Duane Kuiper by making Madlock expendable.

July 20—Bob Knepper beat Steve Carlton 4-1 on the strength of a four-run third inning. Clark hit a two-run homer and Mike Ivie followed with a homer to spark the rally.

August 6—Whitson dazzled the Dodgers 7-1 for his first major league complete game, snapping the Giants' eight-game losing string at Los Angeles.

August 24—McCovey hit his first home run in six weeks and Ivie added a bases-loaded triple in a 5-2 victory over the Cubs. The homer was McCovey's 520th, and his last at Candlestick Park.

Sept. 5—Coach Dave Bristol replaced Joe Altobelli, who was fired as manager after the club slipped to 61-79. The Giants finished the season 10-12 under Bristol.

Dec. 17—The Giants wholeheartedly entered the free agent market by announcing the signing of second baseman Rennie Stennett, catcher Milt May, and outfielder Jim Wohlford.

1980

May 3—Willie McCovey's 521st and final home run snapped an 0-for-15 slump and helped the Giants shade the Expos 3-2 at Montreal. Mac's homer, a 385-foot shot to right center off Scott Sanderson in the fourth, moved him into a tie on the all-time list with boyhood idol Ted Williams.

May 13—Vida Blue fired a four-hit, 5-0 victory over the Pirates, Jack Clark driving in a pair with a single and a home run.

May 17—Darrell Evans smashed his fifth career grand slam to lift Blue to a 4-2 victory over the Cardinals.

May 24—Clark enjoyed his second straight four-hit day, and the Giants edged the Pirates 10-9 in fourteen innings. Jim Wohlford entered the game in the sixth and finished with four hits.

June 9-10—The Longest Night in baseball history. Clark's two-run homer produced a 3-1 victory in a game that finished at 3:11 A.M. in Philadelphia. Steve Carlton had retired twelve straight Giants when the first in a series of rain delays came. The contest consumed 7 hours and 35 minutes from start to finish, but only 2 hours and 36 minutes was used to play baseball.

June 11—Rich Murray, playing his fifth game, belted his first major league homer and finished with three hits and four RBI in a 7-4 victory at Philadelphia.

June 18—The Giants dusted off the Mets 8-5, but the big story oc-curred in Dave Bristol's office long after the game had concluded. The manager and pitcher John Montefusco, who didn't appreciate his removal from the game, became involved in a pushing match and the Count received a black eye in the scuffle.

June 27—Left-hander Jerry Reuss pitched the Dodgers' first no-hitter in ten years, an 8-0 gem at Candlestick Park.

June 29—McCovey's run-scoring double in the bottom of the ninth earned a 4-3 victory over the Dodgers before 50,229 at Candlestick. Rennie Stennett started the rally with a single and Stretch came through off Buddy Castillo with two away.

July 10—McCovey was placed on the voluntary retired list, but not before one last hurrah. His final at bat produced an eighth-inning sacrifice fly off Rick Sutcliffe at Dodger Stadium, giving the Giants a 4-3 lead. They eventually won in the tenth, 7-4, on Milt May's run-scoring single and a two-run single by Stennett.

July 12—John Montefusco and Bill Bordley pitched a wild, 7-4, 10-7 sweep at Cincinnati. Jack Clark hit a three-run homer in the opener and joined Darrell Evans for back-to-back shots in the five-run sixth of the second game.

July 14—Clark's 400-foot homer and Al Hargesheimer's pitching gave the Giants their seventh straight victory, a 5-3 decision over the Reds. San Francisco thereby recorded the first four-game sweep ever by an opponent at Riverfront Stadium.

July 18—Milt May's grand slam was the telling blow in a four-run ninth at St. Louis, giving the Giants an 8-7 victory. Larry Herndon belted two triples and scored three runs.

July 23—The Giants turned on the power in a 14-6 romp over the Cubs. Mike Ivie and Rennie Stennett each clouted four hits among the club's twenty-one, and Clark contributed a three-run homer and four RBI.

Sept. 2—Vida Blue pitched a two-hitter for ten innings, but left the game tied 1-1 in a contest eventually won by the Phillies, 2-1.

Oct. 3—The first triple play in Candlestick Park history involved three rookie infielders for the Giants. San Diego's Dave Cash was the batter and his liner turned into a triple play handled by second baseman Guy Sularz, shortstop Joe Pettini and first baseman Rich Murray.

Dec. 8—The Giants began a busy week of wheeling and dealing at the winter meetings in Dallas. Bob Knepper and Chris Bourjos were sent to Houston for Enos Cabell and a player to be named; John Montefusco and Craig Landis went to Atlanta for Doyle Alexander, and Jerry Martin and Jose Figueroa were obtained from the Cubs for Joe Strain and Phil Nastu. Owner Bob Lurie also pulled a shocker by firing manager Dave Bristol during the meetings.

1981

Jan. 14—Frank Robinson was named manager of the Giants, becoming the first black skipper in the National League.

Feb. 9—Free agent second baseman Joe Morgan was signed by the Giants, Little Joe citing Robinson's presence as a key factor in his decision.

April 20—The Giants acquired outfielder Jeff Leonard and utility man Dave Bergman from Houston for first baseman Mike Ivie, the last great deal executed by General Manager Spec Richardson.

April 28—Right-hander Allen Ripley fired a three-hit, 6-1 victory at Dodger Stadium. Jack Clark cracked a three-run homer and Joe Morgan added a solo shot.

May 9—Billy North, hardly a power hitter, belted a grand-slam homer and a double off Steve Rogers, totaling six RBI in Vida Blue's 8-2 breeze at Montreal.

May 10—North didn't have much time to savor his slugging prowess. One day later, unheralded Expos right-hander Charlie Lea pitched a no-hitter, downing the Giants 4-0 in the second game of a doubleheader at Olympic Stadium.

May 22—Darrell Evans and Jerry Martin pooled their talents for a 6-3, fifteen-inning victory at Houston. Evans' triple and Martin's single gave the Giants a 3-2 lead in the fourteenth, but Houston tied the game in the bottom of the inning. Evans belted a two-run single and Martin added a run-scoring single in the fifteenth.

June 2—The Giants' last hurrah before the strike produced a nine-run fourth and a 15-7 romp over the Reds. Martin had a grand slam and a single in the fourth, and Morgan belted a two-run homer.

July 7—Tom Haller succeeded Spec Richardson as general manager, carrying the title of vice-president of baseball operations. The change occurred during the strike, a period in which the club also released Billy North and Randy Moffitt.

August 9—The All-Star Game at Cleveland marked the resumption of play and Blue was the winner of the Nationals' 5-4 victory. Vida thereby became the only man to win for each league in the All-Star Game.

August 15—Doyle Alexander posted a 5-2 victory at Cincinnati, becoming one of four active major leaguers to defeat all twenty-six existing major league teams.

August 27—Clark's one-out home run in the thirteenth inning defeated the Pirates, 5-4. Clark previously belted a three-run double.

Sept. 3—Doyle Alexander pitched a two-hit, 12-0 rout of the Cubs, retiring the last twenty batters. Evans, Leonard, and Larry Herndon each rapped three hits, and Clark hammered his one-hundredth career homer.

Sept. 4—Clark's two-out homer in the tenth nudged the Cubs, 3-2.

Sept. 6—Blue pitched six hitless innings before Bill Buckner spoiled the no-hit bid with a one-out single in the seventh. Vida settled for a three-hit, 3-0 victory over the Cubs, also slapping a run-scoring single.

Oct. 1—Doyle Alexander downed the Braves for his team-leading eleventh victory. Doyle finished with a 6-0 record and a 2.08 ERA at Candlestick, but announced he wouldn't be back if his contract was not renegotiated. He was traded to the Yankees the next spring.

Nov. 15—Right-hander Ed Whitson was traded to Cleveland for second baseman Duane Kuiper, triggering a rash of winter dealings by Haller. At the winter meetings in Florida, Herndon was swapped to Detroit for pitchers Dan Schatzeder and Mike Chris. One day later, Jerry Martin went to the Royals for pitchers Rich Gale and Bill Laskey.

1982

April 25—Jeff Leonard's grand slam capped a five-run eighth, and the Giants downed the Dodgers 6-3 before 47,808 at Candlestick.

April 28—Rookie Bill Laskey became an instant sensation by pitching a three-hit, 7-0 victory over the Expos shortly after his recall from Phoenix. Champ Summers, acquired in the spring from Detroit, had three singles and a walk.

April 30—The club's flair for late-inning triumphs surfaced in a 5-4 victory over the Mets, who entered the bottom of the ninth leading, 4-2. Jim Wohlford led off with a single, Jeff Ransom walked, and pinch hitter Reggie Smith smashed a three-run homer off Neil Allen.

May 28—Jack Clark snapped a prolonged slump with a three-run homer and a two-run homer off John Candelaria, powering a 10-5 victory at Pittsburgh.

May 29—Clark's grand slam and a two-run homer produced a 9-5 victory at Three Rivers Stadium. The S.F. slugger had eleven RBI and four home runs in two games.

June 1—Clark's pinch single in the eleventh earned a 4-3 victory at St. Louis.

June 5—Right-hander Rich Gale belted a two-run homer off Doug Bird at Chicago to beat the Cubs, 2-1.

June 19—Rookie Chili Davis' grand-slam homer was the big blow in a six-run ninth at Atlanta, downing the Braves, 9-4.

June 29—Rookie left-hander Atlee Hammaker, obtained from Kansas City in a swap for Vida Blue on March 30, pitched a four-hitter and cracked an RBI single in a 3-0 conquest of the Reds.

July 3—Chili Davis' leadoff homer in the fifteenth inning broke a tie and lifted the Giants to a 4-3 victory at San Diego.

July 5—Undaunted by a Veterans Stadium record crowd of 63,501, Laskey pitched the Giants to a 3-1 victory over the Phillies.

July 11—Milt May's tenth-inning homer edged the Expos 8-7 at Montreal. Smith, May, and Summers hit successive home runs in the second inning off Scott Sanderson, the first time the Giants hit three in a row since 1969.

August 1—Frank Robinson was inducted into the Hall of Fame at Cooperstown, N.Y., while coach Jim Davenport handled the club in a weekend series at the Astrodome.

August 3—The Giants, in fourth place and thirteen games behind the Braves, triggered their amazing comeback with a 6-3 victory at Atlanta. Rookie Tom O'Malley's two-run homer was the big blow in a four-run ninth, starting S.F. toward ten straight victories.

August 6—The most stirring victory during the streak found the Giants overcoming a 6-0 lead by Nolan Ryan in the sixth inning to win 7-6 with a three-run ninth. Clark and Smith hit back-to-back homers in the ninth for a tie. Pinch hitter Bob Brenly singled and eventually scored the winning run on a single by pinch hitter Darrell Evans. Clark and Smith each had two solo homers.

August 11—Morgan's walk and Smith's two-run homer in the twelfth edged the Braves 8-6 at Candlestick, giving the Giants ten straight wins and pulling them to within four games of first place.

August 20—The Cardinals were ahead 7-0 after six innings at St. Louis, but the Giants tied it with seven runs in the seventh, featuring a three-run homer by Leonard. Bruce Sutter took over in the eighth and was an 8-7 loser on Evans' triple and May's one-out, run-scoring grounder.

Sept. 4—The Giants did it again, falling behind the Cardinals 4-0 before winning 5-4 with three in the ninth at Candlestick. Leonard started things with a leadoff single, Morgan singled, and Clark clouted a game-winning, three-run homer.

Sept. 24—The Dodgers led 2-0 in the opener of a three-game series at Los Angeles, but Chili Davis' two-run double off Bob Welch in the fifth created a tie. The Giants won 3-2 when Davis singled and scored on Evans' two-out single in the eighth off Steve Howe before 50,606.

Sept. 25—Run-scoring singles by Davis and Morgan knocked home a pair of unearned runs in the eighth, and the Giants shaded the Dodgers 5-4 in front of 51,172 disbelievers.

Sept. 26—A three-run fifth off Burt Hooton carried the Giants to a 3-2 victory and a sweep of the three-game series, leaving S.F. one game out of first place entering the final week of home games. Morgan's walk started the winning rally, Clark followed with a run-scoring double, and Evans hammered a two-run homer. Fred Breining was the winner with help from Al Holland, who had his relief string snapped at 17 2/3 innings and fifty-eight batters without a hit.

Sept. 30—Another improbable victory kept the flag hopes flickering. The Astros were ahead 5-0 entering the seventh, but Ron Pruitt's two-run, two-out single in the bottom of the ninth produced a thrilling, 7-6 victory. It was Pruitt's first hit of the season.

Oct. 3—If the Giants couldn't win, they could do the next best thing—knock the hated Dodgers out of the race. Morgan's three-run homer off Terry Forster in the seventh downed the Dodgers 5-3 and gave the division crown to Atlanta by one game.

Dec. 14—The most controversial swap in General Manager Tom Haller's regime sent Joe Morgan and Al Holland to Philadelphia for pitchers Mike Krukow and Mark Davis, plus minor league outfielder Charles Penigar. The deal was made to assure added pitching depth for the future, but Morgan's leadership qualities contributed to the chemistry of the '82 club and were to be missed in '83.

1983

Feb. 8—The Giants acquired free agent outfielder Joel Youngblood, who was to prove a great addition—as an infielder—during the upcoming season. Youngblood, with no room to play in the outfield, filled in at second and third, and was a virtual regular in the second half, batting .317.

April 17—Left-hander Atlee Hammaker pitched a perfect game for seven innings in the opener of a doubleheader with Cincinnati at Candlestick Park. Johnny Bench's leadoff single snapped the string, but Hammaker finished with a two-hit, 3-0 victory, aided by Jeff Leonard's homer.

April 23—Hammaker fired his second consecutive shutout, a three-hit, 5-0 triumph at Chicago. The Cubs didn't have a hit until Larry Bowa led off the sixth with a single. Chili Davis' two-run homer and a sacrifice fly did most of the offensive damage.

May 14—Darrell Evans, in the midst of a blazing May that would earn him National League Player of the Month honors, belted two home runs for three RBI in an 8-7 victory at Cincinnati, helping the Giants sweep the four-game series.

May 18 — Jack Clark, who entered the game with only four hits in 36 trips with runners in scoring position, belted a run-scoring grounder in the first, a sacrifice fly in the fifth and a grand-slam homer in the seventh at Philadelphia to power a 8-1 romp. The six RBI gave Mike Krukow and Greg Minton plenty of support on a combined six-hitter.

May 26—Picking up where they left off the previous year, the Giants began 1983 play at Dodger Stadium with a 5-3 victory. Leonard connected for a pair of homers off Jerry Reuss to lead the attack. Bill Laskey, National League Pitcher of the Month for May at 6-0, earned the victory with help from Greg Minton.

June 11—Evans, ending a 6-for-41 slump, erupted with four straight hits, including a pair of home runs, to drive in five runs in a 7-6 victory at Atlanta.

June 15—Evans enjoyed the most prodigious slugging performance of his career by belting three home runs at Candlestick to drive in six runs during a 7-1 romp over the Astros. Evans hit a solo shot off Mike LaCoss in the first, a three-run homer off La Coss in the third, and a two-run poke off Vern Ruhle in the seventh for his 250th career homer. It was the club's first three-homer game since Gary Matthews did it on September 25, 1976.

June 18 — The Giants continued to give the Braves trouble by rallying from a 4-0 deficit after five innings to edge Atlanta, 5-4, at Candlestick. Clark's two-run homer in the sixth triggered the comeback and the Giants won it in the bottom of the eighth when Leonard's solo homer followed a two-run blast by Davis.

June 24—Krukow's first major league two-hitter stifled the

Padres, 5-0. He retired twenty-one of the last twenty-two batters after Luis Salazar singled in the third. Salazar also doubled in the first for the other hit. Rookie John Rabb powered the victory with a pair of doubles.

July 15 — Hammaker seemed destined for defeat when the Cardinals scored twice in the eighth for a 4-2 lead, but the Giants rallied for three runs in the bottom of the inning to down the champs, 5-4. Leonard, who had a two-run triple in the third, hit a sacrifice fly for the first run in the eighth and Davis followed with a two-run homer.

July 22—Clark tagged his "cousin" Pirates for five hits in five trips during a 5-3 victory at Pittsburgh. The five Clark singles resulted in the Giants' first five-hit performance since Evans and Terry Whitfield each turned the trick on July 17, 1978.

July 24 — Leonard's second career grand-slam came in the 10th inning at Pittsburgh and produced an 8-5 victory, salvaging a double-header split. Youngblood had a homer, double, single and three RBI.

July 30 — Left-hander Mark Davis made his Giants starting debut a memorable occasion by blanking the Dodgers on seven hits to prevail over Reuss 8-0 at Candlestick.

Aug. 5 — Johnnie LeMaster hit two home runs in a game for the first time as a professional and the Giants rolled to a 7-1 victory over Houston behind Laskey, Minton and Gary Lavelle.

August 10—Evans, returning to the park where he broke into the majors, smashed a three-run, 400-foot home run to center off Terry Forster in the top of the ninth, snapping a tie and propelling the Giants to a 7-4 victory at Atlanta's Fulton County Stadium.

Aug. 15 — Leonard, continuing a torrid August, knocked in four runs with a three-run homer and a triple and Evans blasted a two-run homer among four hits in a 7-3 crunching at Dodger Stadium.

Aug. 23 — Krukow didn't allow an earned run in eight strong innings and the Giants erupted for three runs off ex-teammate Al Holland in the bottom of the eighth for a 3-1 conquest of the Phillies. Steve Nicosia, recently acquired from Pittsburgh in exchange for Milt May, made it 1-1 with a pinch-single and Evans followed with a two-run homer.

August 24—Youngblood's two-run homer off Steve Carlton in the bottom of the ninth snapped a tie and gave the Giants a 5-3 victory and a sweep of the series with Philadelphia at Candlestick. Bob Brenly also belted a two-run homer as the winners posted their first home sweep of a three-game series from the Phillies since June 1-3, 1973.

Sept. 11—Hammaker, though winless since July 10, struck out a career-high fourteen Astros, but was not involved in the decision when the Giants rallied for three runs in the bottom of the ninth to defeat Nolan Ryan, who fanned eleven. No Giants pitcher had struck out more batters since Gaylord Perry's club-record fifteen in 1966. It also was a National League strikeout high for 1983. A two-run single by pinch hitter Dave Bergman tied the game, and Tom O'Malley's pinch single won it.

Sept. 16—Mark Davis extended his streak to eighteen scoreless innings against the Dodgers with a two-hit, 1-0 victory. Davis also singled and scored the only run in the sixth, on Leonard's single off Fernando Valenzuela, who was winless at Candlestick since April of 1981. It was Davis' second major league shutout, both against L.A.

Sept. 18—Youngblood knocked in four runs with a two-run homer and a single, and Breining pitched eight shutout innings in a 6-3 victory for a sweep of the three-game series. It was the first sweep of more than two games against L.A. at Candlestick since June 26-29, 1975, and gave the Giants ten victories in their last thirteen games with the Dodgers.

Oct. 1—Mark Davis continued his mastery over the Dodgers, limiting them to one hit for eight innings before giving way to Gary Lavelle in the ninth during the Giants' 4-1 victory at Los Angeles. Before the Dodgers erupted in the ninth, the left-handed Davis had shut them out in twenty-six consecutive innings. Rookie Chris Smith did the big damage offensively with a two-run double. The Giants also won the season finale on Oct. 2, giving them a 13-5 record against the division champions.

Dec. 20—Manny Trillo, winner of four Gold Gloves, was signed as a free agent to play second base.

1984

Feb. 26 —First baseman Al Oliver, with a .305 lifetime average and eight consecutive .300-plus seasons, was acquired from the Montreal Expos for pitcher Fred Breining and a player to be named.

April 7 — Rookie righthander Jeff Robinson, making the jump from Class A to the majors, fired six innings of shutout ball and allowed only four singles in his major league debut. He also had the game-winning RBI with a grounder to second on his first at bat in an 11-0 rout of the Cardinals.

May 6 — Jack Clark knocked in the first two runs with a homer and a sacrifice fly before singling and scoring the winning run on Dusty Baker's triple in a 3-2 victory at St. Louis. The win enabled the Giants to sweep the Cardinals on the road for the first time since May 6-8, 1966, the final series at old Busch Stadium.

June 13 — Chili Davis, Jeff Leonard, Jack Clark, Al Oliver, Joel Youngblood, Bob Brenly, Brad Wellman and pinch-hitter Duane Kuiper cracked a club-record eight straight hits in a seven-run, fifth-inning rally at Dodger Stadium. The eruption, which included seven singles and Wellman's double, buried the Dodgers, 10-5.

June 16 — Chili Davis slammed a two-run homer in the first inning and added a three-run homer in the fifth to power a 6-3 victory at San Diego.

June 17 — Run-scoring singles by Al Oliver and Jeff Leonard in the 15th inning cracked a tie and earned a 5-3 victory at San Diego after Oliver's single in the eighth created a 3-3 deadlock.

June 27 — Dusty Baker stole second, third and home in the third inning against the Reds, the first player to do so since Pete Rose in 1980. But it took Chili Davis' pinch-hit grand-slam to produce a 14-9 victory for the Giants. Baker, curiously, stole only one other base all season.

June 29 — The game was delayed 57 minutes because of a lighting failure at Candlestick. Then Jeff Robinson put out the Pirates' lights with a five-hit shutout that consumed a mere one hour and 57 minutes.

July 13 — The Giants and the Pirates played 18 innings and 5:11 in the nightcap of a doubleheader at Three Rivers Stadium. The Longest Night concluded on Jason Thompson's bases-loaded single in the 18th, earning a 4-3 Pittsburgh victory. Frank Williams pitched six innings of three-hit shutout relief for the Giants.

Aug. 5 — Danny Ozark's first game as interim manager resulted in a 7-4 victory at Atlanta when Jeff Leonard belted a ninth-inning grand-slam off Donnie Moore. Leonard dedicated the homer to Frank Robinson, who was fired in the late hours the previous night after guiding the club to a 42-64 record.

Aug. 7 — Jeff Leonard belted five hits in five trips and knocked in three runs during a 9-2 romp at The Astrodome.

Aug. 17 — New York Mets rookie Dwight Gooden struck out 12 Giants and Wally Backman's two-run homer in the top of the 10th sent Mike Krukow down to a disheartening 2-0 defeat at Candlestick. Gooden and Krukow were locked in a scoreless duel for nine innings and Krukow finished with a career-high 10 strikeouts.

Aug. 19 — Brad Wellman, a late-inning replacement, walloped a two-run homer off Mets relief ace Jesse Orosco in the bottom of the ninth at Candlestick, lifting the Giants to a dramatic, 7-6 victory in the opener of a doubleheader.

Aug. 24 — The Giants continued to play spoiler against the Mets, sweeping a doubleheader at Shea Stadium. Frank Williams became the first S.F. Giants pitcher to win each end of a doubleheader, working a total of one and two-thirds innings in the 7-6, 6-5 decisions. Greg Minton saved each game.

Aug. 29 — Bob Brenly hit an inside-the-park home run at Montreal in the 11th inning to edge the Expos. Brenly, riding a hot streak, was N.L. Player of the Week, Aug. 20-25, with a .440 average and four homers. His outburst powered a 9-3 road trip, second best in S.F. history.

Sept. 14 — Bob Brenly's two-run homer lifted the Giants to a 3-0 victory at Atlanta. It was his 20th, making him the first Giants catcher to reach that level since Dick Dietz in 1970.

Sept. 16 — Chili Davis smacked two home runs and had four RBI at Atlanta, extending his hitting streak to 18 games, longest on the club since Jack Clark's 26 straight in 1978. Davis was N.L. Player of the Week, Sept. 10-16, with 10 hits in 19 trips, including three homers.

1985

Feb. 1 — Jack Clark finally got his wish when the Giants traded him to St. Louis for lefthander Dave LaPoint, shortstop Jose Gonzalez, first-baseman David Green and utilityman Gary Rajsich. Clark went on to power the Cardinals into the World Series, whereas most of the players the Giants acquired were a disappointment. Gonzalez, perhaps not wishing to be identified with the controversial swap, changed his name to Uribe and became the regular shortstop. The deal came five days after the club sent veteran reliever Gary Lavelle to Toronto for righthander Jim Gott and two minor leaguers.

April 12 — Righthander Mike Krukow posted his first Giants victory at Dodger Stadium, going the distance for a 4-1 decision. The winners scored all of their runs in the third inning, a rally capped by Jeff Leonard's 400-foot, two-run homer to center.

April 19 — In an incident which set the tone for the worst season in Giants history, outfielders Jeff Leonard and Dan Gladden scuffled near the batting cage prior to a 4-2 loss at Cincinnati. Leonard, who provoked the altercation, resigned his team captaincy. Two days later, he called a team meeting to apologize and was reinstated as captain by manager Jim Davenport.

April 26 — The Reds took a 6-1 lead into the bottom of the ninth at Candlestick, but were jolted by a six-run rally in the Giants' greatest comeback of the year. Chili Davis led off with a double and scored on Jeff Leonard's single. Scot Thompson singled and Bob Brenly advanced the runners with a grounder to short. Brad Wellman belted a two-run single, pulling the Giants to within 6-4. With two out, pinch-hitter David Green walked and Dan Gladden smacked a game-winning, three-run homer off Ted Power.

May 5 — Dave LaPoint, a victim of non-support most of the season, figured out the best way to win when he hooked up against his former St. Louis teammates. The southpaw fired a six-hit, 5-0 shutout and made general manager Tom Haller happy by holding Jack Clark hitless in four trips. LaPoint and Jeff Leonard each cracked run-scoring doubles in a three-run fifth off Joaquin Andujar.

May 9 — Atlee Hammaker scattered three singles over eight innings and new relief ace Scott Garrelts struck out five batters the last two innings as the Giants edged the Cubs, 1-0, in 12 innings. The winning rally off Lee Smith started with two outs and none on base. Pinch-hitter Rob Deer singled, Dan Gladden was struck by a pitch and Manny Trillo lined a game-winning single to center.

May 12 — Jim Gott, who didn't bat with the Blue Jays, smashed a pair of solo homers in a 5-4 Giants victory over the Cardinals. Gott became the first Giants pitcher to accomplish the power feat since Dave Koslo in 1949. Reliever Scott Garrelts got the win on David Green's run-scoring single in the bottom of the 10th.

May 18 — The Giants erupted for six runs in the top of the 10th at Shea Stadium to bury the Mets, 8-2. Former teammate Gary Rajsich ended a zero-for-11 slump for the Giants, who had nine of the first 10 batters reach base in the 10th. The rally included a run-scoring double by Chili Davis followed by rookie Chris Brown's two-run homer.

June 11 — Bob Horner's two homers gave Atlanta a 4-0 lead after four innings, but some amazing relief by the Giants manufactured a 5-4 triumph in 18 innings, tying for the club's longest game since 1967. Greg Minton, Scott Garrelts, Mark Davis, Vida Blue and Frank Williams blanked the Braves on three singles over the final 14 innings. The winning rally began with two outs and nobody on base. David Green singled and stole second. After Jeff Leonard was walked intentionally, Bob Brenly lined a run-scoring single to left off Gene Garber, giving the Giants their first lead in 63 innings!

June 14 — Padres righthander Andy Hawkins was 11-0, but he couldn't beat the Giants. Gary Rajsich's force grounder tied it in the bottom of the ninth and David Green's homer off Luis DeLeon with one down in the 11th won it, 5-4.

June 16 — Chris Brown knocked in four runs with a homer, double, and a single as the Giants won the opener of a doubleheader with San Diego, 7-3, before 25,845 at Candlestick. In the nightcap, each team dramatically scored once in the 12th before the Giants won it 5-4 in the 13th on Jeff Leonard's two-out triple and Brown's single.

June 17 — Atlee Hammaker gave his finest post-surgeries performance with a complete-game, four-hit, 4-0 victory over the Reds. Jeff Leonard had a run-scoring single in the first and a solo homer in the sixth.

June 27 — Jeff Leonard became the first Giants slugger since Dave Kingman in 1972 to hit for the cycle during a 7-6 loss at Cincinnati that capped an 0-7 trip. Manager Jim Davenport lost more respect by not fining or reprimanding Leonard for the player's verbal attack on third base coach Rocky Bridges. "What happened in the dugout united 25 guys against Davvy," remarked a player.

June 30 — Vida Blue's 7-4, second-game victory over Houston in a Candlestick Park doubleheader earned him a spot in the rotation. More importantly, it snapped a 10-game losing streak, longest in the club's San Francisco history, and ended a string of 12 straight defeats to the Astros. Blue also registered his 2,000th strikeout during the game.

July 5 — The Giants quieted a crowd of 38,766 at Wrigley Field by posting season highs for hits and runs in a 17-hit, 12-6 romp. The winners erupted for seven runs in the seventh inning for a 10-2 lead. Chris Brown had four hits, including a two-run homer.

Aug. 31 — Dwight Gooden hadn't lost since May 25, winning 14 in a row, and Jim Gott hadn't won since July 2, so 22,887 assembled at Candlestick Park to watch the Mets marvel attempt to continue his mastery of the Giants. Instead, Gott didn't yield an earned run in seven innings and Gooden was handed a 3-2 defeat, making him 20-4. Run-scoring singles by Ron Roenicke and Jose Uribe made it 2-0 after two innings and Chili Davis' sacrifice fly added a run in the eighth.

Sept. 6 — Rookie Chris Brown belted a three-run homer, a two-run double and a run-scoring double among his four hits, crushing the Expos with six RBI in an 8-3 romp. Jose Uribe and Chili Davis hit solo homers for the other runs.

Sept. 18 — Owner Bob Lurie, at a morning press conference, introduced Al Rosen as the club's new president and general manager. Rosen then announced Roger Craig as the field boss. The pair replaced Tom Haller and Jim Davenport, who had guided the Giants to a 56-88 record. The new leaders were treated to a 9-6 victory over the Padres that night.

Oct. 4 — Righthander Roger Mason, acquired from the Tigers in an April swap for Alejandro Sanchez, posted his first National League victory, stopping the Braves on a 10-strikeout, four-hitter, 1-0. It was Mason's initial major league shutout and the first for the Giants since July 18. Doubles by Alex Trevino and pinch-hitter Chris Brown in the bottom of the ninth defeated Rick Mahler.

Oct. 6 — "Bye-bye Love" and "I Left My Heart in San Francisco" played over the sound system in what potentially was the Giants' final game at Candlestick Park. A crowd of 14,537 showed up for the season finale, and was treated to a seven-run, sixth-inning rally by the home club. But Atlanta posted an 8-7 victory that made the Giants the biggest loser in the history of the franchise at 62-100.

Oct. 7 — As promised, Al Rosen began his shakeup by trading Dave LaPoint, Matt Nokes, and Eric King to Detroit for catcher Bob Melvin and pitchers Juan Berenguer and Scott Medvin the day following the conclusion of the season. In the coming months, he also would deal David Green, Manny Trillo, and Alex Trevino, the latter to the Dodgers for Candy Maldonado, Dec. 11.

1986

Jan. 29 — Bay area baseball fans issued a sigh of relief when owner Bob Lurie finally announced the Giants would stay in San Francisco and play at Candlestick Park. The announcement was linked to efforts for a new downtown stadium for the club.

Feb. 12 — Willie Mays concluded a six-year absence from baseball by becoming a special assistant to Al Rosen. Mays would appear in uniform at spring training, along with Hall of Fame-bound Willie McCovey.

April 8 — The new-look Giants made a rousing debut in an 8-3, Opening Night romp at the Astrodome. Will Clark's first major league swing resulted in a home run off Nolan Ryan, Robby Thompson doubled and Candy Maldonado hit a game-winning, three-run triple as a pinch-hitter.

April 9 — Will Clark's double produced the game-winning RBI and Scott Garrelts, now a starter, fired a 4-1 victory. The second straight triumph at the Astrodome doubled the club's 1985 total under glass.

April 20 — Lefthander Vida Blue became the 85th major leaguer to notch 200 victories when a 4-0 collaboration with Jeff Robinson capped a four-game sweep of the Padres before 39,548 paying customers. The Giants mustered only three hits, one of them a two-run homer by Chili Davis.

April 21 — Righthander Roger Mason pitched a three-hitter and Chili Davis cracked a pair of homers in a 5-1 victory that gave the Giants undisputed first place for the first time since Aug. 13, 1978.

April 22 — A seven-run first inning whereby the first nine Giants reached base produced a 10-3 rout of the Dodgers and a six-game winning streak. Chili Davis' two-run double was the big blow in the first and winning pitcher Mike Krukow contributed a run-scoring single.

April 26 — Will (The Thrill) Clark provided just what his nickname implied when his two-out homer in the top of the 10th gave the Giants a 3-2 victory at San Diego.

April 29 — Retread righthander Mike LaCoss, signed as a free agent in spring training, posted his first Giants victory, 2-0, with 7 1/3 scoreless innings against the Cardinals. Chris Brown's two-out double and Jeffrey Leonard's triple gave LaCoss all the support he required. (Leonard had decided to be called Jeffrey instead of Jeff.)

May 13 — San Francisco had blown a 4-0 lead when the host Cubs rallied for five runs in the bottom of the eighth, but pinch-hitter Candy Maldonado's two-out, two-run homer in the ninth vaulted the Giants to a 6-5 victory.

May 25 — Mike LaCoss enjoyed a dream game for a pitcher during an 11-3 romp over the Expos. He fell behind on Tim Wallach's three-run homer in the first and yielded only one hit the next seven innings. He also belted three singles and a double for three RBI to pace a 16-hit attack.

June 3 — Vida Blue was a winner for the first time since April 20 when the Expos were edged at Montreal, 7-6. The price was high because first-baseman Will Clark and centerfielder Dan Gladden suffered injuries that sidelined each for more than one month.

June 8 — The Giants' aggressive brand of ball stole a second-game victory and salvaged a doubleheader split with the Reds. With the score 1-1 in the eighth, successive squeeze bunts by Mike Woodard and Robby Thompson triggered a 3-1 victory. The winning rally also included Jeffrey Leonard's second sacrifice bunt in four years.

June 12 — General manager Al Rosen made his most vital in-season acquisition when the Giants signed utilityman Harry Spilman, recently released by the Tigers. Spilman was 13 for 32 (.406) with nine RBI as a pinch-hitter for his new club.

June 13 — Mike Scott entered the ninth inning with a three-hitter and a 1-0 lead at the Astrodome. Chris Brown walked with one out, Jeffrey Leonard singled and Dave Smith replaced Scott. Chili Davis promptly belted a three-run homer for a 3-1 victory on a combination three-hitter by Mike LaCoss and Mark Davis.

June 15 — Lefthander Bob Knepper had won eight in a row against his former team and topped the N.L. with 10 victories, but the Giants turned on him for a 7-2 triumph. Jeffrey Leonard and Chili Davis powered a 14-hit barrage with three apiece. Davis concluded a six-RBI, .333 spree which earned him N.L. Player of the Week honors.

June 22 — "It seemed like a World Series," crowed manager Roger Craig after a 4-2, 3-2 sweep of the Astros before 47,030 at Candlestick Park wrested first place from Houston. Mike Krukow posted his ninth victory in the opener and reliever Juan Berenguer won the nightcap. Berenguer was N.L. Player of the Week after winning one game and saving three others in five appearances.

June 23 — All 14 Giants who played hit safely and 12 of them scored in a 21-hit, 18-1 demolition of the Padres. It was the most runs for the franchise since an 18-7 drubbing of Cincinnati, Aug. 5, 1965. A five-run first featuring Mike Aldrete's two-run single got things going. Candy Maldonado hit a two-run triple in the five-run seventh. Mike LaCoss coasted to victory on a three-hitter and contributed four RBI with a double and a three-run homer.

July 3 — Mike Krukow, elated upon learning former Phillies teammate Steve Carlton was joining the Giants, fired a three-hit, 1-0 victory over the Cardinals. Randy Kutcher's two-out homer in the sixth took care of the scoring.

July 4 — Steve Carlton ended his silence with a press conference, but new teammates Mike LaCoss and Randy Kutcher stole the show in a 6-1 rout of the Cardinals. Kutcher homered leading off the first and added a two-run single in a five-run fourth. LaCoss, improving to 3-0 against St. Louis, didn't allow a hit after Vince Coleman opened the third with a double, finishing with a five-hitter and his eighth victory.

July 13 — Randy Kutcher hit his sixth homer in 24 major league games and first-baseman Harry Spilman had four RBI with a double and a three-run homer to give the Giants an 11-4 victory and a division lead at the All-Star break for the first time since 1978. Mike LaCoss improved to 9-3.

July 17 — The Giants opened the second half with a 6-4 victory at Wrigley Field, Vida Blue aiding his cause with his first home run since

1979 and Randy Kutcher adding a homer. The win placed the Giants nine games above .500 (49-40) for the first time since 1982 and gave them a two-game lead, biggest of the season.

July 22 — On the short end of a 10-7 decision at Busch Stadium, the Giants lost far more than a game following a bench-clearing brawl with the Cardinals. Upset with Vince Coleman's stolen bases with a 10-2 lead, the Giants responded by hitting the St. Louis speedster with a pitch, triggering the fight. While tackling Coleman, Giants ace Mike Krukow suffered a ribcage injury that cost him three starts and braked the club's momentum.

July 26 — Incomparable Steve Carlton posted his only Giants victory, blanking the host Pirates for seven innings in a 9-0 runaway. Frank Williams and Juan Berenguer completed the shutout. Bob Brenly's two doubles produced four runs. Carlton soon "retired," only to resurface with the White Sox.

Aug. 11 — Catcher Bob Melvin knocked in four runs with a homer and a bases-loaded triple and Bob Brenly added a three-run homer in a 13-4 outburst at Cincinnati made memorable by Pete Rose's last hurrah. Amid rumors that Rose's days as a starter were numbered, the Cincy skipper set a record with the 10th five-hit game of his career, blasting a double and four singles.

Aug. 15 — Mike Krukow posted his first victory since July 12 and lifted his record to 12-6 with a seven-hit, 5-1 decision over the Dodgers. Will Clark knocked in three runs with a pair of homers.

Aug. 20 — Mike Krukow and Don Carman of the Phillies fired a double shutout through nine innings, but the Giants ace was beaten, 1-0, on Juan Samuel's 10th-inning homer. Carman retired the first 24 batters, Bob Brenly ruining the perfect game with a leadoff double in the ninth, the club's only hit.

Aug. 26 — Lefthander Vida Blue pitched his finest game of the season with nothing to show for it, but the Giants emerged with a 1-0 victory over the Expos on pinch-hitter Harry Spilman's 12th-inning single. Blue worked the first nine innings, relinquishing one hit, and Scott Garrelts fired one-hit relief for three innings and was the winner.

Sept. 2 — Mike Krukow capped a brilliant season of pitching against the World Champion Mets when he posted a 4-3 victory at Shea Stadium. Bob Brenly's three-run homer helped Krukow finish 4-0 against New York, a feat no other hurler could claim. In the four victories, two of them over Dwight Gooden, Krukow received 31 runs of support while the Mets scored nine.

Sept. 7 — The fast-charging Krukow pitched a two-hitter, retiring 19 in a row in one stretch, to improve to 15-8 with a 1-0 victory over the Expos. Floyd Youmans, who lost a one-hitter, gave up the only run in the first when Robby Thompson was struck by a pitch and scored on Mike Aldrete's double.

Sept. 14 — Bob Brenly experienced one of the most bizarre games in the history of ANY major leaguer when the Giants hosted the Braves. Brenly's four errors at third base in the fourth inning tied a major league record and staked Atlanta to a 4-0 lead. Brenly then mounted a remarkable personal comeback by homering in the bottom of the fifth for the first Giants run. His two-out, two-run single in the seventh created a 6-6 tie, and Brenly ended the game with a two-out homer in the ninth for a 7-6 victory. "I've never seen anything like that," said manager Roger Craig. Not too many people had.

Sept. 26 — One day after Mike Scott embarrassed the Giants with a division-clinching no-hitter, Mike Krukow continued his march to 20 victories with a three-hit, 3-0 stifling of the Dodgers. Krukow, 19-8, was locked in a scoreless tie until the Giants scored thrice in the eighth with the help of Mike Aldrete's two-run triple.

Sept. 28 — Reliever Greg Minton, of all people, doubled with two outs in the 16th inning and stumbled home on Bob Brenly's single for an incredible, 6-5 victory over the Dodgers. A total of 52 players were used in the five-hour, 45-minute marathon, each team adding to the drama by scoring twice in the 14th. The Dodgers had a 3-0 lead entering the seventh, but homers by Chili Davis and Candy Maldonado helped carry the game into extra innings. Harry Spilman's two-run single in the 14th kept the club alive for Minton's heroics.

Oct. 5 — The Giants, finishing ahead of the Dodgers for the first time since 1971, capped an exciting season with an 11-2 romp in the season finale at Dodger Stadium. Mike Krukow became the club's first 20-game winner since Ron Bryant in 1973 and Candy Maldonado tormented his former team with two homers and six RBI. The final outburst fulfilled a prophecy for Maldonado, who told Krukow at midsummer that the ace would win his 20th on a grand-slam by Candy in Los Angeles.

1987

April 6 — The Giants gave an indication of the dramatics which followed by coming back from a 3–0 deficit to edge the Padres, 4–3, in 12 innings before an Opening Day crowd of 52,020 at Candlestick Park. Mike Krukow fell behind 3–0 in the eighth, but the Giants tied it in the bottom of the inning on a two-run double by Candy Maldonado. With two down in the 12th off reliever Dave Dravecky, singles by Jeffrey Leonard and pinch-hitter Bob Melvin were followed by Chili Davis' run-scoring single, ending the game. "It reminded me a lot of last year," Maldonado said. "We're on a mission and we know what we have to do. We don't have to talk about attitude. We can see it."

April 7 — Trailing 3–2 entering the bottom of the third, the Giants tied it on Melvin's first homer and won it 4–3 when he connected a second time leading off the seventh. "I'd never hit two homers in a major league game before," Melvin said.

April 8 — Chris Brown's two-run homer and the stout pitching of Roger Mason and Scott Garrelts enabled the Giants to sweep the opening series from the Padres with a 2–1 victory. Mason carried a shutout into the eighth and Garrelts registered four outs for his first save. "I have no idea why I was so sharp," said Mason, who struck out six and walked none.

April 9 — With the Dodgers stunned by the Al Campanis fiasco and offering little resistence, the Giants cruised to an 8–1 victory at Los Angeles behind Mark Davis' pitching and two-run homers by Chili Davis and Brown. "We've waited a long time for this," Chili said of the club's 4–0 start. "We have the hitting, pitching and the fielding. We just have to stay healthy."

April 10 — The Giants squandered a 4–0 lead, but rolled to their fifth straight victory, 5–4, on pinch-hitter Harry Spilman's two-out, run-scoring single in the 11th inning at Dodger Stadium. It was a costly victory, however, because Jose Uribe pulled a hamstring scoring the winning run. With two down in the 11th, Uribe lined a single to center off Tim Leary and stole second. Spilman followed with his game-winning hit and Uribe limped to the dugout.

April 13 — Robby Thompson's first career grand-slam and solo homers by Will Clark, Leonard and Melvin powered a 13–6 victory at San Diego. The Giants overcame consecutive home runs by Marvell Wynne, Tony Gwynn and John Kruk to open the Padres' first — the first time that ever happened at the start of a major league game. It was the first four-homer game for S.F. since June 15, 1983. Mason had the ignominious distinction of yielding the Padres' homers.

April 15 — Kelly Down's three-hit shutout gave the Giants a 1–0 victory and their second straight three-game sweep of the Padres. Maldonado accounted for all the scoring with a seventh-inning homer off Storm Davis. "Kelly is my new Mike Scott," manager Roger Craig declared after the club improved to 8–2. "He threw his first shutout, and it's so important to go nine innings."

April 18 — Thompson, pressed into action because the Giants were running out of infielders, doubled and scored the winning run on Clark's 10th-inning single to edge the Braves, 2–1, at Candlestick. The home club entered the bottom of the ninth trailing 1–0, but Leonard's triple and Maldonado's single produced a tie. "Robby's back was really hurting, but he wanted to hang around," Craig explained. "He thought he could bunt, but he didn't think he could swing the bat when we put him in the game in the eighth. That's a great example of intestinal fortitude."

April 20 — The Giants bolted to an 11–3 record, their second fastest start in San Francisco, by downing the Dodgers, 4–3, at Candlestick. Craig played a couple of hunches, substituting Mike Aldrete at first base and Chris Speier at second. Aldrete responded with his first four-hit game and Speier added a solo homer and two singles.

April 26 — With four double plays in a 6–4 victory at Atlanta, the Giants established a major league record with 13 DPs in three consecutive games, helping starter Mark Davis to a 3–0 record. "We're going to get a lot of double plays because of the split-finger fastball," Craig noted.

April 27 — Thompson, Brown and Chili Davis smashed home runs and the Giants notched another DP mark with their 15th in four straight games during a 7–3 rout of the Braves. The previous record was 14, shared by the 1951 White Sox, the 1952 Yankees and the 1955 Reds.

April 30 — The Giants concluded April with a 16–7 record, their best opening month since they went 18–6 in 1973, and became an unblemished 10–0 in one-run decisions with a 5–4 victory at Wrigley Field. It was a tie game until Speier doubled with one out in the ninth off Lee Smith and pinch-hitter Spilman followed with a run-scoring single. Spilman then stole his first base in 411 major league games. "It was a mistake," Spilman said. "It was supposed to be a hit-and-run."

May 1 — Rick Reuschel pitched a four-hitter at Three Rivers Stadium, knocking the Giants out of the division lead with a 4–2 victory. "He didn't give you anything good to hit," said Leonard, whose two hits boosted his batting average to .360.

May 4 — Maldonado became only the fourth S.F. Giant to hit for the cycle and his team overcame a 7–1 deficit to jolt the Cardinals, 10–7, at Busch Stadium. Maldonado's solo homer cut the St. Louis lead to 7–3 in the seventh. When Danny Cox struck Brown on the face with a pitch, fracturing his jaw, the Giants really came to life. Chili Davis' three-run homer was the big blow in a five-run eighth and Maldonado capped the scoring and his cycle with a run-scoring double in the ninth. "When Andre Dawson did it to us the week before in Chicago, I thought to myself that it would be awesome to hit for the cycle," Maldonado said. Added Leonard: "When Cox hit Brownie, it was all over." The Giants had 21 hits.

May 5 — Speier blasted his first grand-slam homer since September of 1972 and added a run-scoring single in a 10–6 drubbing of the Cardinals for a two-game sweep. Leonard belted two doubles and a single, giving him a 24-for-58 spree (.414) and a .376 average.

May 9 — Two unlikely sluggers powered a 9–4 victory over the Pirates at Candlestick. Rookie Mark Wasinger, making his first S.F. start, homered in the first inning and added three doubles, and Speier cracked his second grand-slam in five games. "It's supposed to be a Giants' thing for guys off the bench to play well," Wasinger said. Added Speier: "When you only hit three grand-slams in 15 years, it isn't routine." Atlee Hammaker fired a two-hit shutout over the final five innings for the win.

May 16 — The Giants enjoyed one of their rare 1987 victories over the World Champion Mets when Leonard snapped a tie with a 10th-inning homer off Jeff Innis for a 5–4 triumph before 48,128 at Shea Stadium. "Jeff is the MVP of this league right now," Craig declared.

May 19 — Responding to a tongue-lashing from their manager the previous night, the Giants rode two Leonard homers to a 6–2 victory at Montreal. Leonard also singled in five trips to recapture the league batting lead at .364, and Garrelts retired the only six batters he faced in relief of Mike LaCoss.

May 20 — Chili Davis drilled four singles and the blazing Leonard singled, doubled and tripled to raise his average to .371 in a 9–7 victory at Olympic Stadium. Jeff Robinson was flawless in relief, retiring the last 10 batters.

May 22 — Hammaker pitched six shutout innings for his first victory as a starter and the Giants edged the Phillies, 2–1, for their first win at Veterans Stadium since Aug. 23, 1985. "That was the Atlee of 1983," Leonard remarked after Hammaker retired the first 13 batters before yielding a hit. "He was baffling the hitters by pitching inside and out. They were confused." Added Craig: "Here's to my first win at the Vet as the Giants' manager."

May 24 — LaCoss blanked the Phillies for the first six innings and Thompson broke a tie with a three-run homer in the eighth, giving the Giants a 6–3 victory at Philadelphia. It gave the club a three-game division lead, its biggest since the 1973 club was 3½ games ahead, June 7, 1973. "I'm thrilled to death," Craig said.

May 31 — The Giants enjoyed a rare laugher and concluded an 11–15 May with a 17-hit, 8–0 thrashing of the Expos at Candlestick. Downs pitched a five-hitter for his second shutout and Leonard belted four hits to retake the league lead at .364. The Expos were so hopelessly behind, thirdbaseman Tim Wallach made his pitching debut and faced the minimum three batters in the eighth despite Bob Brenly's fourth single of the game. "You'd love to have a game like this every day," Craig said.

June 6 — Reliever Keith Comstock posted his first Giants' victory with three hitless innings and Maldonado's run-scoring single in the 12th inning earned a 4–3 decision at the Astrodome. Speier led off the 12th with a double, Thompson sacrificed and Maldonado came through following a grounder by Leonard.

June 9 — One night after the Giants alledgedly were demoralized by a 7–6 loss at Riverfront Stadium, they pulled to within two games of the Reds with a 10–2 romp. Clark, who feasted on Cincy pitching all season, led the way with a two-run homer, a two-run double, four RBI and three runs scored. Mark Davis went the distance for the win, snapping a personal four-game losing streak.

June 10 — Solo homers by Kal Daniels off Jim Gott gave the Reds a 2–0 lead, but the Giants roared back to win the series, 9–4, and climbed within one game of Cincinnati. Maldonado's third double of the game knocked in the go-ahead run in a four-run eighth, and the Giants joyfully concluded a 3–3 trip to Houston and Cincy.

June 19 — It was a struggle, but the Giants ended a season-high, six-game losing streak with a 7–6 victory at San Diego. The Padres were ahead 5–0 after six innings behind Dravecky, but the Giants scored thrice in the seventh and four times in the eighth, a rally featuring run-scoring doubles by Maldonado and Chili Davis and a two-run double by Clark off Craig Lefferts.

June 21 — The Giants crushed Eric Show and the Padres, 11–2, amid rumors a deal was in the works involving a San Diego starter. "A guy like Dravecky or Show would win the division for San Francisco," said prophetic San Diego manager Larry Bowa. Rookie Matt Williams enjoyed a two-run homer and the first three-hit game of his career. Brenly became the first Giant to steal home since Joel Youngblood did it at Houston, Aug. 7, 1984.

June 25 — After dropping two games to the Reds to fall 4½ games behind, the Giant salvaged a win in the series with a dramatic, 7–6 victory at Candlestick. Five solo homers by Maldonado, Speier, Aldrete, Thompson and Brenly made it 5–5 until the ninth, when the Reds scored to take a one-run lead. The home club rallied for two in the bottom half on pinch-hitter Youngblood's run-scoring double and Clark's one-out force to centerfielder Eric Davis, who nailed the runner at second in a bizarre finish.

June 28 — Pinch-hitter Spilman roughed up old hunting buddy Nolan Ryan with a three-run homer into the upper deck at Candlestick in the fifth inning, powering an 8–4 victory. Hammaker got the win, but Comstock protected it by facing the minimum 12 batters over the final four innings, yielding one hit. "That was one of the longest homers I've ever seen here," Craig noted. "Nolan probably won't take Harry hunting after that."

July 4 — Saddled with a mediocre 39–40 record following a 5–3 loss to the Cubs at Wrigley, the Giants announced a blockbuster trade that sent Brown, Comstock, Mark Davis and Mark Grant to San Diego in exchange for Dravecky, Lefferts and Kevin Mitchell. "It was tough to trade Chris," general manager Al Rosen said, "but you obviously have to give something to get something. Brown was the key for them, but I like lefthanders — and Dravecky is one of the toughest in the league." That same day, Williams was optioned to Phoenix because Uribe was ready to play and Joe Price was purchased from the Triple-A club. It proved to be the most significant day in the club's title march.

July 5 — Mitchell immediately sweetened the pot for the Giants by smashing a pair of two-run homers at Wrigley, powering a 7–5 victory over the Cubs in his S.F. debut. Speier's two-run, pinch-double in the eighth inning was the winning blow. Price worked two scoreless innings. "I really don't know what happened today," Mitchell said. "I'm tired and I'm still hurting inside over the trade because San Diego is my home."

July 6 — Dravecky blanked the Pirates for the first five innings in his Giants' debut and was rewarded with a 7–5 victory at Three Rivers Stadium. Leonard powered the offense with three hits, including a home run. "Sure there were jitters," Dravecky said. "I normally have butterflies in my stomach before I pitch, anyway. They were just a little bigger tonight. I'm happy with the trade — I picked up 12 games in the standings."

July 8 — Chili Davis crawled out of a hospital bed after a bout with food poisoning and belted a three-run homer in the 14th inning, pacing an 8–4 victory over the Bucs. Jeff Robinson relinquished only one hit over the final 4⅓ innings for the win. "I was swinging the bat good before I went into the hospital, so it's no big deal," Davis said.

July 9 — In a dramatic finish that typified the Giants-Cardinals rivalry in 1987, visiting S.F. scored three times in the top of the 10th for a 6–3 lead, only to have the Redbirds rally for four runs in the bottom half for an improbable 7–6 decision. Aldrete's two-run single capped the top of the 10th, but the Cards bunched four walks with three hits to pull it out. Willie McGee's two-run double was the big blow, and pinch-hitter Jose Oquendo ended the game with a run-scoring single.

July 11 — A crowd of 49,652, fifth largest in Busch Stadium history, watched Garrelts strike out six batters the final 2⅓ innings to seal Downs' 3–1 victory over the Cardinals.

July 19 — Aldrete, on a hot streak ever since he replaced the injured Maldonado in right field, led off the bottom of the eighth with a home run, lifting the Giants to a 4–3 victory over the Cubs at Candlestick. Davis' two-run homer in the first inning helped the winners to a 3–0 lead. "I'm becoming more comfortable with my situation," Aldrete said. "It hasn't gotten to the point where I must play regularly. I'm not an established player. I've just had two hot weeks."

July 21 — Dravecky went the distance with a six-hitter and blanked the Bucs, 7–0, at Candlestick. Aldrete and Brenly hit solo homers and Davis drilled a two-run triple.

July 25 — Pinch-hitter Oquendo, a thorn in the Giants' side all season, hit a two-run homer for a 4–4 tie in the seventh, but Brenly's run-scoring single in the bottom half gave the home club a 5–4 victory over the Cardinals. Garrelts struck out the side in the ninth and earned a save.

July 26 — Clark won the first game with a three-run homer in the 10th and cracked a tie with a solo homer in the fifth inning of the nightcap, powering a 6–3, 5–2 sweep of the Cardinals before 41,256 at Candlestick. The longball show pulled the club to within one game of first-place Cincinnati. "It was their speed versus our power," Clark said. "This is a great confidence-builder."

July 29 — The Giants turned on the power at Dodger Stadium, generating 16 runs out of 16 hits in a 16–2 rout. Krukow went the distance for his second victory of the season and Davis sparked the offense with a three-run homer and a double for five RBI.

August 1 — Clark's two-run homer in the first inning triggered a 7–3 victory in the second game of a Riverfront Stadium series. LaCoss blanked the Reds until the sixth and got the win. "I got some pitches to hit and I did my job," said Clark, who had three hits and three RBI.

August 5 — The Giants were beyond themselves when they concluded a miserable 2–7 trip with a 6–5, 11-inning loss at the Astrodome with the help of a controversial call by umpire Dutch Rennert. The fourth straight defeat knocked the club five games behind the Reds with a 53–55 record. The trip wasn't a total loss, however. Don Robinson was acquired from Pittsburgh, July 31.

August 7 — LaCoss pitched his most important game of the season, stifling the Reds on five hits, 3–1, at Candlestick to ignite the Giants' title push. Clark and Mitchell homered. "That was the game that turned us around," Craig noted.

August 8 — Hammaker, staked to a four-run, first-inning lead, shackled Cincy on a four-hitter for a 5–2 victory that cut the Reds' lead to three games. Clark had a sacrifice fly in the first and a solo homer in the sixth. Maldonado, playing his first game in six weeks while recuperating from a broken thumb, belted a run-scoring double on his first at bat.

August 9 — Krukow and Downs each worked into the ninth inning, helping the Giants to a 3–2, 5–2 sweep of the Reds before 46,434 at Candlestick. The four-game sweep slashed Cincinnati's division lead to one game over S.F. "I've never felt better about this club in my two years here than I do now," Craig declared. "We managed to pick up four games in three days. That's what you call a real Humm-Baby."

August 10 — What did the Giants do for an encore? Plenty. Trailing the Astros 5–4 entering the bottom of the ninth, they got successive home runs from Maldonado and Clark off Dave Meads for a 6–5 shocker at Candlestick. "I feel I'm coming into my own," said Clark, who earned N.L. Player of the Week honors prior to his last-ditch heroics.

August 12 — Turning the tables on Mike Scott, the Giants scuffed the Houston ace with an 8–1 victory that gained a first-place tie for the first time since June 13. Brenly bashed a grand-slam and Hammaker and Don Robinson collaborated on a three-hitter. Clark extended his hitting streak to 10 games, but had his nine-game RBI string snapped.

August 15 — The Giants jumped on Fernando Valenzuela for three runs in the first inning, more than enough for Dravecky's three-hit, 5–0 victory at Candlestick. "That was the best I've seen Dave pitch with us," commented pitching coach Norm Sherry.

August 16 — LaCoss fired a three-hitter over 10 innings and the Giants posted their second straight shutout victory over the Dodgers, 5–0, in front of 52,374, 10th largest baseball crowd in S.F. history. L.A. reliever Tim Leary had two outs in the bottom of the 10th when pinch-hitter Davis lined a single to right and scored on Eddie Milner's double to center. "LaCoss is a money pitcher," Craig said. "We were five games out when we started the homestand. If he doesn't beat the Reds that night, we might be history."

August 19 — The Giants trailed 5–1 after five innings at Shea Stadium, but downed the Mets with a four-run 10th, 10–6. Davis broke the tie with a sacrifice fly, winner Garrelts belted a run-scoring double and Thompson added a two-run single in the 10th off Roger McDowell.

August 21 — In a most significant day on the title trail, the Giants snatched the division lead for good with a 6–3 victory at Montreal and also learned Reuschel would soon be their teammate. "Reuschel already has made us a better club," Craig chortled. "We're already 1–0 with him, and he's not even here yet." Added Rosen: "This gives us a better chance to win it." Two others obtained in trades fittingly were instrumental in the key triumph. Dravecky was the winner and Don Robinson pitched 3⅓ innings of hitless relief. Jeff Robinson was sent to Pittsburgh for Reuschel.

August 24 — Reuschel was staked to three runs in the first inning of his Giants' debut and fired seven strong innings in a 6–1 victory at Philadelphia. "I wanted to get the first one under my belt, and they made it easy for me," Reuschel said.

August 25 — Speier hit a solo homer in the eighth inning, cracking a tie and boosting the Giants to a 3–2 victory at Veterans Stadium. Garrelts retired seven of the eight batters he faced for his 11th victory. "Speier is our MVP," Craig insisted. "A lot of guys have done the job for us, but where would we be without Chris?"

August 26 — Brenly's two-out, two-run homer off Shane Rawley in the top of the ninth accounted for all the runs in the Giants' 2–0 victory at Philadelphia. The three-game sweep sent the club home with a 2½-game division lead. Dravecky and Robinson combined for a five-hit shutout. "That was the only mistake I saw him make all night," Brenly said after belting his 15th homer.

August 29 — The Giants erupted for five runs in the first inning and hammered the Mets, 9–1, behind Hammaker's seven shutout innings. Pinch-hitter Clark's two-run single was the key blow in the opening inning after N.Y. starter Sid Fernandez lasted only two batters because of a shoulder injury. Mitchell singled, doubled and tripled, scoring thrice against his former team.

August 31 — Dravecky pitched a five-hit shutout and Mitchell and Maldonado contributed solo homers in a 5–0 victory over the Expos at Candlestick. It gave the club a 4½-game lead, largest since June 6, 1973.

Sept. 4 — Clark, who repeatedly rose to the occasion during the championship season, hit a one-out homer in the bottom of the 10th for a 3–2 victory over the Phillies at Candlestick.

Sept. 5 — Uribe's two-run homer in the third inning was the big blow off Rawley and the Giants downed the Phillies, 6–3. "The Giants are in a groove," manager Lee Elia observed. "You don't expect Uribe to beat you with a homer, but a different guy is doing it for them every day."

Sept. 6 — Reuschel fired a two-hitter, retiring 27 of 30 batters in a 4–1 conquest of the Phillies. The three-game sweep concluded a 6–3 homestand and built the division lead to 5½ games. "Frankly, I don't see anyone catching us," Brenly said after belting a run-scoring double. "With the pitching we've got, I can't imagine us going into a losing streak. We've always got someone to stop the bleeding."

Sept. 8 — The Giants discouraged a sweep by Houston and maintained their 5½-game lead over the Astros with a crucial, 6–4 victory at the Astrodome. Houston had won the series opener, but Brenly's two-out walk in the ninth, Maldonado's single and Aldrete's two-run double snapped a tie after S.F. had squandered a 4–0 lead. "It was the biggest game of the year," Craig said. "Aldrete showed me he can handle pressure. That was the biggest hit of the year."

Sept. 12 — After dropping the opener of a three-game series at Riverfront, the Giants showed the Reds who's boss with a 7–1 thumping. Reuschel went all the way with a six-hitter and took care of much of the offense with a three-run double. Maldonado and Clark homered.

Sept. 13 — Mitchell homered and doubled for three RBI and the Giants slugged the Reds, 6–1, to return home with a six-game lead over Cincinnati. LaCoss, Lefferts and Robinson took care of the pitching, holding the Reds to six hits.

Sept. 16 — Houston was buried, 7–1, behind Dravecky's four-hitter and four home runs, including a pair of two-run blasts by Clark. The outburst gave Clark 31 homers, most on the Giants since Bobby Bonds hit 39 in 1973.

Sept. 17 — Reuschel's second two-hitter with the Giants and third of the season smothered the Astros, 4–0, at Candlestick and made it an eight-game lead. Brenly's two-run double and run-scoring singles by Aldrete and Maldonado did the bulk of the scoring damage.

Sept. 19 — It was the opener of a two-game series and the Reds desperately needed a sweep to stay alive. They didn't get it. LaCoss registered his team-leading 13th victory and Clark homered in a 5–1 win that knocked Cincy nine games behind with 14 to play.

Sept. 27 — The Braves thought it would be nice if they brought Phil Niekro back for one final start. The Giants enjoyed the nostalgia trip, too, notching a pair of six-run innings in a 15–6 victory that made a victory celebration imminent. Maldonado had a pinch-hit grand-slam and six RBI, and Uribe added a pair of triples among four hits, scoring four times.

Sept. 28 — Davis and Leonard belted their 100th career homers, each as a pinch-hitter, but the night belonged to Robinson as the Giants clinched their first championship since 1971. Robinson worked the final five innings, yielding one run, and cracked a tie with a leadoff homer in the eighth inning for a 5–4 victory. "I think it's fitting that this happened in front of my friends and family in San Diego," said Craig, who earlier in the day became a grandfather again.

Oct. 1 — Jolted by a strong earthquake that shook their downtown hotel in the morning, the Giants mildly succumbed to longtime nemesis Bob Welch's one-hitter at Dodger Stadium, 7–0. The champs were happy to get out of L.A., and later were ecstatic when Welch was traded to the American League.

Oct. 4 — The Giants punctuated the season by doing what they did best. Clark hit a pair of homers for a total of 35 and Davis and Brenly added one apiece, the latter producing a 5–4 victory over the Braves in 10 innings at Candlestick. A crowd of 51,216 set an all-time Giants' single-season attendance mark of 1,917,863. Davis' homer was his career-high 24th, and his last as a Giant. He went to the Angels as a free agent after the season. Brenly's homer was the club's 205th, breaking the former S.F. mark by one.

Oct. 6 — A three-run fifth, featuring a two-run single by winning pitcher Greg Mathews, helped the Cardinals win Game 1 of the National League Championship Series, 5–3, before 55,331 partisans. It was the largest Busch Stadium baseball crowd ever.

Oct. 7 — Dravecky was at the peak of his game with a two-hit, 5–0 victory that squared the series, 1–1. Clark's two-run homer off John Tudor in the second inning was all the support Dravecky needed before a record-equaling crowd of 55,331.

Oct. 9 — The Giants returned home to 57,913 fans, largest baseball crowd in Candlestick history, and quickly jumped to a 4–0 lead behind Hammaker. Jim Lindeman's two-run homer in the sixth triggered a Cardinals' comeback that earned a 6–5 victory. Vince Coleman's two-run single was the big blow in a four-run seventh that proved decisive.

Oct. 10 — With Leonard hitting a record fourth homer in the four successive games, the Giants made it 2–2 in the NLCS with a 4–2 victory before an even larger crowd of 57,997. Krukow went the distance in his finest 1987 performance, scattering nine hits and blanking St. Louis the final seven innings. Thompson's homer opened the S.F. scoring off Danny Cox in the fourth and Leonard's two-run blast gave the winners a 3–2 lead in the fifth. Brenly homered in the eighth.

Oct. 11 — Price became an unexpected hero when he blanked the Cardinals on one hit over the final five innings of a 6–3 victory before a record-scattering crowd of 59,363. It was 3–2 St. Louis before a four-run fourth off Bob Forsch and Ricky Horton represented the Giants' last hurrah of the NLCS. Davis and Clark started the winning rally with singles and Brenly walked, loading the bases. Uribe's two-run single to right gave S.F. a 4–3 lead. Pinch-hitter Aldrete's sacrifice fly and Thompson's triple concluded the Giants' scoring for the remainder of the playoffs.

Oct. 13 — Leonard was the object of attention for a taunting Busch Stadium throng of 55,331, and Tudor responded with a masterful performance, blanking the Giants for 7⅓ innings in a 1–0 gem. Dravecky yielded his only run in post-season competition — 1984 included — but it was enough to edge S.F., 1–0. It was a tainted run, at that, because rightfielder Maldonado lost Tony Pena's liner in the lights leading off the second, and it went for a triple. One out later, the pesky Oquendo hoisted a sacrifice fly to right and Pena eluded Melvin's lunge up the third base line to score. The winners mustered one hit over the final five innings off Dravecky and Robinson while the Giants were stranding five runners in that span.

Oct. 14 — The Giants' scoreless streak was extended to 22 innings by Cox, who thrust the Cardinals into the World Series with an eight-hit, 6–0 victory before another 55,331. Hammaker crumbled in a four-run second. Successive one-out singles by Terry Pendleton, Pena and McGee made it 1–0, and Oquendo landed the crowning blow with a three-run homer. That gave him three career homers, all against the Giants. With two singles in four trips, Leonard tied Terry Puhl (1980) and Ozzie Smith (1985) for the most hits in an NLCS: 10. He also earned the MVP trophy.

Dec. 1 — Brett Butler was signed by the Giants as a free agent, filling the void created by Davis' departure to the Angels. Butler, 30, had played four years with the Indians and was counted on to give S.F. its finest leadoff batter and centerfielder in several years.

2

HISTORY OF THE SAN FRANCISCO GIANTS

When Roger Craig walked into the Giants' lifeless clubhouse, Sept. 18, 1985, he must have wondered what he was getting into as the newly-appointed manager of a demoralized baseball team going nowhere.

The players did some wondering, too. Who was this tall drink of water with the wide-brimmed hat and cowboy boots, and what could he possibly do to inject hope into a dead horse, one heading toward a franchise-record 100 defeats?

"I couldn't believe the attitude on the Giants when I took over that day," Craig recalled. "All I saw in the clubhouse was guys cleaning guns and thinking about hunting season. It definitely was a country-club atmosphere."

General manager Al Rosen, who also took charge that fateful September day and hired Craig, also didn't like what he saw. A major house-cleaning was imperative, as was a significant attitude adjustment.

Well, the party soon was over and a celebration was about to begin, one which culminated in a division championship merely two years later. By soaring from 62–100 to 90–72, the Giants became only the fourth team in major league history since 1900 to finish first during a full season two years following a 100-loss disaster.

"I don't think any of us who were here in 1985 could imagine we'd win the division two years later," veteran catcher Bob Brenly said. "Naturally, there was skepticism when Al and Roger took over, but their optimism gave us hope and we gained confidence by winning in 1986."

The first thing Craig and Rosen did was remove all doubt regarding who was in charge of a tattered bunch of players lacking in self-esteem. But when clubhouse leaders like Jeffrey Leonard, Mike Krukow and Brenly fell in line, the others followed.

"I bought their act from the start," said Leonard, who immediately began towing the line by wearing his baseball cap in the conventional manner. "We needed direction and we could tell Roger and Al were serious about winning."

Since actions speak louder than words, the Giants and their followers needed physical evidence. That came the following spring, when Craig boldly predicted victory and the players justified that faith with the club's first winning (13–8) April since 1973.

Clark, Thompson promoted

There was risk involved. Craig took a gamble by starting two rookies from the lower minors, firstbaseman Will Clark and secondbaseman Robby Thompson. That precocious pair and ex-Dodger outfielder Candy Maldonado represented the most significant changes from the 1986 debacle.

"Roger didn't convince us overnight," Krukow noted. "There were no major trades, and we came to camp with basically the same people as we had in 1985, and he still insisted we were going to win. I'm sure some guys thought he was crazy."

"There was skepticism, but our confidence came from Roger. We started winning, and suddenly we realized we were competitive. We opened on the road against two teams (Houston and Los Angeles) which had beaten the daylights out of us in 1985."

"We won both series and took it from there," Krukow said. "We were the bratty child who needed discipline. Roger did it by paying attention to detail and not playing favorites. We had a manager who could think more than one inning ahead."

The revived Giants also had a new battle cry. The inspirational play of journeyman catcher Brad Gulden during spring training prompted Craig to nickname him Humm-Baby. The monicker quickly caught on, and the term soon became the symbol of the club's new spirit.

"The biggest reason for our early success was what we called a humm-baby attitude," Craig recalled. "I saw a bunch of hungry players eager to win. Before we took the field at Houston for the opener, I told them we had a chance to win the whole thing, and I meant it." .

Craig's confidence rubbed off instantly. The Giants used the quick start as a springboard toward the division lead by the All-Star break. The 1986 Giants remarkably spent 47 days in first place before injuries to key players like Leonard and Clark exacted their toll.

Still, the club finished 83–79, becoming only the eighth major league team since 1900 to post a winning record one year after losing 100 games. Moreover, the Giants developed a personality that was the essence of Humm-Babyism, an aggressive and opportunistic brand of ball that suddenly perked interest and commanded attention.

Masters of execution

The 1986 Giants were masters of execution, scoring 18 runs on squeeze bunts, drastically reducing errors and stealing 147 bases, most for the franchise since 1919. Those little things meant a lot, translating into 40 come-from-behind victories, 26 attained on the final at bat.

"I'm proud of the guys for finishing above .500 under the circumstances," noted Craig, referring to an inordinate number of injuries. "The players showed a lot of character and determination. We also had great play off our bench, which helped to pick up the slack."

Maldonado exemplified the humm-baby spirit by establishing a club record with 17 pinch hits, four of them homers, before Leonard's wrist injury made him a regular, Aug. 10. Despite limited duty as a starter, Maldonado belted 18 homers and had a team-high 85 RBI en route to Giants' MVP honors.

The powerful Puerto Rican crowned his and the club's turnaround year with two homers and six-RBI in a season-ending romp at Dodger Stadium. The longball demonstration rewarded Krukow with his 20th victory, a first for the Giants since Ron Bryant won 24 games in 1973.

By convincingly transforming a whimpering and whining loser into a contender, the Giants gained newfound respectability. "You ain't seen nothing yet" was Craig's winter theme, and he boldly predicted a championship season. The manager realistically had some reservations.

"If we stay healthy, we can contend," Craig predicted during the off-season, fully aware that six of the Giants' everyday players were coming off surgery. "My biggest concern is that our injuries heal sufficiently to allow us to play up to our potential."

Reasonably healthy, the Giants bolted to a 5–0 start and turned it into a 16–7 April. The robust hitting of outfielders Leonard (.354), Maldonado (.326) and Chili Davis (.302) was augmented by the stout pitching of Mark Davis (3–0, 2.19) and Jeff Robinson (2–0, 1.86, 4 saves).

Double the pleasure

The other elements of success included a defense that established major league double-play records during a weekend series at Atlanta, and a bench that capably filled the gaps when regulars were sidelined. Rookie shortstop Matt Williams took over when Jose Uribe was injured in early April, and the club didn't skip a beat afield.

Pitching problems primarily were responsible for an 11–15 May in 1987, yet the club remained in the thick of the race behind the blazing bat of Leonard, who overcame four surgeries to bat .390 with 13 doubles and seven home runs in the final 24 games of the month.

"The worst trade I ever made at Houston was letting Jeff get away to the Giants—he's incomparable in terms of value to this team, on and off the field," Rosen declared. Added Craig: "Jeff is the MVP of the league right now."

Maldonado was right behind. From May 2 till June 10, sweet-swinging Candy batted .381 with 13 doubles, eight homers and 28 RBI. "I always dreamed of playing as a regular, so I'm just making the best of my opportunity,'' Maldonado humbly pointed out.

But Maldonado broke his right ring finger on a fielding play during an 11-16 June and the sagging Giants entered the traditional halfway point of the season, July 4, looking more like a pretender than a contender at 39-40. ''I felt we were better than a .500 club, and I couldn't understand why we were playing .500 ball so long,'' Rosen said.

The general manager did something about it. He celebrated the Fourth of July by sending up a flare, trading Chris Brown, Mark Grant, Mark Davis and Keith Comstock to San Diego for Kevin Mitchell, Dave Dravecky and Craig Lefferts.

''We have a lot better shot at winning it now,'' Craig said enthusiastically. The players had a similar reaction, pointing to the dependability of proven veterans like Dravecky and Lefferts, as compared to the inconsistency of talented youngsters like Davis and Grant.

The stunning swap provided an instant fix. Mitchell made his Giants' debut at Wrigley Field, July 5, and promptly belted two home runs to power a 7-5 victory. The next day, Dravecky was a 7-5 winner at Pittsburgh. The club's confidence level suddenly was raised a few notches.

But the Giants' character had to survive one more stern test. It came during a trip to Los Angeles, Cincinnati and Houston. The club flunked. It went 2-7 and limped home with four straight defeats coming on home runs by opponents on their final at bats. A controversial call by an umpire in the final game at Houston merely added fuel to the flames.

If the Giants were to crumble and drop out of the race, that demoralizing trip provided the perfect opportunity. As is Craig's way, the team turned something negative into a positive motivating force.

The pivotal series

The Giants were frustrated and angry when they returned from Houston with a 53-55 record, trailing the first-place Reds by five games entering a four-game series with Cincinnati at Candlestick Park, Aug. 7.

''We've tried team meetings and everything else,'' Craig noted, ''so now we'll see if anger can motivate them.'' Three days later, the manager had his answer. Mike LaCoss pitched a five-hit, 3-1 victory in the opener. The next day, Atlee Hammaker pinned a 5-2 defeat on the Reds.

In a Sunday doubleheader before 46,434, Krukow and Kelly Downs fired 3-2 and 5-2 victories that completed an exhilarating four-game sweep and pulled the Giants to within one game of the division leaders.

''That series was our season,'' Krukow summed up. ''Had we lost those four games, we would have been nine down and pretty much out of it. You bet what happened in Houston motivated us. Things got serious.''

Craig also noted the difference. ''That Cincinnati series was the turning point,'' the manager said. ''Something happened to the club after that trip. There was an intensity I hadn't seen before. Everything sort of came together.''

That stirring sweep was followed by three wins in four games with the Astros, a feat that landed the Giants in a first-place tie. "We're on a roll," Craig noted. "We're healthy and we're playing well. We're a different ballclub now, and the other teams know it."

By the time a record, 9–2 homestand had concluded with two wins in three games with the Dodgers, the Giants were atop the division for good. Successive shutouts by Dravecky and LaCoss crowned the achievement, yet it was the slugging of Clark which commanded most of the attention.

Clark's slugging spree

The sophomore slugger batted .440 with eight homers and 18 RBI in a 14–game stretch while the Giants were making their move. He was especially devastating against the Reds and the Astros, accumulating 19 of his 35 homers and 47 of his 91 RBI against the club's prime opposition.

"Will has exceeded our expectations," Rosen said. "Big league pitching doesn't tear him apart. He's going to be awesome. There's no question he has superstar potential. Some guys are born to play ball. Will is a natural."

Clark's well-timed batting binge, which included at least one RBI in nine straight games, coincided with solid offensive production from supersub Mike Aldrete and Mitchell, the biggest bargain of all in Rosen's flurry of summer trading activity.

Aldrete batted .352 and Mitchell .381 during an 18–11 August that fueled a long-awaited championship. "The more I see Aldrete, the more I realize I'm going to have to find a place for him to play," Craig said. "And, frankly, I didn't realize how good Mitchell was when we made the trade. He's going to have a great future with us."

Dravecky was the most effective pitcher on the club in August, going 3–0 with a 2.08 ERA. He also had two new teammates who would profoundly affect the outcome of the division race. Reliever Don Robinson was acquired from Pittsburgh, July 31, and Rick Reuschel came from the benevolent Bucs, Aug. 21.

"Al did his job—now I've got to do mine," a beaming Craig said when Reuschel became the final piece in the puzzle. "There's no question Al gave us what we needed most. He picked up the entire team. He's our MVP. We're going to win this thing if I don't mess it up."

At the time of the Reuschel swap, the Giants were 63–59. With Big Daddy firing a pair of two-hitters and going 5–3, the club went 27–13 down the stretch. Reuschel, Dravecky, Robinson and Lefferts were a combined 20–12 with 11 saves in their new surroundings.

Reuschel, Dravecky deliver

The week of Aug. 31–Sept. 6 underscored their effectiveness in a homestand with the Mets, Phillies and Expos. Dravecky was 2–0 with a 0.63 ERA, earning N.L. Pitcher of the Week honors. Reuschel was 2–0 with a 1.69 ERA, hurling his league-leading 10th complete game.

"I can't see us blowing it with that kind of pitching—there's always someone to go out there and stop the bleeding," remarked Brenly, who joined in the heroics with a two-run, ninth-inning homer off Shane Rawley at Philadelphia, Aug. 26. The blast capped a 6–3 trip and gave the Giants their first season sweep at the Phillies' park since 1964.

That the Giants were a team of destiny seemed evident against the Phils at Candlestick, Sept. 5. Rawley, the league's top winner, was beaten again, this time on an unlikely game-winning homer by Uribe and brilliant relief by Kelly Downs, who blossomed in the bullpen after Scott Garrelts fractured a finger.

The Giants on Sept. 7 embarked on their final crucial trip of the season, taking a 5½–game lead on a six-game swing through Houston and Cincinnati. The trip opener featured a scuffball controversy while Mike Scott retired the final 26 batters in a 4–2 Astros' victory.

A three-game sweep would have slashed the S.F. lead to 2½ games, but that notion was dashed when Aldrete entered the game with a pinch-single in the eighth and delivered a two-run double with two down in the ninth for a dramatic, 6–4 victory, Sept. 8.

"You feel the pressure," Aldrete said. "The only difference is how you react to it. You can't let it get to you. Some people thrive on it." Aldrete definitely did, batting a league-leading .412 with runners in scoring position and topping the Giants with a .325 average.

After the Giants dropped the opener at Cincinnati, Reuschel and LaCoss posted easy victories and the club returned home with a 3–3 split on the trip and a six-game lead. When LaCoss beat the Reds at Candlestick, Sept. 19, the winning streak had reached seven games and the division lead was a season-high nine games over Cincinnati.

"We're playing like a championship team," Craig said. "We're getting good pitching, great defense, timely hitting and a new hero every day. We're getting closer and closer."

San Diego celebration

The suspense ended at San Diego, Sept. 28. Chili Davis and Leonard each belted his 100th career home run, as pinch-hitters, but Robinson was the undisputed hero. His leadoff homer off Lance McCullers in the top of the eighth cracked a tie and made him a 5–4 winner, clinching the club's first title since 1971.

"This feels even better than I thought it would," a champagne-drenched owner Bob Lurie said. Added Rosen: "I thought it would be a race to the wire, but this club wouldn't let that happen."

Craig was equally ecstatic. As a resident of the San Diego area and as a former manager of the Padres, he relished his homecoming. On a day when be became a grandfather once again, the Giants' real Humm-Baby regarded the victory celebration as most appropriate.

"It's kind of nice how it all worked out," Craig said amid the clubhouse jubilation. "Maybe this was the way it was meant to be. I got a chance to win it in front of about 20 friends and relatives. I've never been happier. This is what Humm-Baby is all about."

The Giants finished the season a solid 90–72, going 37–17 since that fateful early August trip. They were 46–28 after the All-Star break, the only N.L. West team to play above .500 in that span. They set a franchise record with 183 double plays, an S.F. mark with 205 home runs and led the majors with a 3.68 ERA.

It was a team of balance, a blend of old and new. "A lot of guys put their egos aside for the good of the team," Leonard noted. That was apparent. The biggest winner on the pitching staff was LaCoss at 13–10. Nobody enjoyed a superstar season, except perhaps Clark.

By belting 35 homers and batting .308, the colorful Clark established himself as one of the game's brightest stars. Yet he was no more significant down the stretch than the persistent Aldrete, or Mitchell, who batted .306 after joining the Giants and finished with 22 homers.

Among the old guard, Leonard batted .280; Maldonado batted .292 with 85 RBI for a two-year total of 170 in only 251 games; Chili Davis hit a career-high 24 homers, and Chris Speier was voted the team's most inspirational player for his exemplary work off the bench.

Uribe and Robby Thompson were the defensive glue that meant so much to the pitchers. LaCoss was a dazzling 4–0 against the Reds, his former team. Hammaker, at 10–10, proved he could pitch effectively again. Don Robinson posted a career-high 19 saves. Garrelts was 11–7 with one dozen saves.

Leonard's NLCS triumph

The National League Championship Series almost was anti-climactic for a team which had gone so long without winning anything. Still, the Giants carried the Cardinals to a seventh game, missing a trip to their first World Series since 1962 by going scoreless the final 22 innings.

Dravecky's two-hit, 5–0 victory in Game 2 squared the series and returned the club to adoring fans at Candlestick. A 4–0 lead was squandered in a 6–5 loss in Game 3, but the Giants bounced back for a 4–2 victory behind Krukow and Leonard's fourth homer in as many games.

When Joe Price's five innings of one-hit relief and a Mitchell homer powered a 6–3 victory in Game 5, the confident Giants headed for St. Louis with a 3–2 edge. But Dravecky lost a 1–0 heartbreaker on a ball rightfielder Maldonado lost in the lights and the Cardinals ended dream season with a 6–0 triumph in Game 7.

"The best thing that could have happened to this team was spending that final night in St. Louis," Krukow said. "All we could hear were those horns blaring. I took that noise home with me this winter as a reminder."

Leonard didn't forget, either. He was the MVP of the NLCS and its central figure, yet the prize was a small consolation. "Every player loves that kind of attention," Leonard said, "but I would have traded it all for a pennant. It was a rough winter because there's a big difference between winning and going all the way."

Craig spent the winter working on his mountain retreat near San Diego and reminding people the Giants' job was unifinished, too. "We smelled the roses, but we didn't pluck them," the AP Manager of the Year said. "It's going to be different in 1988 because we're a better club and we're confident."

Part of that confidence was attributed to the winter acquisition of free agent Brett Butler, giving the club a solid centerfielder and its finest leadoff batter in several years. Butler did nothing to discourage that notion while batting .385 during the first week of the season.

Craig also was enthused about having Uribe and Thompson healthy from the start. The Giants definitely seemed stronger up the middle with Butler in center and Uribe and Thompson contributing to 17 double plays in the first 15 games.

The pitching quality was evident immediately. After each of the five starters took a turn, they had a combined 0.96 ERA and had limited the Dodgers and the Padres to a .164 average. Instead of worrying about trading for pitching help during the course of the season, Craig was well-armed from the start. Reuschel began the year 5-1.

The Giants, like most N.L. clubs, sagged offensively the first six weeks of the season, yet Clark and Mitchell were ahead of their 1987 home run paces, Thompson was leading the club in hitting, Youngblood became the majors' early pinch-hit leader.

As a team, the Giants' only constant was stout pitching. It flourished in mid-May with the first three-game sweep of the powerful Mets since 1983, a series in which great starting pitching by Downs, Krukow, and LaCoss helped to contain New York to fifteen hits and three earned runs.

With more than 1.2 milion tickets sold by Opening Day—a higher number than the total season attendance in 15 of the previous 20 years!—the 1988 Giants obviously were generating a lot of excitement, a feeling created by the club's promise of a great future.

Considering their solid core of young talent, the Giants are hopeful of sustaining success similar to that of the early San Francisco teams with Hall of Famers Willie Mays, Willie McCovey and Juan Marichal continuing the legacy established by the franchise in New York.

A rich tradition

It's a rich tradition, one which began with 10 pennants and three world championships directed by John McGraw. Bill Terry took it from there and posted three pennants and one world title in a five-year span, 1933–37. Those clubs featured Hall of Famers like Christy Mathewson, Mel Ott, Travis Jackson, Fred Linstrom, Frankie Frisch, Carl Hubbell and Terry.

The post-War years began a new era of Giants' success, including a league record 221 home runs in 1947. Four years later, Bobby Thomson's memorable playoff homer against Brooklyn's Ralph Branca became one of baseball's magic moments, the shot heard 'round the world.

Leo Durocher's Giants failed against the Yankees in that subway World Series, but they pulled off one of the greatest upsets in 1954 by stunning the Indians in four straight games. Rosen, the architect of the 1987 success, was the thirdbaseman on that Cleveland club, one which set an American League record with 111 victories.

By then, Mays already was a budding superstar, but he wouldn't be New York's darling for long. When Walter O'Malley became serious about moving to a larger stadium than Ebbets Field and eventually decided on sprawling Los Angeles, Horace Stoneham indicated he'd be interested in following the Dodgers to the West Coast.

On Aug. 19, 1957, Stoneham sent shock waves through Manhattan, the Bronx and Staten Island, too. The Giants were moving to San Francisco. Asked if he felt badly about taking the Giants from the kids of New York, Stoneham replied: "I feel bad about the kids, but I haven't seen many of their fathers at games recently."

Stoneham made dwindling attendance his escape clause. Only 11,606 attended the wake when the Giants played their final game at the Polo Grounds, Sept. 29, 1957. Dusty Rhodes, hero of the 1954 World Series, gounded out to punctuate a 9–1 defeat to the Pirates. Fans cried and Mrs. John McGraw tearfully said: "New York will never be the same." Nothing is.

San Francisco embraces rookies

There was excitement and enthusiasm in the winter of 1957-58 because the Bay Area, a cradle for future major leaguers, finally was going to have a team of its own. But there also was a degree of apprehension. Proud Californians didn't want a hand-me-down. They didn't need a team with emotional ties to New York.   •

It was for that reason, more than anything, that Willie Mays wasn't embraced immediately as the leader of the Giants. It was important for the club to develop a local identity, and the timing couldn't have been better for Horace Stoneham, who spent some of his youth in California's gold country.

Stoneham made the transition smoothly, setting a fine example. "I don't even miss Broadway," chortled Horace, who regarded San Francisco, surrounded on three sides by water, as a mini-Manhattan — but with crisp, clean air and a lack of congestion.

Stoneham also had a fruitful farm system which was to prove a blessing in the franchise's fresh start. The 1958 squad featured no less than six rookies who played a prominent role in helping the Giants firmly plant Bay Area roots: Orlando Cepeda, Jim Davenport,

Bob Schmidt, Willie Kirkland, Felipe Alou, and Leon Wagner.

Mays batted a career-high .347 with twenty-nine homers and ninety-six RBI, but he was treated like a Communist at an American Legion rally. So far as many Bay Area fans were concerned, there was only one great center fielder. Joe DiMaggio was born in crossbay Martinez and reared in San Francisco sandlots, so there was some resentment of Mays' intrusion.

Giants fans needed a new hero, and they got one in the powerful Cepeda, who earned the adoration with a team-leading .312 average, twenty-five home runs, ninety-six RBI, and Rookie of the Year distinction. The slick-fielding, clutch-hitting Davenport also became an instant hit. Schmidt was the regular catcher and Wagner batted .317 as a part-timer.

The rookies created a solid base for the club, which maintained its tradition of tape-measure home runs, late-inning rallies, and prodigious slugging feats. The Giants didn't skip a beat while switching from the Polo Grounds to Seals Stadium. The Bay Bombers, win or lose, made the game exciting.

They lived by the home run, and they died by it, a trend which was to continue under the Stoneham ownership. Beginning with the 8-0 victory over the Dodgers in the 1958 opener, the Giants featured a power-packed attack that laid the cornerstone for the club's Bay Area future.

The '58 Giants averaged almost five runs per game, led the league with 652 RBI, and boasted of nine hitters with ten or more home runs. The club also captured the fans' fancy with some amazing comebacks, like the May game with Pittsburgh in which the Giants entered the bottom of the ninth behind 11-1 before proudly emerging 11-10 losers.

The June Swoon

That year the Giants began another tradition, the June Swoon. The club entered the jinx month in first place with a 27-17 record, only to go 10-16 in June and fall to third, where it ultimately finished with an 80-74 record.

The Giants also enhanced their popularity by winning sixteen of twenty-two games with the arch-rival Dodgers, something they hadn't been able to do as well since 1937. They also attracted 1,272,625 paying customers in a park with a capacity of 22,900, a successful season in every sense of the word.

"If we had any kind of pitching, we would have won the pennant by a dozen games," declared Stoneham, who had little to go with Johnny Antonelli (16-13) and league ERA leader Stu Miller (2.47). Horace, however, attacked the problem straight on by trading for Sam Jones and Jack Sanford prior to the 1959 season.

Jones pitched in fifty games, going 21-15 with a league-leading

2.83 ERA; Sanford won fifteen games, and Antonelli was 19-10, but the Giants had to stop printing World Series tickets in 1959 when the Dodgers and the Braves zoomed past the Bay Bombers in September, entering a playoff before Los Angeles won the pennant.

Mays, as usual, was outstanding with thirty-four homers, 104 RBI, and a .313 average, but he was once again upstaged by Cepeda, who belted twenty-seven homers, drove in 105 runs, and batted .317. Then something happened that challenged Cepeda's popularity and ultimately led to the Baby Bull's controversial departure, the arrival of another imposing slugger.

The 1959 Giants avoided a June Swoon and took the league lead until a late July slump. Something was needed to give the club a boost, and Pacific Coast League batting leader Willie McCovey proved an instant elixir, just as Mays had been when he jumped from Minneapolis to New York eight years earlier.

McCovey, a gangly first baseman batting .377 at Phoenix, made his debut against Robin Roberts and the Phillies on July 30 and proceeded to crush four hits, including a pair of triples. The Giants went on to win eight of the next nine games, with McCovey powering the surge. They built a four-game lead on August 23 and held a two-game lead with eight games remaining in the season.

But the Giants didn't yet learn to win the big games. They dropped a three-game series to the Dodgers and fell to third place with five games to go. They had to be content with an 83-71 record, another exciting race, a pitching turnaround, and a young stable of sluggers that was the envy of the National League. McCovey finished with a .354 average and was named Rookie of the Year.

"Best young lineup"

"It was the best young lineup in baseball," Bill Rigney, who was the Giants manager in 1958-60, recalled. "You didn't play for one run because you knew you had to get a lot. I don't remember us bunting much. The Polo Grounds created the Giant's image. Horace lived by the home run. He seldom got involved in other areas.

"I really thought we had a dynasty going with that 1958 club. They were all such marvelous young hitters. Mays, of course, was outstanding, but Orlando was the best young right-handed hitter I ever managed. He had phenomenal power.

"One of our biggest problems in those early years was who to play," Rigney said. "I had guys like Alou, Kirkland, and Wagner on the bench. Then McCovey came up, and we had difficulty finding room for him. Those lineups were as feared as any in the league. There were headaches because you never could score enough runs, but it also was a lot of fun."

Well, most of the time. The 1960 Giants sagged to fifth place, a skid accelerated by an 11-16 June. Rigney was fired, with the team 33-25 and in third place June 18. Interim manager Tom (Clancy) Sheehan couldn't apply the brakes, going 46-50. The Giants' first bad trade of the San Francisco era made Don Blasingame the second baseman and leadoff hitter, but he batted .235 and was gone one year later.

On a positive note, the Giants moved into Candlestick Park and set a franchise attendance record of 1,795,356, one which still stands twenty-six years later. They also received solid seasons from Mays, Cepeda, and Jones, and introduced a third great rookie in three years when Juan Marichal was promoted from Triple-A a few days after Rigney's departure and proceeded to one-hit the Phillies in his debut.

The Candlestick wind immediately became a topic of conversation, but the conditions actually weren't much better at Seals Stadium. In fact, Antonelli's angry reaction to a pair of wind-aided homers at Seals Stadium quickly put him in disfavor with the natives and contributed to his departure from the Giants. The lefty was swapped, along with Willie Kirkland, to Cleveland for Harvey Kuenn in 1961.

Kuenn had adjustment problems in 1961, but rookie manager Alvin Dark had enough offense to keep the club in contention much of the year. The fans warmed to Mays, who belted four home runs in one game and finished with forty round trippers, 123 RBI, and a .308 average. But Cepeda was still the top dog with forty-six homers, a league-leading 146 RBI, and a .311 average.

Stu Miller, who was forced into a balk by a wind gust during the All-Star Game at Candlestick, was the Giants' biggest winner, going 14-5 in relief with seventeen saves and a 2.66 ERA. That someone out of the bullpen was the staff "ace" strongly suggests why the club didn't finish higher than third despite a solid 85-69 record.

Trading for a pennant

But Dark was placing the pieces together and a winter swap gave the Giants the pitching that would make the difference in 1962. Giving up nothing of consequence, the club acquired Billy Pierce and Don Larsen from the White Sox, which added up to twenty-one victories and one dozen saves on the most successful Giants team in fifty years, the biggest winner at 103-62 since the 1913 club won 101.

Pierce, a crafty left-hander, was unbeaten at Candlestick Park; Sanford won twenty-four games, including sixteen in a row; Miller saved nineteen games; Billy O'Dell, unspectacular when acquired in 1961, was a nineteen-game winner; and Marichal had his first of several solid seasons at 18-11. The Giants, at last, had a pitching staff to match their offense.

Mays was the home-run king with forty-nine, knocking in 141 runs and batting .304; Cepeda batted .306 with 35 homers and 114 RBI; Kuenn batted .304 with nine game-winning RBI; Davenport enjoyed his finest season at .297; Felipe Alou batted .316 with twenty-five homers and ninety-eight RBI; McCovey blasted twenty homers in merely 229 at bats; and catchers Tom Haller and Ed Bailey pooled talents for thirty-five homers and one hundred RBI.

Despite the Giants' greatness, evidence supports the contention that it was more a case of the Dodgers losing the pennant than the Giants winning it. After all, Los Angeles lefty Sandy Koufax had piled up fourteen victories by mid-July and had to stop pitching the rest of the way because of a circulatory problem in his fingers.

When Koufax was knocked from the rotation, the Dodgers led the Giants by two games. The lead increased to 5 1/2 games when L.A. visited San Francisco for a three-game series. The Giants found a way to slow down Maury Wills on his record swath of 102 stolen bases. When the Dodgers arrived at Candlestick, they found the infield extensively watered down between first and second.

"An aircraft carrier wouldn't have run aground .... They found two abalone under second base," mused Jim Murray of the *Los Angeles Times*. Another Southland scribe suggested Giants groundskeeper Matty Schwab be named Most Valuable Player after the Giants slowed down the Dodgers with a sweep that pulled them to within 2 1/2 games of first place.

The Dodgers were eager to avenge that series loss to Swamp Fox Dark when the Giants visited Dodger Stadium for a four-game series the first week of September. The Giants entered trailing by 3 1/2 games, but won three out of four to climb to within 1 1/2 games.

Kuenn's clutch hit

Dark regarded the final game of the series as the most important game he ever managed. It was 5-5 in the top of the ninth when Kuenn batted for Haller with the bases loaded and smoked a three-run double off Ron Perranoski. The Giants' winning streak reached seven, so they were only one-half game out of first place on September 11.

The Dodgers, who had been in first place most of the way, lost five out of nine on the road, but the Giants couldn't capitalize. They dropped six in a row on the road, and with thirteen games remaining, they were four games out. "The Giants is dead," was written, but Dark was a picture of determination. "We aren't through," he insisted. "The race will go down to the last day."

They remained four out with seven games to go. While the Giants won two out of three at home from the Cardinals, the Dodgers lost two of three to Houston, so their lead was two games with three remaining. Rain washed out the Giants' game with Houston on the final Friday, but St. Louis edged the Dodgers 3-2, to slice their lead to 1 1/2.

In a doubleheader with Houston the following day, the Giants cut the lead to one by romping 11-5 in the first game behind Sanford's twenty-fourth victory with home runs by McCovey, Haller, and Cepeda. But the enthusiasm dimmed when Bob Bruce downed the Giants in the nightcap, 4-2. The Dodgers, however, obliged by losing to the Cardinals 2-0 and remaining only one game up with one to go.

The final day was dripping with drama and tension. Giants announcers Russ Hodges and Lon Simmons were listening to the Los Angeles broadcast and relaying the information to their audience. While O'Dell and Miller held Houston to one run, a home run by Bailey had the clubs tied until Mays smashed a home run in the eighth for a 2-1 victory. Many spectators remained at Candlestick, though, because the Cardinals and the Dodgers had only completed five innings of a scoreless tie. Then Gene Oliver homered in the ninth and the Cardinals held on to win 1-0, thereby creating a tie. Bedlam erupted throughout the Bay Area. The Giants would not quit. They would not die. They forced a playoff, as they did in 1951.

And, like '51, there were vivid reminders of a glorious past. Leo Durocher, now a Dodgers coach, reportedly brought the same T-shirt he had worn in the '51 playoff finale to the '62 opener. Dark, who was Leo's captain in 1951 an 1954, was asked if he brought any memento of Bobby Thomson's memorable game. "Yeah," Dark replied, "Willie Mays!"

The playoff opener at Candlestick was an 8-0 rout powered by Mays' two home runs and Pierce's thirteenth straight victory at home. The Dodgers, scoreless in three straight games, overcame a 5-0 deficit, won the second game at Los Angeles 8-7, and had the homefield advantage entering the final playoff game.

A two-run homer by Tommy Davis helped the Dodgers take a 4-2 lead into the fateful ninth. Pinch hitter Matty Alou led off with a single and one-out walks to McCovey, and Felipe Alou loaded the bases. Mays' single off pitcher Ed Roebuck's glove made it 4-3 and left the bases bulging.

Davvy downs Dodgers

Stan Williams replaced Roebuck and the slumping Cepeda lofted a sacrifice fly to right, creating a tie. A wild pitch advanced Mays and Bailey was walked intentionally, loading the bases with two outs. Davenport then walked on five pitches, forcing home the go-ahead run in a 6-4 triumph. Pierce then retired the Dodgers in the bottom half to place a lock on the Giants' first, and only, San Francisco pennant.

The Giants were bubbling over, but they were drained. Cepeda, when asked if he was ready for the World Series opener the next day, jokingly said, "Who we playing?" Cepeda wasn't far from the truth, because the clash with the Yankees was regarded as anti-climactic following such a gut-wrenching final few weeks.

Giants fans probably felt the same way. On the club's flight to the Bay Area following the stirring playoff clincher, approximately 75,000 people jammed into S.F. International Airport and spilled onto the field. There was a delay of close to one hour before the circling airplane could land and taxi to a maintenance area, away from the swarming public.

"In all my born years, I've never seen anything like this," said Giants general manager Chub Feeney. "It certainly wasn't this way when we won in 1951." But this was a Bay Area hungry for its first professional champion. The Giants provided that hope in dramatic fashion, and perhaps for the first time, finally had cut their emotional ties to New York.

The World Series was much closer than anyone could have expected, and rainouts added to the buildup, extending it to thirteen days before the Giants finally succumbed on their final at bats in the seventh game, October 16. The two clubs simply traded victories after the Yankees won the opener 6-2 at Candlestick Park.

Sanford's three-hitter and McCovey's home run produced a 2-0 victory in Game 2. The Yankees won two out of three at New York; San Francisco's only victory came in Game 4, when Chuck Hiller hit the first National League grand slam in Series history en route to a 7-3 victory in relief by ex-Yankee Larsen.

When action shifted back to Candlestick, Pierce maintained his mastery at Candlestick with a three-hit, 5-2 victory over Whitey Ford, setting the stage for the final duel between Ralph Terry and Sanford. The Yankees scored on a double-play grounder in the fifth and Terry took a two-hit, 1-0 shutout into the frenzied ninth.

Pinch hitter Matty Alou beat out a bunt single and went to third on Mays's two-out double to right. That brought up McCovey, who homered off Terry in Game 2. Teeing off on a 1-1 pitch, McCovey lined a rope that second baseman Bobby Richardson grabbed slighty to his left. It wasn't a difficult chance, but the ball was struck with such ferocity that a couple of inches either way may have meant a game-winning hit instead of a season-ending out.

Tears of joy

There was temporary dejection, but the 1962 Giants had made a city proud. There was sadness, but many more tears of joy. According to Art Rosenbaum and Bob Stevens, who authored *The Giants of San Francisco* in 1963, a disconsolate McCovey was in a downtown nightclub many hours after the game.

Duke Ellington's orchestra spotted Stretch and saluted him with one of The Duke's classics, changing the title to "You Hit it Good, and That Ain't Bad," an appropriate tribute to a great day, win or lose.

The Giants figured 1962 was the beginning of a string of pennants. They seemingly had it all, particularly power. McCovey erupted to stardom in 1963 with forty-four homers and 102 RBI, as did Marichal at 25-8, a 2.41 ERA, and a no-hitter. Mays, Cepeda, and Felipe Alou also were solid, but others tailed off sharply, especially Davenport and Pierce, who lost his magic and went 3-11.

It added up to a third-place finish at 88-74, and an improved 90-72 in 1964 couldn't keep the Giants out of fourth in Dark's final year as manager. · The '64 season featured Mays' forty-seven homers, Marichal's twenty-one victories, and a thirty-one-homer rookie season for Jim Ray Hart. But McCovey slumped badly and it seemed the club's chemistry wasn't right with Cepeda and Stretch each better suited to playing first base.

When Cepeda was injured most of the 1965 season, McCovey returned to first base and clouted thirty-nine home runs. Mays was the MVP a second time, hitting a career-high fifty-two home runs. Hart avoided the sophomore jinx with a .299 average and ninety-six RBI, Marichal was 22-13, and rookie manager Herman Franks, once a catcher with the club in New York, guided the Giants to their first of five consecutive second-place finishes.

Franks came closest to going all the way in his first two seasons, the Giants finishing two games behind the Dodgers in 1965 and 1 1/2 in back of their primary nemesis the following year. A lack of pitching depth frequently was blamed for the near misses, and it could be argued the club failed to win the pennant despite a 95-67 finish in '65 because Marichal missed some turns following his altercation with John Roseboro at Candlestick on August 22.

Regardless, the Giants soared into the lead in mid-September on the strength of a fourteen-game winning streak, but the Dodgers later won thirteen in a row and the Giants were beaten despite a solid September. Convinced that pitching was the difference, Cepeda was swapped to St. Louis in May of 1966 for left-hander Ray Sadecki.

The controversial swap placed great pressure on Sadecki, who was a flop in his first season with the Giants. But the club stayed close with a 93-68 record in 1966 because Marichal and Gaylord Perry combined for forty-six victories, and Mays (thirty-seven homers), McCovey (thirty-six), Hart (thirty-three), and Haller (twenty-seven) supplied a lot of punch.

It actually was a two-team battle between the Dodgers and the Pirates most of the way, but the Giants finished fast, swept a three-game series at Pittsburgh, and hurdled the Bucs for second. Another great trade prior to the 1967 season bolstered the pitching when Mike McCormick was acquired from the Senators.

McCormick comes back

McCormick, who came west with the Giants in 1958, won the Cy Young Award with a 20-10 season. Unfortunately, Perry had a tough-luck, 15-17 campaign, and an injury limited Marichal to fourteen victories. But even with Mays showing advancing age (.263, twenty-two homers), the club went 21-7 down the stretch to finish with a strong record, though languishing 101/2 games behind St. Louis.

The club's personality began to change in 1968. The skills of Mays and Hart were diminishing, so only McCovey (thirty-six homers, 105 RBI) and rookie Bobby Bonds were ascending offensive forces. The 88-74 finish behind the Cardinals was attributed to a club-record (S.F.) 2.71 ERA. Marichal was 26-9 with a 2.43 figure and Bobby Bolin went 10-5 with a 1.99 ERA.

Franks announced in mid-season that he was retiring if the Giants didn't win, but the second-place rut continued under Clyde King in the first two-division alignment in 1969. King was 90-72 as a rookie skipper, keeping the team close until a ten-game Atlanta winning streak outlasted the Giants by three games.

McCovey developed into a bona fide superstar in '69, winning MVP honors with a .320 average, forty-five homers, and 126 RBI. In his first full season as a major leaguer, Bonds produced thirty-two homers and 90 RBI, but there was a big dropoff thereafter. Marichal and Perry combined for forty victories, and again there wasn't much support.

So the Giants completed the sixties by averaging 91.4 victories the last five years and having little to show for it but individual glory and consistent runner-up status. Those were great teams to watch, full of stars and excitement, but annual high expectations led to disappointment. There always seemed to be something missing, especially defensively.

"Those were good terms, or else we wouldn't have been winning so many games," Franks recalled, "but the main reason we didn't win a couple of pennants was our double-play combination. I can still remember several games we blew because we couldn't turn a double play. We could have used a left-handed reliever, too."

Hal Lanier, whose father, Max, pitched for the Giants in New York, was among those infielders in the late sixties. His version of why pennants were elusive: "We just weren't fundamentally sound. The Giants always waited for the home run. We could hit the long ball with anyone and we had some pretty good pitching, but we never seemed to do the little things we needed to do in the close games."

A lack of execution continued to be a Giants' malady in the seventies and eighties, but there was to be one more bright moment, in 1971, before the demise of the Stoneham Empire nearly cost Bay Area fans their beloved Giants.

Year of The Fox

Following a 19-23 start in 1970, King was fired and replaced by Charlie Fox who like Franks, was a New York Giants catcher. The club went 67-53 under Fox, McCovey once again was the league's most dangerous hitter (thirty-nine homers, 126 RBI), and Perry notched twenty-three victories. But the best was yet to come.

Fox did his best managing in 1971 guiding a mixture of youngsters and veterans to the Western Division title by one game over the hated Dodgers. For the first time since 1876, a team went all the way without a .300 hitter or a twenty-game winner; as a result, Fox was named Manager of the Year.

Bolting to an 18-5 start, the Giants took the lead on April 12 and never looked back. Bonds was the major offensive threat with thirty-three homers and 102 RBI, and Marichal topped the pitchers with eighteen wins, including a 5-1 decision over the Padres on the final day, clinching the division crown.

The Pirates were pounded to defeat nine times in twelve regular-season meetings, and Perry beat them 5-4 in the playoff opener. But the Bucs jolted the Giants in the next three games to advance to the World Series. One year later, the club was to begin a slide from which it never really recovered, posting a losing record (69-86) in 1972 for the first time in the Giants' Bay Area history.

It also marked the first time the incomparable Mays didn't finish the season with the club. Willie was traded to the Mets, primarily to save Stoneham from paying his salary, but there were two other factors that had a far greater impact on the club: McCovey's broken arm and an atrocious trade engineered by Fox, sending Perry to the Indians for Sudden Sam McDowell. Granted, Perry didn't relate well to the younger players on the squad, but McDowell definitely wasn't the answer. Perry went on to win a Cy Young Award and three hundred games, but McDowell became not so sudden and was out of baseball.

Whereas 1971 was known as The Year of the Fox, 1973 definitely was The Year of the Bonds. The Giants' regression was delayed one year simply because Bonds did everything right in an 88-74 season, including All-Star Game MVP honors. He was regarded as the finest talent in the league after belting thirty-nine homers and swiping forty-three bases.

McCovey returned to form with twenty-nine homers, Gary Matthews batted .300 and was Rookie of the Year, and left-hander Ron Bryant enjoyed a dream season at 24-12. *The Sporting News* honored Bonds and Bryant as Player and Pitcher of the Year, re-spectively, the first time one club had two players so honored by the publication.

The Giants fell to 72-90 in 1974 and Wes Westrum, yet another ex-Giants catcher, replaced Fox at mid-season. The club was going with youth now that McCovey and Marichal were gone, but there were four managers in four years and little success except for flashes of brilliance like Ed Halicki's no-hitter and John Montefusco's Rookie of the Year distinction, each in 1975.

The bottom almost fell out on the club in 1975 despite a respectable 80-81, third-place finish under Westrum. The 1974-75 combined seasons' attendance was 1,042,916, as Stoneham was running out of money even though the high-salaried superstars were gone. In January of 1976, Stoneham sold his beloved Giants to Labatt's Breweries of Toronto, ending fifty-seven years of ownership by his family.

Lurie to the rescue

It seemed the National League would beat the American League to the Canadian city, but San Francisco Mayor George Moscone received a temporary restraining order against the move. The hunt began for new owners who would keep the club in the Bay Area. Bob Lurie, son of a wealthy San Francisco financier, pulled out his checkbook. But Lurie, a member of the Giants Board of Directors for most of the Stoneham years in San Francisco, couldn't do it alone, so a search was made for a partner as the league deadline approached. March 2 was the target date, but that morning Lurie was still without an angel. But with Mayor Moscone serving as an intermediary, Lurie was placed in contact with Arizona cattleman Bud Herseth, who ultimately saved the Giants' bacon.

Within minutes of the 5 P.M. deadline imposed by the league, Lurie and Herseth had pooled resources to save the Giants for San Francisco. Mayor Moscone, informing the Bay Area media of the good news, summed up the successful, last-ditch effort by declaring, "Bobby Thomson lives!"

Lurie and Herseth didn't have time to bask in the glory of their heroic deed. They had to field a winner and give the fans reason to return to Candlestick Park. Rigney was rehired as manager, but there were no young lions as he had enjoyed in 1958. Montefusco came closest to that status, pitching a no-hitter, but he was merely 16-14 and the Giants finished fourth at 74-88.

There was a one-game improvement in 1977, but things were looking up under rookie manager Joe Altobelli. Lurie, who was about to buy out Herseth and become sole owner, had the good judgment to sign McCovey, who went to spring training as a nonroster player after being released by the crossbay A's. Willie's presence rekindled a spark.

McCovey batted .280 and slammed twenty-eight home runs for Comeback of the Year honors. Bill Madlock, acquired in the off season, batted .302. Rookie Jack Clark gave a hint of what was to come and reliever Gary Lavelle had a 2.06 ERA and a club-record twenty saves.

Blue crosses the bridge

The Giants finally climbed out of their rut in 1978, more than doubling attendance with 1,740,477 customers, leading the league much of the season, and finishing third at 89-73. Altobelli was named Manager of the Year and general manager Spec Richardson, who masterminded the preseason swap that brought Vida Blue from the A's, was selected the top executive.

Vida Blue was the catalyst for the club's resurgence, going 18-10 with a 2.79 ERA. Fellow lefty Bob Knepper was right behind at 17-11, 2.63. Madlock batted .309, and new addition Mike Ivie followed at .308. But Clark, only twenty-two years old, was the big gun with a .306 average, twenty-five home runs, ninety-eight RBI, and a club-record forty-six doubles. He also set a Giants' record with a twenty-six-game hitting streak, surpassing Freddie Lindstrom's, Don Mueller's and McCovey's twenty-four.

When the 1979 club didn't live up to its predecessor, Madlock was swapped in mid-season (and pushed the Pirates to a championship), and Altobelli was replaced by third base coach Dave Bristol in September. Ivie and Clark carried the offense and McCovey, who passed Mel Ott on the career-home-run list, swatted .393 as a pinch hitter.

Blue bounced back in 1980 and Clark and Darrell Evans did some damage offensively, but the club plunged to fifth at 75-86 and Bristol was relieved of his duties during the winter meetings. Frank Robinson was named as his replacement in January, becoming the first black manager in the National League, a distinction he received in the American League in 1975.

The 1981 season was ripped apart by the strike, which proved to be a boon for the Giants. They were 27-32 prior to the walkout and 29-23 following the resumption of play, finishing 56-55 overall. Newcomer Doyle Alexander was the pitching ace at 11-7, and the offensive load was carried by Clark and Evans, with Jeff Leonard coming up from the minors and enjoying a blazing second half with a .307 average. Milt May batted .310.

The upward trend continued in '82. By virtue of the strongest second half in the league, the Giants posted an 87-75 record and finished third, two games out of the division lead. This was done despite a complete revamping of the starting rotation by general manager Tom Haller, who replaced Richardson during the 1981 strike.

Haller replaced veterans like Alexander and Blue with rookies like Bill Laskey and Atlee Hammaker, who combined for twenty-five victories. Clark responded with his finest season, belting twenty-seven homers and knocking in 103 runs. Free agent Reggie Smith provided eighteen homers and a .284 average, while Joe Morgan contributed leadership and a team-leading .289 average. Greg Minton posted a club-record thirty saves.

In a controversial off-season swap, Morgan and reliever Al Holland were sent to Philadelphia for right-hander Mike Krukow and two minor league prospects, and Smith elected to play in Japan. Evans compensated for Smith's absence by switching to first base and enjoying this finest season with the Giants while ranked among the league leaders in many offensive categories.

Leonard developed into a solid slugger and an outstanding left fielder, and Johnnie LeMaster had his greatest all-around season at shortstop. Free agent Joel Youngblood made a big contribution in the infield and outfield, Lavelle returned to eminence as a reliever, and Laskey and Hammaker continued to flash brilliance.

The collapse of '84

But Clark and Chili Davis slumped miserably, Minton was a shadow of his former self, and the injury-riddled Giants were slightly out of sync most of the 1983 season. A poor second half dropped the club near the basement and had the front office talking about sweeping changes for the rebuilding process over the winter months. That 1984 would become the losingest season in the Giants' San Francisco history was disguised by an 18-9 spring training record, best in the Cactus League. With Darrell Evans signing with Detroit as a free agent, the Giants filled their first base void by acquiring veteran Al Oliver from Montreal during spring training.

But the early enthusiasm was dampened by a 7-16 April, and by the time a productive offense got into gear, the pitching was in disarray. The Giants fell 10 games behind on May 1, at the end of a nine-game losing streak, and they never recovered.

By the All-Star break, the club trailed by 16 games at 33-50, and five straight losses at the start of the second half suggested the early slump was no fluke. With the club 22 games in arrears, Aug. 4, Bob Lurie fired Frank Robinson with two years remaining on his contract and coach Danny Ozark took over on an interim basis.

The Giants improved slightly, going 24-32 under the former Phillies manager, yet couldn't escape a last-place finish because of a 4-12 nosedive down the stretch. The highlight of Ozark's tenure was a 9-3 swing through New York, Montreal and Phildelphia, Aug. 24-Sept. 2, the club's most successful East Coast trip ever.

Oliver batted .298, but failed to provide the required punch (zero homers, 34 RBI in 91 games), so he was swapped to Philadelphia. Jack Clark was off to his finest start, but a knee injury ended his season June 26, when he was batting .320 with 11 homers and 44 RBI in 57 games. But the injury proved to be a blessing in disguise and paved the way for the winter trade of the moody slugger.

A great, young outfield

With Clark shelved, outfielder Dan Gladden was promoted from Phoenix, where he was batting .397. The feisty Gladden batted .351 in 86 major league games, joining Chili Davis (.315) and Jeff Leonard

(.302) to give the Giants a trio of young flyhawks who collectively batted .319 and augured well for the future.

Davis, Leonard and catcher Bob Brenly each had at least 20 home runs and 80 RBI for an offense that ranked second in batting (.265) and fourth in runs scored in the National League. But that pop couldn't compensate for the worst pitching (4.39 ERA) and the worst defense (173 errors) in the league.

Among the starters, only Mike Krukow had reasonable success at 11-12. Rookie Jeff Robinson made the jump from Class-A to the rotation and tailed off following a quick start. Atlee Hammaker did not pitch until June 26 following rotator cuff surgery, winning twice.

Reliever Gary Lavelle set an all-time Giants record with his 635th game, breaking Christy Mathewson's mark, and worked in 77 games in what was to be his final season with the club. Greg Minton had a team-leading 19 saves and rookie Frank Williams was 9-4, performing an oddity by winning each end of a doubleheader, Aug. 24, at New York.

Following the dismal 1984, it generally was felt the Giants couldn't be any worse in 1985, but they were. The only non-expansion franchise to avoid losing 100 games had its streak snapped in a 62-100 campaign rife with dissension and disappointment. It was a Murphy's Law season in which everything which could go wrong did.

Improvement was expected because personable Jim Davenport was an easygoing sort who was to be the antithesis of the demanding Robinson. Moreover, the club acquired two regulars (first-baseman David Green and shortstop Jose Uribe) and a starting pitcher (Dave LaPoint) for Clark, who was not missed during Gladden's rookie spree.

A 7-12 April which included a seven-game losing streak set the tone for the season. And while Clark and the Cardinals were heading toward a pennant, Green batted .080 during his first 21 games and became a scapegoat — much as was the case with Ray Sadecki in the Orlando Cepeda swap.

Green recovered to bat .318 after July 1, but it was too late. Public opinion and Oliver-like production (five homers, 20 RBI) cooked his goose and he virtually was given away at season's end. LaPoint, pitching in bad luck, lost 17 games and also was sent packing. Uribe survived, leading the club with 147 games played and fielding solidly.

Green wasn't alone. Leonard, Davis and Brenly also tailed off sharply from their 1984 success, and Gladden was a bust at the leadoff spot. Nothing seemed to click in a season which found the club plunging from second to last in batting (.233) and also finishing at the bottom in runs scored.

The lone bright spot in the offense was rookie third-baseman Chris Brown, who broke in with a team-leading .271 average and a career-high 16 home runs while making only 10 errors. But he had little help on a club which had nobody knock in more than 62 runs or any starting pitcher post more than eight victories.

From the morass of despair emerged two significant pitching performances. Scott Garrelts was switched from a starter to the bullpen and promptly became one of the best in the bigs with a 9-6 record, a 2.30 ERA and 13 saves. Vida Blue returned to the mound following a one-year exile and was 8-8 for a club which finished 38 games below .500.

Rosen, Craig welcomed

There also was a silver lining around the dark cloud that hovered the entire season. The situation became so bleak, Lurie was compelled to make a sweeping change that would profoundly affect the future of the club. On Sept. 18, the owner gave the Giants much-needed new direction by replacing general manager Tom Haller and Davenport with Al Rosen and Roger Craig, respectively.

For the first time in several years, the Giants had a plan for success and the leadership to implement it. The club finished 6-12 under Craig, who "saw a lot of things I didn't like" and quickly worked with Rosen to rectify them. The plan would bear fruit one year later, but not before a winter of uncertainty regarding the club.

Lurie, intent on not playing at Candlestick Park in 1986, considered playing home games in Oakland or in Denver until a downtown stadium were built. It wasn't until Jan. 29, 1986, that Giants fans knew for sure that the club once again would call San Francisco home. What followed was one of the most exciting seasons in recent Giants history.

Craig boldly gave starting jobs to rookies Will Clark (first base) and Robby Thompson (second base) during spring training. The club bolted to a 10-4 start and enjoyed its first winning April (13-8) since 1973, acquiring Craig's confidence and Hum-Baby attitude.

Despite myriad roster moves (a total of 61!) and constant lineup juggling because of injuries, the Giants remained in contention most of the season. With a 48-40 record, they topped the division at the All-Star break for the first time since 1978. The club led or shared first place 47 days.

An injury which sidelined Leonard the final two months cost the club dearly, but it still showed a 21-game improvement from 1985, the greatest one-year turnaround in S.F. history and the most by the franchise since 1954. The Giants also became only one of 10 teams since 1900 to post a winning record (83-79) after losing 100 the previous year.

Character and confidence exemplified the club's turnaround. There were 40 come-from-behind victories, including 26 on the final at bats. The Giants avoided a June Swoon with a 16-12 record and were 16-11 in September without help from Leonard or Brown, who missed most of the final month with a shoulder injury.

Individually, Krukow's 20-win season stood out and typified the comeback character of the club. Injured in a St. Louis scuffle after the All-Star break, the veteran righthander missed a few turns. But he turned a 6-0 September (earning N.L. Pitcher of the Month honors) into the first 20-win season for the club since Bryant in 1973.

Righthander Mike LaCoss helped the club to its first-half lead by going 9-3 before fading. Garrelts began the season as a starter, but returned to the bullpen and again established himself as a premier reliever. His 13-9 record and 3.11 ERA ranked behind Krukow's 20-9 and 3.05 marks.

Candy was dandy

The offensive resurgence was powered by newcomer Candy Maldonado, whose 17 pinch hits set a club record. When Leonard was sidelined, Maldonado became a regular down the stretch and finished with a team-leading 18 home runs and 85 RBI in only 133 games and 405 at bats.

Clark and Thompson made a big impact and were instant favorites of the fans. Clark missed one month with an elbow injury and batted a solid .287. Thompson was named *The Sporting News* Rookie Player of the Year after batting a career-high .271 and exhibiting a hard-nosed style of play reminiscent of Eddie Stanky.

Brown was the team battting leader at .317, tailing off after entering his first All-Star Game with a .338 average. Davis made his second All-Star appearance, knocking in 55 runs at the time, but added only 15 thereafter in a second-half slump (and disenchantment with Candlestick Park) that stamped him prime winter trade bait.

In addition to the attitude adjustment created by Rosen and Craig, the factors most responsible for the club's improvement were deft execution and production off the bench. The Giants, devoid of consistent power, emphasized the little things and registered 18 squeeze bunts among 101 sacrifices. They also set a San Francisco record with 148 stolen bases.

Giants pinch-hitters topped the majors with 10 homers and 59 RBI. Maldonado led the league with four homers and 20 RBI in a pinch. Joel Youngblood's 16 hits also surpassed the previous mark of 14 (Duane Kuiper, 1982) and Harry Spilman, acquired in mid-June, came through with 13 hits and a .406 average off the bench.

3

1987
STATISTICS

SAN FRANCISCO GIANTS
1987 DAY-BY-DAY RECORD

GAME	DATE	D/N	OPP	WINNER/LOSER	W/L	SCORE	RECORD	POS	G +/-	CLUB
1	4/6	D	S.D.	J. Robinson (1-0) / Dravecky	W	4-3 (12)	1-0	T1	---	Cin/Hou
2	4/7	N	S.D.	LaCoss (1-0) / Whitson	W	4-3	2-0	T1	---	Hou
3	4/8	D	S.D.	Mason (1-0) /Hawkins	W	2-1	3-0	T1	---	Hou
4	4/9	D	@L.A.	Davis (1-0) / Welch	W	8-1	4-0	1	+ 0.5	Hou
5	4/10	N	@L.A.	Garrelts (1-0) / Leary	W	5-4 (11)	5-0	1	+ 0.5	Hou
6	4/11	D	@L.A.	HERSHISER / KRUKOW (0-1)	L	1-5	5-1	3	- 0.5	Hou
7	4/12	D	@L.A.	Valenzuela / LaCoss (1-1)	L	5-7	5-2	T2	- 1.5	Hou
8	4/13	N	@S.D.	Gott (1-0) / Dravecky	W	13-6	6-2	T2	- 0.5	Hou
9	4/14	N	@S.D.	Grant (1-0) / Wojna	W	3-2	7-2	T1	- .079	Cin
10	4/15	N	@S.D.	DOWNS (1-0) / Davis	W	1-0	8-2	1	+ 0.5	Hou
	4/16		OFF DAY					1	+ 0.5	Hou
11	4/17	N	Atl.	SMITH / Krukow (0-2)	L	0-2	8-3	T1	- .051	Cin
12	4/18	D	Atl.	Garrelts (2-0) / Garber	W	2-1 (10)	9-3	T1	- .050	Cin
13	4/19	D	Atl.	J. Robinson (2-0) / Assenmacher	W	4-3	10-3	1	+ 0.5	Cin
14	4/20	N	L.A.	Davis (2-0) / Hershiser	W	4-3	11-3	1	+ 0.5	Cinn
15	4/21	N	L.A.	Howell / Garrelts (2-1)	L	8-11 (10)	11-4	1	+ 0.5	Cin
16	4/22	N	L.A.	Valenzuela / Krukow (0-3)	L	3-5	11-5	1	+ 0.5	Cin/Hou
	4/23		OFF DAY					T1	---	Cin/Hou
17	4/24	N	@Atl.	Minton (1-0) / Acker	W	7-5	12-5	T1	---	Cin
18	4/25	D	@Atl.	Garber / Garrelts (2-2)	L	3-5	12-6	2	- 1	Cin
19	4/26	D	@Atl.	Davis (3-0) / Palmer	W	6-4	13-6	2	- 1	Cin
20	4/27	N	@Atl.	Downs (2-0) / Mahler	W	7-3	14-6	2	- 0.5	Cin
21	4/28	D	@Chi.	KRUKOW (1-3) / Sutcliffe	W	6-2	15-6	1	+ 0.5	Cin
22	4/29	D	@Chi.	Maddux / Mason (1-1)	L	4-8	15-7	1	+ 0.5	Cin
23	4/30	D	@Chi.	Garrelts (3-2) / Smith	W	5-4	16-7	1	+ 0.5	Cin
24	5/1	N	@Pit.	REUSCHEL / Davis (3-1)	L	2-4	16-8	2	- 0.5	Cin
25	5/2	N	@Pit.	Smiley / DOWNS (2-1)	L	0-1	16-9	2	- 0.5	Cin
	5/3		@Pit.	RAINED OUT				2	- 0.5	Cin
26	5/4	N	@St.L.	LaCoss (2-1) / Dawley	W	10-7	17-9	2	- 0.5	Cin
27	5/5	D	@St.L.	Garrelts (4-2) / Mathews	W	10-6	18-9	2	- 0.5	Cin
28	5/6	N	Chi.	Sanderson / Davis (3-2)	L	4-9	18-10	2	- 0.5	Cin
29	5/7	N	Chi.	LaCoss (3-1) / Lynch	W	11-1	19-10	T1	- .012	Cin
30	5/8	N	Pit.	Downs (3-0) / Fisher	W	4-2	20-10	T1	- .012	Cin
31	5/9	D	Pit.	Hammaker (1-0) / Walk	W	9-4	21-10	1	+ 1	Cin
32	5/10	D	Pit.	Robinson / Garrelts (4-3)	L	1-4 (11)	21-11	1	+ 1	Cin
	5/11		OFF DAY					1	+ 0.5	Cin
33	5/12	N	St.L.	Magrane / Davis (3-3)	L	5-6	21-12	1	+ 0.5	Cin
34	5/13	D	St.L.	Soff / J. Robinson (2-1)	L	6-7	21-13	2	- 0.5	Cin
	5/14		OFF DAY					2	- 1	Cin
35	5/15	N	@N.Y.	Fernandez / Krukow (1-4)	L	3-8	21-14	2	- 1	Cin
36	5/16	N	@N.Y.	Garrelts (5-3) / Innis	W	5-4 (10)	22-14	T1	---	Cin
37	5/17	D	@N.Y.	Cone / Hammaker (1-1)	L	4-6	22-15	T1	---	Cin
38	5/18	N	@Mon.	HEATON / Downs (3-2)	L	2-7	22-16	2	- 0.5	Cin
39	5/19	N	@Mon.	LaCoss (4-1) / Youmans	W	6-2	23-16	1	+ 0.5	Cin
40	5/20	N	@Mon.	J. Robinson (3-1) / St. Claire	W	9-7	24-16	1	+ 0.5	Cin
	5/21		OFF DAY					1	+ 1	Cin
41	5/22	N	@Phi.	Hammaker (2-1) / Carman	W	2-1	25-16	1	+ 2	Cin
42	5/23	N	@Phi.	Bedrosian / J. Robinson (3-2)	L	8-9	25-17	1	+ 2	Cin
43	5/24	D	@Phi.	LaCoss (5-1) / Tekulve	W	6-3	26-17	1	+ 3	Cin
44	5/25	D	N.Y.	Leach / Grant (1-1)	L	7-8	26-18	1	+ 2	Cin
45	5/26	N	N.Y.	Sisk / J. Robinson (3-3)	L	2-3	26-19	1	+ 1	Cin

GAME	DATE	D/N	OPP	WINNER/LOSER	W/L	SCORE	RECORD	POS	G +/-	CLUB
46	5/27	D	N.Y.	McDowell / J. Robinson (3-4)	L	3-4	26-20	1	+1	Cin
	5/28		OFF DAY					1	+1	Cin
47	5/29	N	Mon.	Heaton / LaCoss (5-2)	L	4-10	26-21	T1	---	Cin
48	5/30	D	Mon.	Youmans / KRUKOW (1-5)	L	4-6	26-22	2	+1	Cin
49	5/31	D	Mon.	DOWNS (4-2) / Sebra	W	8-0	27-22	2	-1	Cin
50	6/1	N	Phi.	Hammaker (3-1) / Carman	W	9-2	28-22	T1	---	Cin
51	6/2	N	Phi.	Ritchie / Davis (3-4)	L	2-7	28-23	2	-1	Cin
52	6/3	D	Phi.	LaCoss (6-2) / Ruffin	W	4-1	29-23	2	-1	Cin
	6/4		OFF DAY					2	-1	Cin
53	6/5	N	@Hou.	Scott / Krukow (1-6)	L	1-6	29-24	2	-2	Cin
54	6/6	N	@Hou.	Comstock (1-0) / Andersen	W	4-3 (12)	30-24	2	-2	Cin
55	6/7	D	@Hou.	Ryan / Hammaker (3-2)	L	0-3	30-25	2	-2	Cin
56	6/8	N	@Cin.	Franco / Garrelts (5-4)	L	6-7	30-26	2	-3	Cin
57	6/9	N	@Cin.	DAVIS (4-4) / Pacillo	W	10-2	31-26	2	-2	Cin
58	6/10	D	@Cin.	Comstock (2-0) / Gullickson	W	9-4	32-26	2	-1	Cin
59	6/11	N	S.D.	DOWNS (5-2) / Show	W	1-0	33-26	T1	---	Cin
60	6/12	N	S.D.	WHITSON / LaCoss (6-3)	L	0-4	33-27	T1	---	Cin
61	6/13	D	S.D.	Hawkins / Hammaker (3-3)	L	2-11	33-28	2	-1	Cin
62	6/14	D	S.D.	DRAVECKY / Davis (4-5)	L	1-4	33-29	2	-2	Cin
	6/15		OFF DAY					2	-2	Cin
63	6/16	N	@Atl.	ALEXANDER / Downs (5-3)	L	2-7	33-30	3	-1.5	Cin
64	6/17	N	@Atl.	Mahler / J. Robinson (3-5)	L	1-6	33-31	3	-2.5	Cin
65	6/18	D	@S.D.	Davis / Hammaker (3-4)	L	1-3	33-32	3	-3.5	Cin
66	6/19	N	@S.D.	J. Robinson (4-5) / McCullers	W	7-6	34-32	3	-2.5	Cin
67	6/20	N	@S.D.	Jones / J. Robinson (4-6)	L	4-10	34-33	3	-2.5	Cin
68	6/21	D	@S.D.	Downs (6-3) / Show	W	11-2	35-33	3	-2.5	Cin
	6/22		OFF DAY					3	-2.5	Cin
69	6/23	N	Cin.	Robinson / Hammaker (3-5)	L	1-4	35-34	3	-3.5	Cin
70	6/24	D	Cin.	Franco / Garrelts (5-5)	L	4-5 (10)	35-35	3	-4.5	Cin
71	6/25	N	Cin.	Garrelts (6-5) / Murphy	W	7-6	36-35	3	-3.5	Cin
72	6/26	Nd	Hou.	Knepper / LaCoss (6-4)	L	6-9	36-36	3	-4.5	Cin
73	6/27	D	Hou.	Deshaies / Downs (6-4)	L	5-6	36-37	3	-4.5	Cin
74	6/28	D	Hou.	Hammaker (4-5) / Ryan	W	8-4	37-37	3	-3.5	Cin
75	6/29	N	Atl.	SMITH / Grant (1-2)	L	0-1	37-38	3	-4	Cin
76	6/30	N	ATl.	J. Robinson (5-6) / Alexander	W	5-2	38-38	3	-4	Cin
77	7/1	D	Atl.	MAHLER / LaCoss (6-5)	L	3-8	38-39	3	-5	Cin
	7/2		OFF DAY					3	-4.5	Cin
78	7/3	D	@Chi.	Downs (7-4) / Moyer	W	3-1	39-39	3	-4.5	Cin
79	7/4	D	@Chi.	Sutcliffe / Hammaker (4-6)	L	3-5	39-40	3	-5.5	Cin
80	7/5	D	@Chi.	Price (1-0) / Lynch	W	7-5	40-40	3	-5.5	Cin
81	7/6	N	@Pit.	Dravecky (4-7) / Dunne	2/	7-5	41-40			
82	DH	N	@Pit.	LaCoss (7-5) / Drabek	W	7-4	42-40	3	-4	Cin
83	7/7	N	@Pit.	Gideon / Price (1-1)	L	4-6 (11)	42-41	3	-4	Cin
84	7/8	N	@Pit.	J. Robinson (6-6) / Gideon	W	8-4 (14)	43-41	3	-3	Cin
85	7/9	N	@St.L.	Horton / Garrelts (6-6)	L	6-7 (10)	43-42	3	-4	Cin
86	7/10	N	@St.L.	Tunnell / Lefferts (2-3)	L	5-7 (13)	43-43	3	-4	Cin
87	7/11	N	@St.L.	Downs (8-4) / Magrane	W	3-1	44-43	3	-3	Cin
88	7/12	D	@St.L.	Horton / Hammaker (4-7)	L	2-3	44-44	3	-3	Cin

● ●

ALL-STAR BREAK — RECORD 44-44

● ●

GAME	DATE	D/N	OPP	WINNER/LOSER	W/L	SCORE	RECORD	POS	G +/-	CLUB
89	7/16	N	Chi.	Moyer / Dravecky (4-8)	L	1-4	44-45	3	-3	Cin
90	7/17	N	Chi.	Sutcliffe / Downs (8-5)	L	1-5	44-46	3	-4	Cin
91	7/18	D	Chi.	HAMMAKER (5-7) / Maddux	W	9-2	45-46	3	-4	Cin
92	7/19	D	Chi.	Garrelts (7-6) / Sanderson	W	4-3	46-46	2	-3	Cin
93	7/20	N	Pit.	Fisher / LaCoss (7-6)	L	6-7	46-47	2	-4	Cin
94	7/21	N	Pit.	DRAVECKY (5-8) / Kipper	W	7-0	47-47	2	-4	Cin
95	7/22	D	Pit.	REUSCHEL / Downs (8-6)	L	0-4	47-48	2	-4	Cin
	7/23		OFF DAY					3	-4.5	Cin
96	7/24	N	St.L.	Hammaker (6-7) / Horton	W	4-3	48-48	3	-3.5	Cin
97	7/25	D	St.L.	Garrelts (8-6) / Dawley	W	5-4	49-48	2	-2.5	Cin
98	7/26	D	St.L.	Garrelts (9-6) / Worrell	W	6-3 (10)	50-48			
99	DH	D	St.L.	LaCoss (8-6) / Mathews	W	5-2	51-48	2	-1	Cin
100	7/27	N	@L.A.	Leary / Garrelts (9-7)	L	5-6 (12)	51-49	2	-1.5	Cin
101	7/28	N	@L.A.	Hershiser / Hammaker (6-8)	L	2-4	51-50	2	-2.5	Cin
102	7/29	N	@L.A.	Krukow (2-6) / Honeycutt	W	16-2	52-50	2	-2.5	Cin
	7/30		OFF DAY					2	-2	Cin
103	7/31	N	@Cin.	Robinson / Dravecky (5-9)	L	2-9	52-51	2	-3	Cin
104	8/1	D	@Cin.	LaCoss (9-6) / Gullickson	W	7-3	53-51	2	-2	Cin
105	8/2	D	@Cin.	Montgomery / J. Robinson (6-7)	L	4-5 (11)	53-52	2	-3	Cin
106	8/3	N	@Hou.	Agosto / Price (1-2)	L	3-5 (13)	53-53	2	-3	Cin
107	8/4	N	@Hou.	Heathcock / Lefferts (2-4)	L	4-5	53-54	3	-4	Cin
108	8/5	N	@Hou.	Andersen / J. Robinson (6-8)	L	5-6 (11)	53-55	3	-5	Cin
	8/6		OFF DAY					3	-5	Cin
109	8/7	N	Cin.	LaCOSS (10-6) / Gullickson	W	3-1	54-55	3	-4	Cin
110	8/8	N	Cin.	HAMMAKER (7-8) / Browning	W	5-2	55-55	2	-3	Cin
111	8/9	D	Cin.	Krukow (3-6) / Power	W	3-2	56-55			
112	DH	D	Cin.	Downs (9-6) / Hoffman	W	5-2	57-55	2	-1	Cin
113	8/10	N	Hou.	D. Robinson (7-6) / Meads	W	6-5	58-55	2	-1	Cin
114	8/11	N	Hou.	Heathcock / LaCoss (10-7)	L	3-7	58-56	2	-1	Cin
115	8/12	D	Hou.	Hammaker (8-8) / Scott	W	8-1	59-56	T1	---	Cin
116	8/13	D	Hou.	Lefferts (3-4) / Childress	W	7-6 (11)	60-56	T1	---	Cin
117	8/14	N	L.A.	Hillegas / Downs (9-7)	L	3-4	60-57	2	-0.5	Cin
118	8/15	D	L.A.	DRAVECKY (6-9) / Valenzuela	W	5-0	61-57	T1	---	Cin

GAME	DATE	D/N	OPP	WINNER/LOSER	W/L	SCORE	RECORD	POS	G +/−	CLUB
119	8/16	D	L.A.	LaCOSS (11–7) / Welch	W	1–0 (10)	62–57	T1	---	Cin
	8/17		OFF DAY					T1	---	Cin
120	8/18	N	@N.Y.	Gooden / Hammaker (8–9)	L	2–7	62–58	T1	---	Cin
121	8/19	N	@N.Y.	Garrelts (10–7) / McDowell	W	10–6 (10)	63–58	1	+ 1	Cin
122	8/20	D	@N.Y.	Cone / Downs (9–8)	L	4–7	63–59	T1	---	Cin
123	8/21	N	@Mon.	Dravecky (7–9) / Martinez	W	6–3	64–59	1	+ 1	Cin
124	8/22	N	@Mon.	Burke / Lefferts (3–5)	L	4–5 (10)	64–60	1	+ 0.5	Hou
125	8/23	D	@Mon.	Downs (10–8) / Sebra	W	5–3	65–60	1	+ 0.5	Hou
126	8/24	N	@Phi.	Reuschel (9–6) / Ruffin	W	6–1	66–60	1	+ 0.5	Hou
127	8/25	N	@Phi.	Garrelts (11–7) / Gross	W	3–2	67–60	1	+ 1.5	Hou
128	8/26	N	@Phi.	D. Robinson (8–6) / RAWLEY	W	2–0	68–60	1	+ 2.5	Hou
	8/27		OFF DAY					1	+ 2.5	Hou
129	8/28	N	N.Y.	GOODEN / LaCoss (11–8)	L	0–4	68–61	1	+ 2.5	Hou
130	8/29	D	N.Y.	Hammaker (9–9) / Fernandez	W	9–1	69–61	1	+ 3.5	Hou
131	8/30	D	N.Y.	Aguilera / Reuschel (9–7)	L	3–5	69–62	1	↓ 3.5	Hou
132	8/31	N	Mon.	DRAVECKY (8–9) / Martinez	W	5–0	70–62	1	+ 4.5	Hou
133	9/1	N	Mon.	Reuschel (10–7) / Youmans	W	14–4	71–62	1	+ 5.5	Hou
134	9/2	D	Mon.	Perez / LaCoss (11–9)	L	3–7	71–63	1	+ 4.5	Hou
	9/3		OFF DAY					1	+ 4.5	Hou
135	9/4	N	Phi.	D. Robinson (9–6) / Ritchie	W	3–2 (10)	72–63	1	+ 4.5	Hou
136	9/5	D	Phi.	Dravecky (9–9) / Rawley	W	6–3	73–63	1	+ 4.5	Hou
137	9/6	D	Phi.	REUSCHEL (11–7) / Toliver	W	4–1	74–63	1	+ 5.5	Hou
138	9/7	N	@Hou.	SCOTT LaCoss (11–10)	L	2–4	74–64	1	+ 4.5	Hou
139	9/8	N	@Hou.	D. Robinson (10–6) / Andersen	W	6–4	75–64	1	+ 5.5	Hou
140	9/9	N	@Hou.	Ryan / Hammaker (9–10)	L	2–4	75–65	1	+ 4.5	Hou
	9/10		OFF DAY					1	+ 5	Hou/Cin
141	9/11	N	@Cin.	Rasmussen / Dravecky (9–10)	L	3–4	75–66	1	+ 4	Cin
142	9/12	N	@Cin.	REUSCHEL (12–7) / Toliver	W	7–1	76–66	1	+ 5	Cin
143	9/13	D	@Cin.	LaCoss (12–10) / Browning	W	6–1	77–66	1	+ 6	Cin
144	9/14	N	S.D.	Lefferts (4–5) / McCullers	W	4–3	78–66	1	+ 6.5	Hou
145	9/15	N	S.D.	Hammaker (10–10) / Nolte	W	13–3	79–66	1	+ 7	Cin
146	9/16	D	Hou.	DRAVECKY (10–10) / Scott	W	7–1	80–66	1	+ 7.5	Cin
147	9/17	D	Hou.	REUSCHEL (13–7) / Darwin	W	4–0	81–66	1	+ 8	Cin
	9/18		OFF DAY					1	+ 8	Cin
148	9/19	D	Cin.	LaCoss (13–10) / Browning	W	5–1	82–66	1	+ 9	Cin
149	9/20	D	Cin.	Murphy / D. Robinson (10–7)	L	6–10	82–67	1	+ 8	Cin
150	9/21	N	L.A.	Welch / Downs (10–9)	L	2–4	82–68	1	+ 7.5	Cin
151	9/22	N	L.A.	Valenzuela / Dravecky (10–11)	L	3–4	82–69	1	+ 6.5	Cin
152	9/23	N	L.A.	Lefferts (5–5) / Hershiser	W	8–7	83–69	1	+ 7.5	Cin
	9/24		OFF DAY						+ 7	Cin
153	9/25	N	@Atl.	Krukow (4–6) / Glavine	W	9–2	84–69	1	+ 7	Cin
154	9/26	N	@Atl.	Puleo/Reuschel (13–8)	L	5–10	84–70	1	+ 7	Cin
155	9/27	D	@Atl.	Price (2–2) / Cary	W	15–6	85–70	1	+ 7	Cin
156	9/28	N	@S.D.	D. Robinson (11–7) / McCullers	W	5–4	86–70	1	+ 7	Cin
157	9/29	N	@S.D.	Downs (11–9) / Jones	W	5–3	87–70	1	+ 7	Cin
158	9/30	N	@L.A.	Krukow (5–6) / Belcher	W	3–0	88–70	1	+ 7	Cin
159	10/1	N	@L.A.	WELCH / Reuschel (13–9)	L	0–7	88–71	1	+ 6	Cin
160	10/2	N	Atl.	Coffman / Dravecky (10–12)	L	4–6	88–72	1	+ 6	Cin
161	10/3	D	Atl.	Downs (12–9) / Clary	W	6–3	89–72	1	+ 6	Cin
162	10/4	D	Atl.	Bockus (1–0) / Acker	W	5–4 (10)	90–72	1	+ 6	Cin

1987 GIANTS STATISTICS

PLAYER	AVG.	G	AB	R	H	2B	3B	HR	RBI-GW	SH	SF	HP	BB-IBB	SO	SB-CS	GDP	E
ALDRETE	.325	126	357	50	116	18	2	9	51 8	4	2	0	43 5	50	6 0	6	3
BRENLY	.267	123	375	55	100	19	1	18	51 8	3	6	3	47 3	85	10 7	5	9
CLARK	.308	150	529	89	163	29	5	35	91 11	3	2	5	49 11	98	5 17	2	13
DAVIS	.250	149	500	80	125	22	1	24	76 5	0	4	2	72 15	109	16 8	8	7
Left-handed	.244	-	316	-	77	16	0	10	42 3	0	3	1	53 10	60	- -	5	-
Right-handed	.261	-	184	-	48	6	1	14	34 2	0	1	1	19 5	49	- -	3	-
LEONARD	.280	131	503	70	141	29	4	19	63 6	0	5	2	21 6	68	16 7	17	7
MALDONADO	.292	118	442	69	129	28	4	20	85 12	0	7	6	34 4	78	8 8	9	5
MELVIN	.199	84	246	31	49	8	0	11	31 6	0	2	0	17 3	44	0 4	7	1
MILNER	.252	101	214	38	54	14	0	4	19 4	1	0	0	24 3	33	10 9	2	1
MITCHELL (TOT)	.280	131	464	68	130	20	2	22	70 6	0	1	2	48 4	88	9 6	10	15
MITCHELL (SF)	.306	69	268	49	82	13	1	15	44 4	0	0	2	28 1	50	9 6	5	7
SPEIER	.249	111	317	39	79	13	0	11	39 5	1	1	3	42 5	51	4 7	3	4
SPILMAN	.267	83	90	5	24	5	0	1	14 2	0	2	0	9 0	20	1 1	3	2
THOMPSON	.262	132	420	62	110	26	5	10	44 2	6	0	8	40 3	91	16 11	8	17
URIBE	.291	95	309	44	90	16	5	5	30 3	5	1	1	24 9	35	12 2	1	13
Left-handed	.308	-	211	-	65	12	5	2	18 1	4	1	0	18 5	24	- -	0	-
Right-handed	.255	-	98	-	25	4	0	3	12 2	1	0	1	6 4	11	- -	1	-
WILLIAMS	.188	84	245	28	46	9	2	8	21 0	3	1	1	16 4	68	4 3	5	9
YOUNGBLOOD	.253	69	91	9	23	3	0	3	11 0	0	1	1	5 0	13	1 1	3	0
DOWNS	.143	41	56	1	8	1	0	0	6 1	7	1	0	1 0	23	0 1	0	3
DRAVECKY (TOT)	.143	49	56	8	1	0	0	0	0 0	4	0	0	4 0	27	1 1	0	2
DRAVECKY (SF)	.132	18	38	3	5	1	0	0	0 0	2	0	0	3 0	18	1 0	0	1
GARRELTS	.200	65	10	1	2	1	0	0	2 0	0	0	0	0 0	5	0 0	0	1
HAMMAKER	.123	31	57	0	7	0	0	0	3 0	2	0	0	1 0	22	0 0	1	0
Left-handed	.115	-	26	-	3	0	0	0	0 0	0	0	0	0 0	14	- -	0	-
Right-handed	.129	-	31	-	4	0	0	0	3 0	2	0	0	1 0	8	- -	1	-
KRUKOW	.167	30	54	1	9	2	0	0	7 1	5	0	0	2 0	27	0 0	0	1
LaCOSS	.060	39	50	2	3	0	0	0	3 0	4	0	1	2 0	16	0 0	1	2
LEFFERTS (TOT)	.286	77	7	0	2	1	0	0	1 0	0	0	0	0 0	4	0 0	0	2
LEFFERTS (SF)	.250	44	4	0	1	1	0	0	1 0	0	0	0	0 0	2	0 0	0	1
PRICE	.167	20	6	1	1	0	0	0	1 0	0	0	0	0 0	3	0 0	0	0
REUSCHEL (TOT)	.139	34	79	8	11	3	0	1	10 1	7	0	0	5 0	26	1 0	1	2
REUSCHEL (SF)	.105	9	19	1	2	1	0	0	5 0	1	0	0	1 0	3	0 0	1	0
ROBINSON (TOT)	.222	69	18	2	4	1	0	1	2 1	0	0	0	1 0	4	0 0	0	0
ROBINSON (SF)	.273	25	11	2	3	1	0	1	1 1	0	0	0	0 0	2	0 0	0	0
GIANTS	.260	162	5608	783	1458	274	32	205	731 83	55	35	39	511 73	1094	126 96	99	129
OPPONENTS	.255	162	5518	669	1407	235	28	146	624 67	74	36	27	547 86	1038	132 86	146	135

PITCHER	W	L	ERA	G	GS	CG	GF	SHO	SV	IP	H	R	ER	HR	BB-IBB	SO	WP	BK
DOWNS	12	9	3.63	41	28	4	4	3	1	186.0	185	83	75	14	67 11	137	12	4
DRAVECKY (TOT)	10	12	3.43	48	28	5	8	3	0	191.1	186	82	73	18	64 7	138	2	1
DRAVECKY (SF)	7	5	3.20	18	18	4	0	3	0	112.1	115	43	40	8	33 3	78	1	0
GARRELTS	11	7	3.22	64	0	0	43	0	12	106.1	70	41	38	10	55 4	127	5	1
HAMMAKER	10	10	3.58	31	27	2	1	0	0	168.1	159	73	67	22	57 10	107	8	7
KRUKOW	5	6	4.80	30	28	3	0	0	0	163.0	182	98	87	24	46 6	104	3	3
LaCOSS	13	10	3.68	39	26	2	4	1	0	171.0	184	78	70	16	63 12	79	6	1
LEFFERTS (TOT)	5	5	3.83	77	0	0	22	0	6	98.2	92	47	42	13	33 11	57	6	3
LEFFERTS (SF)	3	3	3.23	44	0	0	14	0	4	47.1	36	18	17	4	18 6	18	1	1
PRICE	2	2	2.57	20	0	0	5	0	1	35.0	19	10	10	5	13 2	42	1	0
REUSCHEL (TOT)	13	9	3.09	34	33	12	0	4	0	227.0	207	91	78	13	42 3	107	7	0
REUSCHEL (SF)	5	3	4.32	9	8	3	0	1	0	50.0	44	28	24	1	7 2	27	2	0
ROBINSON (TOT)	11	7	3.42	67	0	0	54	0	19	108.0	105	42	41	7	40 6	79	7	1
ROBINSON (SF)	5	1	2.74	25	0	0	17	0	7	42.2	39	13	13	1	18 3	26	1	0
GIANTS	90	72	3.68	162	162	19	143	10	38	1471.0	1407	669	601	146	547 86	1038	59	25
OPPONENTS	72	90	4.34	162	162	14	148	8	40	1462.2	1458	783	705	205	511 73	1094	55	21

1987 CHAMPIONSHIP SERIES

After running away with their first division crown in 16 years, the 1987 Giants were supremely confident entering the NLCS. With Dave Dravecky firing a shutout in Game 2 and Mike Krukow and Joe Price also pitching stoutly, the Giants forged a 3–2 series edge entering the final two games at St. Louis. The Cardinals held them scoreless in those games, and for the final 22 innings, to shatter some World Series dreams. Jeffrey Leonard, who set a record with four homers in the first four games, earned a consolation prize: the MVP trophy.

1987 PLAYOFF BOXES

GAME 1 — Oct. 6 at Busch Stadium

SAN FRANCISCO	AB	R	H	RBI	ST. LOUIS	AB	R	H	RBI
Thompson, 2b	3	2	0	0	Coleman, lf	3	0	1	1
Mitchell, 3b	4	0	1	0	Smith, ss	3	1	1	0
Leonard, lf	4	1	2	1	Herr, 2b	4	0	0	0
Maldonado, rf	4	0	1	2	Driessen, 1b	4	1	2	0
Davis, cf	3	0	0	0	McGee, cf	4	1	2	1
Clark, 1b	4	0	1	0	Pendelton, 3b	4	1	1	1
Brenly, c	4	0	0	0	Ford, rf	4	0	1	0
Uribe, ss	4	0	1	0	Pena, c	3	1	1	0
Reuschel, p	1	0	0	0	Mathews, p	1	0	1	2
Lefferts, p	0	0	0	0	Worrell, p	0	0	0	0
Speier, ph	1	0	0	0	Dayler, p	0	0	0	0
Garrelts, p	0	0	0	0					
Melvin, ph	1	0	0	0					
TOTALS	**33**	**3**	**7**	**3**	**TOTALS**	**30**	**5**	**10**	**5**

				R	H	E
San Francisco ..	1 0 0	1 0 0	0 1 0	—	3	7	1
St. Louis.......	0 0 1	1 0 3	0 0 x	—	5	10	1

E—Driessen, Uribe. DP—San Francisco 1, St. Louis 1. LOB—San Francisco 6, St. Louis 6. 2B—Maldonado, Driessen 2. 3B—Smith. HR—Leonard. SB—Clark. Sac—Mathews 2, Reuschel.

PITCHING SUMMARY

San Francisco	IP	H	R	ER	BB	SO
Reuschel (L)	6	9	5	5	2	1
Lefferts	1	1	0	0	1	0
Garrelts	1	0	0	0	0	2
St. Louis						
Matthews (W)	7.3	4	3	2	1	7
Worrell	0.3	2	0	0	1	0
Dayley (save)	1.3	1	0	0	0	1

Umpires—Kibler, Engel, Quick, Montague, Gregg and Pallone. Time—2:34. Attendance—55,331.

GAME 2 — Oct. 7 at Busch Stadium

SAN FRANCISCO	AB	R	H	RBI	ST. LOUIS	AB	R	H	RBI
Thompson, 2b	5	0	0	0	Coleman, lf	3	0	0	0
Mitchell, 3b	5	0	0	0	Smith, ss	3	0	0	0
Leonard, lf	4	2	3	1	Herr, 2b	4	0	1	0
Maldonado, rf	4	2	2	0	Pendleton, 3b	3	0	0	0
Davis, cf	3	1	0	0	McGee, cf	3	0	0	0
Milner, pr-cf	0	0	0	0	Lindeman, 1b	3	0	1	0
Clark, 1b	3	1	2	2	Oquendo, rf	2	0	0	0
Melvin, c	3	0	0	0	Pena, c	2	0	0	0
Uribe, ss	4	0	1	0	Tudor, p	2	0	0	0
Dravecky, p	4	0	1	0	Pagnozzi, ph	1	0	0	0
					Forsch, p	0	0	0	0
TOTALS	**35**	**5**	**10**	**3**	**TOTALS**	**26**	**0**	**2**	**0**

				R	H	E
San Francisco ..	0 2 0	1 0 0	0 2 0	—	5	10	0
St. Louis.......	0 0 0	0 0 0	0 0 0	—	0	2	1

E—Smith. DP—San Francisco 2. LOB—San Francisco 6, St. Louis 3. 2B—Uribe. HR—Clark, Leonard. Sac—Milner.

PITCHING SUMMARY

San Francisco	IP	H	R	ER	BB	SO
Dravecky (W)	9	2	0	0	4	6
St. Louis						
Tudor (L)	8	10	5	3	2	6
Forsch	1	0	0	0	0	2

Umpires—Montague, Pallone, Gregg, Quick, Engel and Kibler. Time—2:33. Attendance—55,331.

GAME 3 — Oct. 9 at Candlestick Park

ST. LOUIS	AB	R	H	RBI	SAN FRANCISCO	AB	R	H	RBI
Coleman, lf	4	1	1	2	Thompson, 2b	2	0	0	0
Smith, ss	5	1	3	0	Spilman, ph	1	1	1	1
Herr, 2b	4	0	0	0	Mitchell, 3b	5	0	1	0
Lindeman, 1b	3	1	1	3	Leonard, lf	3	1	1	1
McGee, cf	4	0	1	0	Maldonado, rf	4	0	0	0
Pena, c	4	0	1	0	Davis, cf	3	1	1	0
Oquendo, rf-3b	4	1	1	0	Milner, cf	1	0	0	0
Lawless, 3b	2	0	1	0	Clark, 1b	4	1	2	1
Ford, ph-rf	1	1	1	0	Brenly, c	4	1	1	1
Magrane, p	1	0	0	0	Uribe, ss	4	0	0	0
Clark, ph	1	0	0	0	Hammaker, p	3	0	0	0
Forsch, p	0	0	0	0	Robinson, p	0	0	0	0
Driessen, ph	1	0	1	1	Lefferts, p	0	0	0	0
Johnson, pr	0	1	0	0	LaCoss, p	0	0	0	0
Worrell, p	1	0	0	0	Aldrete, ph	1	0	0	0
TOTALS	**35**	**6**	**11**	**6**	**TOTALS**	**35**	**5**	**7**	**4**

				R	H	E
St. Louis.......	0 0 0	0 0 2	4 0 0	—	6	11	1
San Francisco ..	0 3 1	0 0 0	0 0 1	—	5	7	4

E—Mitchell, Herr. DP—San Francisco 2. LOB—St. Louis 6, San Francisco 6. 2B—Davis, Brenly, Clark. 3B—McGee. HR—Leonard, Lindeman, Spilman. SB—Thompson, Herr, Johnson. Sac—Herr. SF—Lindeman.

PITCHING SUMMARY

St. Louis	IP	H	R	ER	BB	SO
Magrane...........	4	4	4	2	2	3
Forsch (W)........	2	1	0	0	0	1
Worrell (save)	3	2	1	1	0	4
San Francisco						
Hammaker	6	7	3	3	0	4
Robinson (L)	0	3	3	3	0	0
Lefferts	1	1	0	0	0	0
LaCross	2	0	0	0	2	1

HB—Leonard (Forsch). WP—Magrane. Umpires—Pallone, Gregg, Quick, Engel, Kibler and Montague. Time—3:27. Attendance—57,913.

GAME 4 — Oct. 10 at Candlestick Park

ST. LOUIS	AB	R	H	RBI	SAN FRANCISCO	AB	R	H	RBI
Coleman, lf	4	0	2	1	Milner, cf	4	0	0	0
Smith, ss	4	0	0	0	Mitchell, 3b	4	1	2	0
Herr, 2b	4	0	1	0	Leonard, lf	2	1	1	2
Driessen, 1b	3	0	0	0	Clark, 1b	4	0	2	0
McGee, cf	4	0	1	0	Aldrete, rf	4	0	1	0
Pendleton, 3b	4	0	1	0	Brenly, c	4	1	2	1
Ford, rf	4	1	1	0	Thompson, 2b	4	1	1	1
Pena, c	3	1	2	0	Uribe, ss	4	0	0	0
Cox, p	3	0	1	1	Krukow, p	2	0	0	0
TOTALS	**33**	**2**	**9**	**2**	**TOTALS**	**32**	**4**	**9**	**4**

				R	H	E
St. Louis.......	0 2 0	0 0 0	0 0 0	—	2	9	0
San Francisco ..	0 0 0	1 2 0	0 1 x	—	4	9	2

E—Thompson, Clark. DP—San Francisco 4. LOB—St. Louis 5, San Francisco 7. 2B—Mitchell, Clark. HR—Thompson, Leonard, Brenly.

PITCHING SUMMARY

St. Louis	IP	H	R	ER	BB	SO
Cox (L)	8	9	4	4	3	6
San Francisco						
Krukow (W)	9	9	2	2	1	3

Umpires—Gregg, Quick, Engel, Kibler, Montague, Pallone. Time—2:23. Attendance—57,997.

GAME 5 — Oct. 11 at Candlestick Park

ST. LOUIS	AB	R	H	RBI	SAN FRANCISCO	AB	R	H	RBI
Coleman, lf	4	1	2	0	Thompson, 2b	2	1	1	1
Smith, ss	2	0	0	1	Mitchell, 3b	3	1	2	2
Herr, 2b	3	0	0	1	Leonard, lf	4	0	0	0
Driessen, 1b	3	0	0	0	Maldonado, rf	4	0	1	0
Lindeman, ph-1b	1	0	0	0	Davis, cf	3	1	1	0
McGee, cf	4	0	2	0	Milner, cf	1	0	0	0
Pendleton, 3b	4	1	1	0	Clark, 1b	3	1	1	0
Morris, rf	2	0	0	0	Brenly, c	1	1	0	0
Forsch, p	0	0	0	0	Uribe, ss	4	1	1	2
Horton, p	0	0	0	0	Reuschel, p	1	0	0	0
Lawless, ph-rf	2	0	0	0	Aldrete, ph	0	0	0	1
Pena, c	2	1	1	0	Price, p	1	0	0	0
Mathews, p	1	0	1	0					
Ford, rf	0	0	0	0					
Oquendo, ph-rf	2	0	0	0					
Dayley, p	0	0	0	0					
TOTALS	**30**	**3**	**7**	**2**	**TOTALS**	**28**	**6**	**7**	**6**

				R	H	E
St. Louis	1 0 1	1 0 0	0 0 0	—	3	7	0
San Francisco	1 0 1	4 0 0	0 0 x	—	6	7	1

E—Reuschel. DP—St. Louis 1, San Francisco 1. LOB—St. Louis 4, San Francisco 5. 2B—Coleman, Thompson. HR—Mitchell. SB—Thompson, Mitchell, Uribe. Sac—Smith. SF—Herr, Smith, Aldrete.

PITCHING SUMMARY

St. Louis	IP	H	R	ER	BB	SO
Mathews	3	2	2	2	2	3
Forsch (L)	0	3	4	4	1	0
Horton	3	2	0	0	0	2
Dayley	2	0	0	0	2	2
San Francisco						
Reuschel	4	6	3	2	0	1
Price (W)	5	1	0	0	1	6

HB—Thompson (Dayley). WP—Reuschel. Umpires—Quick, Engle, Kibler, Montague, Pallone and Gregg. Time—2:48. Attendance—59,363.

GAME 6 — Oct. 13 at Busch Stadium

SAN FRANCISCO	AB	R	H	RBI	ST. LOUIS	AB	R	H	RBI
Thompson, 2b	3	0	0	0	Coleman, lf	4	0	0	0
Mitchell, 3b	4	0	1	0	Smith, ss	4	0	0	0
Leonard, lf	3	0	1	0	Herr, 2b	3	0	2	0
Maldonado, rf	3	0	0	0	Lindeman, 1b	3	0	2	0
Aldrete, ph-rf	1	0	0	0	Pendleton, 3b	3	0	0	0
Davis, cf	4	0	0	0	Pena, c	3	1	1	0
Clark, 1b	3	0	0	0	McGee, cf	3	0	0	0
Melvin, c	3	0	3	0	Oquendo, rf	2	0	0	1
Milner, pr	0	0	0	0	Worrell, p-rf	0	0	0	0
Robinson, p	0	0	0	0	Tudor, p	2	0	0	0
Spilman, ph	0	0	0	0	Morris, rf	1	0	0	0
Speier, ph	1	0	0	0	Dayley, p	0	0	0	0
Uribe, ss	3	0	1	0					
Dravecky, p	2	0	0	0					
Brenly, ph-c	1	0	0	0					
TOTALS	**31**	**0**	**6**	**0**	**TOTALS**	**28**	**1**	**5**	**1**

				R	H	E
San Francisco	0 0 0	0 0 0	0 0 0	—	0	6	0
St. Louis	0 1 0	0 0 0	0 0 0	—	1	5	0

E—none. DP—none. LOB—San Francisco 8, St. Louis 4. 3B—Pena. Sac—Uribe. SF—Oquendo.

PITCHING SUMMARY

San Francisco	IP	H	R	ER	BB	SO
Dravecky (L)	6	5	1	1	0	8
Robinson	2	0	0	0	0	1
St. Louis						
Tudor (W)	7.3	6	0	0	3	6
Worrell	1	0	0	0	0	2
Dayley (save)	0.7	0	· 0	0	0	1

Umpires—Engle, Kibler, Montague, Pallone, Gregg and Quick. Time—3:09. Attendance—55,331.

GAME 7 — Oct. 14 at Busch Stadium

SAN FRANCISCO	AB	R	H	RBI	ST. LOUIS	AB	R	H	RBI
Aldrete, rf	4	0	0	0	Coleman, lf	4	1	1	0
Mitchell, 3b	4	0	1	0	Smith, ss	4	0	1	0
Leonard, lf	4	0	2	0	Herr, 2b	5	0	2	2
Clark, 1b	4	0	1	0	Lindeman, 1b	3	0	0	0
Davis, cf	4	0	0	0	Driessen, ph-1b	1	0	0	0
Brenly, c	3	0	1	0	Pendleton, 3b	1	1	1	0
Speier, 2b	3	0	0	0	Lawless, ph-3b	2	0	1	0
Uribe, ss	3	0	2	0	Pena, c	4	1	2	0
Hammaker, p	0	0	0	0	McGee, cf	4	1	2	1
Milner, ph	1	0	1	0	Oquendo, rf	2	2	1	3
Price, p	0	0	0	0	Cox, p	3	0	1	0
Downs, p	0	0	0	0					
Thompson, ph	1	0	0	0					
Garrelts, p	0	0	0	0					
Lefferts, p	0	0	0	0					
LaCoss, p	0	0	0	0					
Spilman, ph	1	0	0	0					
Robinson, p	0	0	0	0					
TOTALS	**32**	**0**	**8**	**0**	**TOTALS**	**33**	**6**	**12**	**6**

				R	H	E
San Francisco	0 0 0	0 0 0	0 0 0	—	0	8	1
St. Louis	0 4 0	0 0 2	0 0 x	—	6	12	0

E—Davis. DP—St. Louis 3. LOB—San Francisco 5, St. Louis 9. 2B—McGee. HR—Oquendo. SB—Coleman, Pena. Sac—Cox.

PITCHING SUMMARY

San Francisco	IP	H	R	ER	BB	SO
Hammaker (L)	2	5	4	4	0	3
Price	0.7	2	0	0	0	1
Downs	1.3	1	0	0	0	0
Garrelts	1.7	2	2	2	4	2
Lefferts	0	1	0	0	0	0
LaCoss	1.3	1	0	0	1	1
Robinson	1	0	0	0	0	2
St. Louis						
Cox (W)	9	8	0	0	0	5

WP—Garrelts. PB—Brenly. Umpires—Kibler, Montague, Pallone, Gregg, Quick and Engle. Time—2:59. Attendance—55,331.

NLCS STATISTICS
GIANTS' BATTING

Player	AVG	G	AB	R	H	2B	3B	HR	RBI	GW	BB	SO	SB	CS	E
Aldrete	.100	5	10	0	1	0	0	0	1	0	0	2	0	0	0
Brenly	.235	6	17	3	4	1	0	1	2	0	3	7	0	0	0
Clark	.360	7	25	3	9	2	0	1	3	1	3	6	1	1	1
C. Davis	.150	6	20	2	3	1	0	0	0	0	1	4	0	0	1
Leonard	.417	7	24	5	10	0	0	4	5	1	3	4	0	0	0
Maldonado	.211	5	19	2	4	1	0	0	2	0	0	3	0	0	0
Melvin	.429	3	7	0	3	0	0	0	0	0	1	1	0	0	0
Milner	.143	6	7	0	1	0	0	0	0	0	0	3	0	0	0
Mitchell	.267	7	30	2	8	1	0	1	2	0	0	3	1	0	1
Speier	.000	3	5	0	0	0	0	0	0	0	0	2	0	0	0
Spilman	.500	3	2	1	1	0	0	1	1	0	0	0	0	0	0
Thompson	.100	7	20	4	2	0	1	1	2	0	5	7	2	2	1
Uribe	.269	7	26	1	7	1	0	0	2	1	0	4	1	1	1
Downs	---	1	0	0	0	0	0	0	0	0	0	0	0	0	0
Dravecky	.167	2	6	0	1	0	0	0	0	0	0	1	0	0	0
Garrelts	---	2	0	0	0	0	0	0	0	0	0	0	0	0	0
Hammaker	.000	2	3	0	0	0	0	0	0	0	0	2	0	0	0
Krukow	.000	1	2	0	0	0	0	0	0	0	1	0	0	0	0
LaCoss	---	2	0	0	0	0	0	0	0	0	0	0	0	0	0
Lefferts	---	3	0	0	0	0	0	0	0	0	0	0	0	0	0
Price	.000	2	1	0	0	0	0	0	0	0	0	1	0	0	0
Reuschel	.000	2	2	0	0	0	0	0	0	0	0	1	0	0	1
D. Robinson	---	3	0	0	0	0	0	0	0	0	0	0	0	0	0
Giants	.239	7	226	23	54	7	1	9	20	3	17	51	5	4	6
Opponents	.260	7	215	23	56	4	4	2	22	4	16	42	4	4	3

GIANTS' PITCHING

Pitcher	W	L	ERA	G	GS	CG	SHO	SV	IP	H	R	ER	HR	BB	SO
Downs	0	0	0.00	1	0	0	0	0	1.1	1	0	0	0	0	0
Dravecky	1	1	0.60	2	2	1	1	0	15.0	7	1	1	0	4	14
Garrelts	0	0	6.75	2	0	0	0	0	2.2	2	2	2	0	4	4
Hammaker	0	1	7.88	2	2	0	0	0	8.0	12	7	7	2	0	7
Krukow	1	0	2.00	1	1	1	0	0	9.0	9	2	2	0	1	3
LaCoss	0	0	0.00	2	0	0	0	0	3.1	1	0	0	0	3	2
Lefferts	0	0	0.00	3	0	0	0	0	2.0	3	0	0	0	1	0
Price	1	0	0.00	2	0	0	0	0	5.2	3	0	0	0	1	7
Reuschel	0	1	6.30	2	2	0	0	0	10.0	15	8	7	0	2	2
D. Robinson	0	1	9.00	3	0	0	0	0	3.0	3	3	3	0	0	3
Giants	3	4	3.30	4	4	2	1	0	60.0	56	23	22	2	16	42
Opponents	4	3	2.95	7	7	2	2	3	61.0	54	23	20	9	17	51

4

THE GREAT
SAN FRANCISCO
GIANTS

Hall of Famers Significantly Associated with the Giants	Year Elected to Hall of Fame
Christy Mathewson	1936
John McGraw	1937
Roger Bresnahan	1945
Jim O'Rourke	1945
Buck Ewing	1946
Joe McGinnity	1946
Frank Frisch	1947
Carl Hubbell	1947
Mel Ott	1951
Bill Terry	1954
Tim Keefe	1964
Monte Ward	1964
Dave Bancroft	1971
Rube Marquard	1971
Ross Youngs	1972
Monte Irvin	1973
George Kelly	1973
Mickey Welch	1973
Roger Connor	1976
Fred Lindstrom	1976
Amos Rusie	1977
Willie Mays	1979
Travis Jackson	1982
Juan Marichal	1983
Hoyt Wilhelm	1985
Willie McCovey	1986

Other Hall of Famers Who Played for the Giants	Year Elected to Hall of Fame
Willie Keeler	1939
Rogers Hornsby	1942
Dan Brouthers	1945
Mike"King" Kelly	1945
Jesse Burkett	1946
Ray Schalk	1955
Edd Roush	1962
Burleigh Grimes	1964
Joe Medwick	1968
Waite Hoyt	1969
Jake Beckley	1971
Warren Spahn	1973
Casey Stengel	1974
Hack Wilson	1979
Duke Snider	1980
Ernie Lombardi	1986

SKETCHES OF THE
SAN FRANCISCO GREATS

Willie Mays

Willie Mays unquestionably was the greatest all-around player in Giants history, displaying his extraordinary skills for six seasons in New York and for fifteen more in San Francisco. He was hailed for his consummate excellence in all facets of the game, but is best remembered for his home runs, all but fourteen of his 660 coming as a member of the Giants.

The Say Hey Kid, as he was known in his New York days, tied John Mize's club record with fifty-one home runs in 1955 and set a new standard by blasting fifty-two for San Francisco ten years later. He became the National League's first 30-30 man by belting thirty-six homers and stealing forty bases in 1956. One year later, he became the first man to do it twice.

Mays, who wore No. 24, was purchased from the Birmingham Black Barons for $14,000 in 1950 at age nineteen. One year later he was in the bigs, helping the Giants win a miracle pennant. Following two years in the military service, he returned to New York in 1954 and parlayed an MVP season into victory in the World Series, one best remembered for his catch of Vic Wertz's long fly to center. Mays won the batting title that year at .345.

Although Willie was a hero in New York, he was greeted with skepticism when the Giants moved west in 1958. Despite a career-high .347 average that maiden season, the Bay Area fans didn't fully accept Mays until his slugging feats rewarded San Francisco with its only pennant winner in 1962. He hit forty-nine homers and knocked in a career-high 141 runs that year.

Mays's one last gasp of glory for the Giants came at age forty, when his hot first half gave the 1971 club the division lead en route to the title. One year later, Mays was traded to the Mets and his beloved New York, where he went out in style by appearing in the 1973 World Series. It's been many years since he last wore a Giants uniform, but the incomparable Mays still tops the San Francisco Giants in all offensive categories except batting average, games played, and home runs.

Juan Marichal

Nobody did it better than the Dominican Dandy. Juan Marichal simply was the finest pitcher to wear a San Francisco uniform, winning 104 more games than anyone else in the Giants' West Coast history. Marichal was 238-140 with the Giants, including fifty-two shutouts and a 2.84 earned run average over fourteen seasons.

Marichal required only 2½ years of minor league seasoning before he joined the Giants to stay with a one-hit debut against the Phillies in 1960. He had his first great season in 1963 with a 25-8 record and a 2.41 ERA plus a no-hitter against Houston (the Giants' first since 1929!), and a sixteen-inning, 1-0 victory over Warren Spahn of the Braves.

That season began a string of six twenty-win campaigns in seven years, the exception being 1967, when injury deprived him of approximately one dozen starts and restricted him to a 14-10 record. Contemporaries Bob Gibson, Sandy Koufax, and Don Drysdale received more attention in the sixties, but none could match Juan's 191 victories for the decade.

Marichal was the complete pitcher, a right-handed Spahn with his high-kicking delivery. Others were faster and had sharper-breaking pitches, but none could master their repertoire like Juan could. His ability to nick the corners with all of his vast assortment of pitches baffled hitters. Durability was another Marichal asset — he completed sixteen games in a row en route to a 26-9 season in 1968.

Orlando Cepeda

The Baby Bull enjoyed only seven full seasons in the Giants' livery, yet he made the greatest impact on the San Francisco franchise in the shortest amount of time. Nobody, not even the great Mays, took the Bay Area by storm as Orlando Cepeda did in his and the Giants' rookie year in San Francisco. Anxious fans desperately wanted a new hero and Cepeda won their hearts with a .312 average, twenty-five home runs, and Rookie of the Year honors.

The Puerto Rican powerhouse won batting titles in his first two minor league seasons for Kokomo (.393) and St. Cloud (.355) before using Triple-A Minneapolis as a stepping stone to the majors. Cepeda smacked a home run in his first big league game, the historic Giants-Dodgers West Coast inaugural, and was dear to the hearts of Bay Area fans ever since that sensational debut.

He already was an All-Star Game performer by 1959, and in 1961 he enjoyed one of the finest seasons in the club's history. Cepeda set a San Francisco record in 1961 with 142 runs batted in and led the National League with forty-six home runs, a career high. Despite a late-season slump, he helped the Giants to the 1962 pennant with thirty-five homers and 114 RBI.

Cepeda never hit below .297 in his seven full seasons with the club, and his .308 career average with the Giants is the highest in the history of the franchise on the West Coast. Mays, at .301, is the only other player to post a lifetime mark above .300. But Cepeda was deemed expendable in 1966 when it finally was determined that neither he nor Willie McCovey could play anywhere but first base.

Willie McCovey

The presence of Willie McCovey made the trading of Cepeda to St. Louis tolerable, because Stretch proved beyond a doubt that if one of the popular youngsters had to go, the Giants made the correct decision. As soon as Cepeda departed, McCovey settled at first base, brought consistency to his game, and blossomed into one of the greatest sluggers in history.

McCovey became the most popular player in the club's West Coast history, enjoying a career that spanned four decades and produced 521 home runs. He hit 469 of those with the Giants, ten more than Mays accumulated in a San Francisco uniform.McCovey retired in 1980 with eighteen grand-slam home runs, more than anyone in National League history.

But it was a rocky path to stardom for No. 44. He made a big splash as a rookie in 1959, batting .354 with thirteen home runs in fifty-two games in 1959 and earning Rookie of the Year distinction. One year later, he struggled and was returned to the minors. When he rejoined the Giants, his playing time was reduced by Cepeda's presence, yet he helped the Giants to the 1962 flag with a .293 average and twenty home runs in only 229 at bats in 1962.

Stretch was used as a left fielder in 1963, responding with a club-record forty-four home runs at that position and tying Hank Aaron for the league lead. There was a woeful slump in 1964, but by 1965 an upward trend began that earned the big fellow MVP honors in 1969 with forty-five homers, 126 RBI, and a .320 average.

McCovey was the most feared slugger in the league during his peak years. In 1969-70, for instance, he totaled eighty-four homers and 252 RBI despite a staggering 258 walks. He was swapped to San Diego in 1974, but his heart remained in San Francisco. In 1977, Willie Mac was signed by the Giants as a free agent and said "thank you" with twenty-eight home runs as the Comeback Player of the Year. To some, he'd never left.

Gaylord Perry

Some might argue that Gaylord Perry doesn't belong among the Giants greats, but the 300-game winner spent more complete seasons (eight) with San Francisco than with any other club. Only Marichal has better numbers in most of the S.F. pitching lists, which show Gaylord with 134 victories and a 2.96 ERA.

Perry, a $90,000 bonus baby, made it to the big leagues to stay in 1964; a performance at New York, May 31, 1964, started him on the road to stardom. It was the second game of the longest doubleheader in history and Perry worked ten innings, striking out nine, to gain the victory in the Giants' 8-6, twenty-three-inning decision. That was the first time, by Gay's admission, that he used his so-called "spitter."

Perry always pitched in Marichal's shadow and was a tough-luck hurler for the Giants. In 1967-68, for instance, his ERAs were 2.61 and 2.44, yet his combined record was 31-32. His first great season with the Giants was 1966, when Gaylord went 21-8 and set a San Francisco strikeout record with fifteen against the Phillies on July 22. That was the most strikeouts by a Giants pitcher since Christy Mathewson's sixteen in 1904.

He fired the second no-hitter in S.F. history by shackling the Cardinals in 1968, won nineteen games with a 2.49 ERA in '69, and enjoyed his finest Giants season in 1970, topping the National League with a 23-13 record. He aided the club's 1971 pennant drive with sixteen victories, added one more in the playoffs, and was traded to Cleveland for Sam McDowell in one of the more controversial and ill-fated swaps in Giants history. Perry won more games (twenty-four) for the Indians in '72 than McDowell did in his S.F. career.

Bobby Bonds

Though Bobby Bonds enjoyed an excellent career and played with many teams, he's best remembered for his first seven years with the Giants, a time in which he attained stardom while teammates like Willie Mays and Willie McCovey were in the twilight of their success. Bonds, in fact, was in the spotlight as "the next Mays" as soon as he belted a grand-slam home run off the Dodgers' John Purdin in the speedy slugger's major league debut, June 25, 1968.

Bonds blended the rare combination of speed and power into some outstanding seasons, yet he never escaped the shadow of Mays. He also had a penchant for the strikeout, so observers constantly wondered what more he could have achieved by making more contact. Under the circumstances, his accomplishments were staggering.

In his first full major league season in 1969, Bonds joined the exclusive 30–30 club by hitting 32 home runs and swiping 45 bases. Mays had been the only player in baseball history to do it twice, and Bobby tied for that honor with 39 homers and 43 stolen bases in 1973, his finest all-around season. That year, he also set a major league mark with 11 homers as the leadoff batter in a game.

Bonds became the last Giant to register 200 hits when he did it in 1970, setting San Francisco standards with 134 runs scored and 663 at bats that year. In 1971, his 102 RBI helped the club to its first division title. In 1973, he was named N.L. Player of the Year by The Sporting News and also was the All-Star Game MVP. He led the league in runs (131) and total bases (341) that season, but played only one more year with the Giants before Horace Stoneham swapped him to the Yankees for Bobby Murcer.

Jack Clark

When Jack Clark's playoff homer thrust the Cardinals into the 1985 World Series, the moody slugger attained national recognition. But Giants' fans already knew he was something special when he established two all-time franchise records in 1978, his second full season as a big leaguer. Blessed with quick wrists, Clark belted a record 46 doubles that year and also hit safely in 26 straight games.

"The bat feels like a wand—I swing it and I get hits," Clark innocently explained during his banner season, one which included a .306 batting average for a club which contended much of the season. Greatness was predicted for a youngster who was signed as a pitcher in the 13th round of the 1973 draft. Nothing was said about his hitting. So much for scouting.

Clark sparkled again in 1982, reaching career highs with 27 home runs and 103 RBI, becoming the first Giant to surpass 100 since Bonds in 1971. Then injuries began taking their toll, limiting his participation with the Giants and the Cardinals the last five years, through 1987. He was headed for a big year in 1984, for instance, when injury enabled him to play merely 57 games. He already had 44 RBI and was batting .320 in his final year with San Francisco.

Although he had the ability to become one of the most popular players in San Francisco history, Clark's constant harping about Candlestick Park and the club's losing trend during his career led to unhappiness and triggered the controversial trade to S. Louis prior to 1985. The Cards reaped immediate benefits, yet when Clark opted for free agency and went to the Yankees in 1988, the Giants still had star shortstop Jose Uribe from that deal.

Vida Blue

There's no doubt Vida Blue had his greatest years as a member of the crossbay A's, yet it was his presence on the 1978 Giants that lifted the club from its doldrums and made it respectable once again. Thanks to a blockbuster trade involving seven Giants during spring training, the club finally acquired a stopper, March 15, 1978.

Blue, then 28, was an immediate sensation in the National League following a 124–86 beginning with the A's. The veteran lefty kept the Giants in contention with an 18–10 record and a 2.79 earned run average, winning 10 straight games in one stretch. For his efforts, he was named N.L. Pitcher of the Year by The Sporting News.

That season, he also became the first pitcher in history to start an All-Star Game with each league. Three years later, with a victory at Cleveland, Blue became the first pitcher to win an All-Star Game for each league. The next spring, however, he was traded to Kansas City in a swap that brought Atlee Hammaker to San Francisco.

Following his well-documented involvement with drugs, Blue mounted a comeback. The Giants gave him an opportunity, and he responded with an 8–8 record in 1985, at age 36. He concluded an excellent major league career by going 10–10 with the Giants, including his 200th victory, in 1986. Blue finished with 209 triumphs, 72 of them with the Giants.

Will Clark

It could be argued that WIll Clark hasn't had enough experience to be included in this section, yet a long and successful major league career seems to be a foregone conclusion for this precocious power-hitter, a former U.S. Olympian and the outstanding collegiate player in America in 1985.

Will The Thrill has captivated Giants' fans ever since his first major league swing produced a home run off Nolan Ryan at the Astrodome in 1986. Making the jump from 65 games in Double-A to the big leagues, Clark enjoyed a solid rookie season, one marred only by a wrist injury. One year later, he already was regarded among the premier firstbasemen in the game.

If Clark's 1987 success is merely the tip of the iceberg, a Hall of Fame career is within the realm of possibility. When he batted .308 with 35 home runs for the division champions, Clark became the first S.F. slugger to hit .300 with at least 30 homers since Willie McCovey (.320–45) did it in his MVP season of 1969.

Clark's 35 homers were the most by a Giant since Bobby Bonds belted 39 in 1973. While the Giants were making their push toward a title down the stretch, he tied an S.F. record with at least one RBI in nine straight games, Aug. 3–11. He crowned an exemplary sophomore season by batting .360 against the Cardinals in the NLCS. A thrill, indeed.

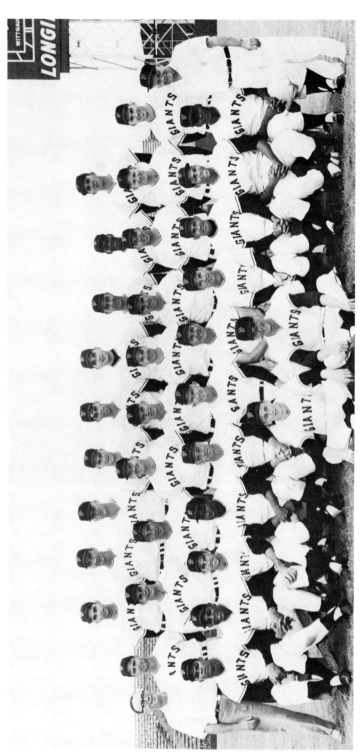

San Francisco's first Giants, 1958, l. to r. (top row) Ramon Monzant, Hank Sauer, Bob Schmidt, Bob Speake, Eddie Bressoud, John Antonelli, Ray Jablonski, Valmy Thomas, Mike McCormick; (middle row) Eddie Logan, Don Johnson, Paul Giel, Nick Testa, Al Worthington, Jackie Brandt, Stu Miller, Danny O'Connell, Gordon Jones, Whitey Lockman, Daryl Spencer, Doc Bowman; (bottom row) Felipe Alou, Willie Mays, Jim Davenport, Willie Kirkland, Wes Westrum, Bill Rigney, Herman Franks, Sa ty Parker, Ruben Gomez, Orlando Cepeda, Bill White; (batboys) Roy McKercher and Frank Iverlich

WILLIE MAYS . . . after move to S.F. in 1958

ORLANDO CEPEDA . . . rookie listened to records

SEALS STADIUM . . . first home of the San Francisco Giants, 1958–59

Willie Mays (right) posed with Stan Musial at Seals Stadium

Rookie Willie McCovey's powerful swing at Seals Stadium, 1959

CANDLESTICK PARK...a capacity crowd at new home of the Giants

ALVIN DARK...managed N.L. champs in 1962

FELIPE ALOU...a .316 average in 1962

STU MILLER . . . won 14 in relief in 1961

SAD SAM JONES . . . a 21-game winner in 1959

Giants' Murderers Row of early Sixties, (from left) Willie McCovey, Willie Mays and Orlando Cepeda terrorized N.L. pitchers

BILLY PIERCE . . . contributed 16 wins in 1962   JACK SANFORD . . . Giants' 1962 ace at 24–7

FELIPE ALOU . . . slid into Dodgers' catcher John Roseboro

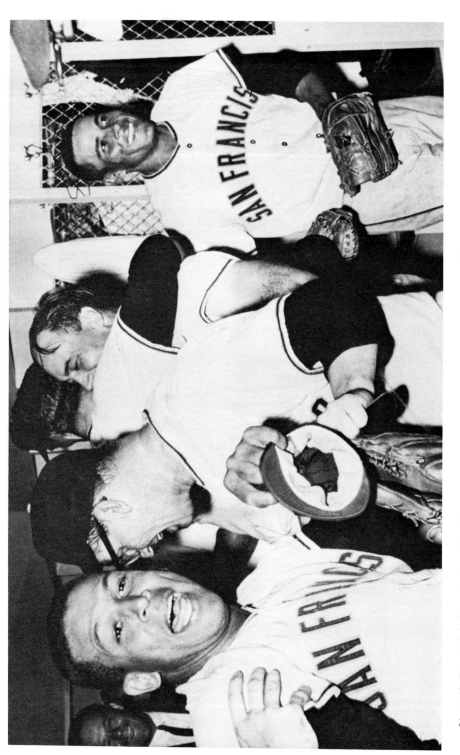

Giants (left to right) Orlando Cepeda, Bob Nieman, Chuck Hiller (being hugged) and Jose Pagan were in a joyous mood following pennant-clinching 6–4 playoff victory at Los Angeles in 1962 (Associated Press photo)

Chuck Hiller watched the flight of the ball after becoming the first N.L. player ever to hit a grand-slam in a World Series game. The blow occurred at Yankee Stadium in 1962 (Associated Press photo)

1962 champions, l. to r. (top row) Jim Davenport, Willie Mays, Bob Bolin, Harvey Kuenn, Manny Mota, Bob Nieman; (second row) Don Larsen, Ed Bailey, Tom Haller, Juan Marichal, Felipe Alou, Willie McCovey, Mike McCormick; (third row) Eddie Logan, Jim Duffalo, Whitey Lockman, Larry Jansen, Alvin Dark, Wes Westrum, Jack Sanford, Orlando Cepeda, Doc Bowman; (bottom row) Stu Miller, Billy Pierce, Ernie Bowman, Chuck Hiller, Ernie Reddick, Matty Alou, Jose Pagan, Billy O'Dell, Joe Pignatano

Willie McCovey belted a three-run homer to down the Cubs, 6–4, at wide-open Candlestick Park in 1965. That's Jesus Alou heading for third and Willie Mays approaching second

Willie Mays, as he looked in the mid-Sixties, when his consistent excellence carried the club to perennial second-place finishes

Willie Mays rapped out one of his 2,992 career hits

Stylish righthander Juan Marichal was the winningest N.L. pitcher in the Sixties, posting 20-victory seasons six of seven years, 1963–69. He's the biggest winner in S.F. history with 238

GAYLORD PERRY ... began 300-win career with Giants

JIM RAY HART ... blasted 139 homers in first five years

Hal Lanier (left), who managed Houston to a division title in 1986, beat the throw to Mets' catcher Jerry Grote in 1966

A grim moment in Candlestick Park history found Juan Marichal (27) attacking Dodgers' catcher John Roseboro with a bat as coach Charlie Fox and Sandy Koufax looked on

Lefthander Mike McCormick rejoined the Giants in 1967 and promptly was the N.L.
Cy Young Award winner with a 22–10 record and a 2.85 earned run average

HERMAN FRANKS . . . four straight runners-up, 1965–68

CLYDE KING . . . managed 90–72 Giants of 1969

CHARLIE FOX . . . Year of the Fox brought title in 1971

WES WESTRUM . . . guided Stoneham Era's last hurrah in 1975

Gaylord Perry displayed the 1970 form which produced a 23–13 record, including four straight September shutouts

Bobby Bonds, who bounced around the majors after leaving S.F., enjoyed his finest season with the 1973 Giants, belting 39 homers, stealing 43 bases and knocking in 96 runners. He also was the All-Star Game MVP

1971 division champions, l. to r. (top row) Eddie Logan, Mike Murphy, Willie Mays, Jerry Johnson, Bobby Bonds, Jim Barr, Tito Fuentes, Steve Hamilton, Jim Ray Hart, Jim Willoughby, Willie McCovey, Fran Healy, Ha Lanier, Al Wylder, Chris Arnold, Dave Rader, Doc Hughes, Rich Robertson; (middle row) Frank Bergonzi, Dick Dietz, Russ Gibson, Ozzie Virgil, John McNamara, Wes Westrum, Charlie Fox, Larry Jansen, Alan Gallagher, Don McMahon, Gaylord Perry; (bottom row) Chris Speier, Juan Marichal, Frank Duffy, Steve Sockolov, Jim Saunders, Ron Bryant, Don Carrithers, Steve Stone, John Cumberland, Jimmy Rosario

JIM DAVENPORT...greatest third baseman in S.F. history

CHRIS SPEIER...rookie whiz sparked 1971 title

JUAN MARICHAL...at dusk of a Hall of Fame career

DAVE KINGMAN...29 homers in 1972

GEORGE FOSTER...a bad trade for Giants

GARY MATTHEWS...Rookie of the Year in 1973

GARRY MADDOX...a .319 hitter in 1973

These four starters (clockwise from top left), Bob Knepper, Jim Barr, John Montefusco and Vida Blue, posed by the Golden Gate Bridge for a Sporting News cover after getting the 1978 Giants off to a fast start. Newcomer Blue won 18 games and Knepper added 17

BILL MADLOCK...batted .309 in 1978

FRANK ROBINSON...first black manager in N.L.

JACK CLARK...blowing bubbles during spring training exercises

JACK CLARK...Giants' most feared slugger, 1978–84, in batting cage

WILLIE McCOVEY...finished with 521 homers, 1980

ROGER CRAIG...a Hum Baby success in 1986

JEFFREY LEONARD . . . club's leader of the mid-Eighties

MIKE KRUKOW . . . a 20-game winner in 1986

BOB BRENLY . . . team homer leader in 1985

CHILI DAVIS . . . a switch-hitter with power

CHRIS BROWN . . . batted .317 in 1986

SCOTT GARRELTS . . . club's new relief ace

WILL CLARK . . . jumped from Class-A to majors

ROBBY THOMPSON . . . rookie sensation of 1986

JEFF ROBINSON...six wins and 10 saves prior to Aug. 21 trade

RICK REUSCHEL...five victories after joining Giants

DAVE DRAVECKY . . . 7–5, 3.20 in second half for S.F.

MIKE ALDRETE...batting leader at .325

MATT WILLIAMS...top 1987 rookie

JOE PRICE...bargain-basement lefty

KELLY DOWNS...12 wins and a save

JOSE URIBE and ROBBY THOMPSON . . . key combination for a frachise-record 183 double plays

CANDY MALDONADO...solid first season as a regular

BOB BRENLY . . . congratulated at home plate after his 10th-inning home run defeated the Braves, 5–4, in the final regular-season game. It was the club's 205th, establishing a San Francisco record.

THE OLD GUARD . . . outfielders Chili Davis (left) and Jeffrey Leonard trotted off the field as the season drew to a close. Each belted his 100th career homer in the division-clinching victory at San Diego, Sept. 28.

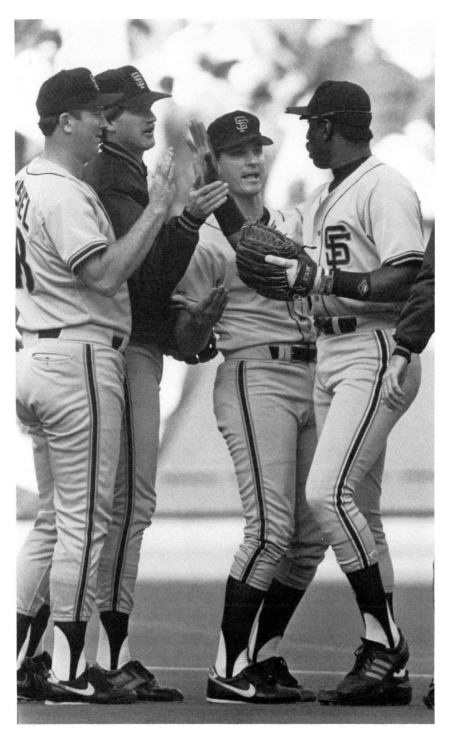

JUBILANT GIANTS... Following a Game 2 NLCS victory, Giants' (left to right) Rick Reuschel, Kelly Downs, Dave Dravecky and Jeffrey Leonard celebrated Dravecky's two-hit, 5–0 triumph at St. Louis.

JEFFREY LEONARD ... Giants' leader in a reflective mood

MIKE KRUKOW . . . in afterglow of Game 4 NLCS victory

RICK REUSCHEL . . . treasure from Pirates

DON ROBINSON . . . division-clinching hero

HARRY SPILMAN . . . big bopper off bench

JOEL YOUNGBLOOD . . . good in a pinch

CHILI DAVIS...hit career-high 24 homers in final season with Giants

JEFFREY LEONARD . . . a hearty welcome following record NLCS homer

JEFFREY LEONARD . . . adoring fans demand a curtain call

DELIRIOUS DUO ... Joe Price and Will Clark celebrate final out

MIKE LaCOSS...team-high 13 victories

CRAIG LEFFERTS...gave bullpen a boost

KEVIN MITCHELL....306 with Giants

BOB MELVIN...a well-armed catcher

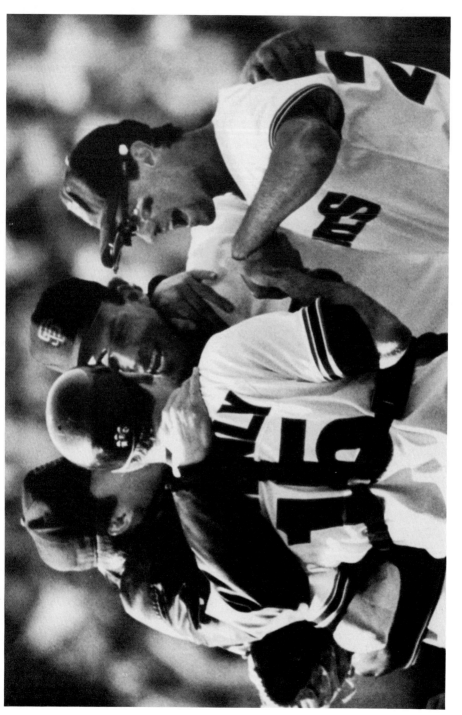

FINAL FLING...after taking a 3–2 NLCS lead on a Game 5 victory, their last of 1987, the Giants' (left to right) Atlee Hammaker, Bob Brenly, Joe Price and Will Clark whooped it up at Candlestick Park.

ROGER CRAIG . . . the real Humm-Baby worked on his image

DIVISION CHAMPIONS . . . the 1987 Giants, who gave the club its first division title in 16 years, posed at Candlestick Park early in the season. Back row, left to right, Jeffrey Leonard, Chili Davis, Candy Maldonado, Scott Garrelts, Jim Gott, Bob Brenly, Bob Melvin, Kelly Downs, Mile LaCoss, Jeff Robinson, Greg Minton, Atlee Hammaker, Mark Davis, Mike Krukow and Joel Youngblood. Middle row, left to right, Mike Murphy, Dirk Smith, Mark Letendre, Matt Williams, Mark Grant, Gordy MacKenzie, Bob Lillis, Norm Sherry, Roger Craig, Bill Fahey, Don Zimmer, Jose Morales, Chris Speier, Harry Spilman, Greg Lynn, Dennis Perry. Front row, left to right, Dan Culbertson, Bill Fanaca, Mike Woodard, Robby Thompson, Mark Wasinger, Jose Uribe, Mike Aldrete, Will Clark, Eddie Midyett and Mark Mullane.

5

THE 1962 GIANTS

The 1962 Giants established a San Francisco record with 103 victories, including a pair of playoff triumphs which placed the franchise into the World Series for the only time in its Bay Area history. The Giants were four games behind the Dodgers with 13 games remaining, but managed a tie to force a playoff. Willie Mays powered an attack which lead the league in batting, runs and home runs. He hit a league-leading 49 home runs and was among seven Giants batting above .292. Mays knocked in 141 runs and Orlando Cepeda added 114 RBI for a formidable attack that supported stout pitching. Righthander Jack Sanford was tops at 27–7, including 16 consecutive victories, and Stu Miller saved 19 games. How the 1962 Giants did it:

CHAMPIONSHIP SEASON OF 1962

APRIL (15–5)

Game	Date	Opponent	Score	Winner	Loser	W–L	GB/GA
1	April 10	Milwaukee	6–0	Marichal (1–0)	Spahn	1–0	+ 1
2	April 11	Milwaukee	3–1	O'Dell (1–0)	Willey	2–0	+ 1
3	April 12	Milwaukee	8–4	Sanford (1–0)	Buhl	3–0	+ 1
4	April 13	Cincinnati	7–2	Pierce (1–0)	O'Toole	4–0	+ 1
5	April 14	Cincinnati	13–6	Larsen (1–0)	Ellis	5–0	+ 1
6	April 15	Cincinnati	3–4	Purkey	Marichal (1–1)	5–1	+ 1
7	April 16	Los Angeles	19–8	O'Dell (2–0)	Williams	6–1	+ 2
8	April 17	Los Angeles	7–8	Drysdale	McCormick (0–1)	6–2	+ 1
9	April 18	@Milwaukee	4–6	Spahn	Miller (0–1)	6–3	+ 1
10	April 19	@Milwaukee	7–6	Marichal (2–1)	Burdette	7–3	+ 1
11	April 21	@Cincinnati	8–6	Larsen (2–0)	Brosnan	8–3	+ 1
12	April 22	@Cincinnati	4–6	Jay	Sanford (1–1)	8–4	+ 1
13	April 23	@Cincinnati	4–1	Pierce (2–0)	O'Toole	9–4	+ 1
14	April 24	@Pittsburgh	3–7	McBean	Marichal (2–2)	9–5	Tie
15	April 25	@Pittsburgh	8–3	Perry (1–0)	Friend	10–5	+ 1
16	April 27	Chicago	5–4	Miller (1–1)	Anderson	11–5	+ ½
17	April 28	Chicago	11–2	Marichal (3–2)	Lary	12–5	+ ½
18	April 29	Chicago (1)	7–0	Sanford (2–1)	Hobbie	13–5	
19	April 29	Chicago (2)	6–0	Pierce (3–0)	Curtis	14–5	+ 2½
20	April 30	Pittsburgh	4–1	Perry (2–0)	Mizell	15–5	2½

MAY (20–10)

Game	Date	Opponent	Score	Winner	Loser	W–L	GB/GA
21	May 1	Pittsburgh	4–2	O'Dell (3–0)	Veale	16–5	+2½
22	May 2	Pittsburgh	3–2	Marichal (4–2)	Francis	17–5	+3½
23	May 3	Pittsburgh	8–4	Sanford (3–1)	Haddix	18–5	+4
24	May 4	@Chicago	11–6	Pierce (4–0)	Ellsworth	19–5	+5
25	May 5	@Chicago	8–12	Schultz	Duffalo (0–1)	19–6	+4
26	May 6	@Chicago	7–3	O'Dell (4–0)	Buhl	20–6	+4½
27	May 8	@St. Louis	4–3	Marichal (5–2)	Jackson	21–6	+5
28	May 9	@St. Louis	3–7	Simmons	Sanford (3–2)	21–7	+4
29	May 10	@St. Louis	6–0	O'Dell (5–0)	Gibson	22–7	+4
30	May 11	@Houston	0–7	Farrell	Perry (2–1)	22–8	+3
31	May 12	@Houston	11–0	Marichal (6–2)	Woodeshick	22–8	+4
32	May 13	@Houston	7–2	Sanford(4–2)	Johnson	24–8	+4
33	May 15	St. Louis	6–3	Pierce (5–0)	Simmons	25–8	+4
34	May 16	St. Louis	7–2	Marichal (7–2)	McDaniel	26–8	+4
35	May 17	St. Louis	0–1	Gibson	O'Dell (5–1)	26–9	+3
36	May 18	Houston	*2–3	Johnson	Sanford (4–3)	26–10	+3
37	May 19	Houston	10–2	McCormick (1–1)	Witt	27–10	+4
38	May 20	Houston (1)	5–6	Bruce	Marichal(7–3)	27–11	
39	May 20	Houston (2)	7–4	Pierce (6–0)	Woodeshick	28–11	+4½
40	May 21	@Los Angeles	1–8	Koufax	O'Dell (5–2)	28–12	+3½
41	May 22	@Los Angeles	1–5	Williams	Sanford (4–4)	28–13	+2½
42	May 23	Philadelphia	7–10	Mahaffey	McCormick (1–2)	28–14	+1½
43	May 24	Philadelphia	7–4	Miller (2–1)	McLish	29–14	+1½
44	May 25	Philadelphia	10–7	Pierce (7–0)	Hamilton	30–14	+1½
45	May 26	New York	*7–6	Larsen (3–0)	Hook	31–14	+1½
46	May 27	New York (1)	7–1	Sanford (5–4)	Craig	32–14	
47	May 27	New York (2)	6–5	Duffalo (1–1)	Anderson	33–14	+1½
48	May 30	@Phila. (1)	4–3	Miller (3–1)	Short	34–14	
49	May 30	@Phila. (2)	5–2	McCormick (2–2)	Hamilton	35–14	+1½
50	May 31	@Philadelphia	1–2	Mahaffey	O'Dell (5–3)	35–15	+½

JUNE (16–13)

Game	Date	Opponent	Score	Winner	Loser	W–L	GB/GA
51	June 1	@New York	9–6	Pierce (8–0)	Craig	36–15	Tie
52	June 2	@New York (1)	10–1	Sanford (6–4)	Hook	37–15	
53	June 2	@New York (2)	6–4	O'Dell (6–3)	Anderson	38–15	+1½
54	June 3	@New York	6–1	Marichal (8–3)	Miller	39–15	+2½
55	June 5	@Chicago	11–4	O'Dell (7–3)	Buhl	40–15	+2
56	June 6	@Chicago	*3–4	Ellsworth	Larsen (3–1)	40–16	+½
57	June 7	@Chicago	3–4	Cardwell	Pierce (8–1)	40–17	+½
58	June 8	@St. Louis	4–8	Gibson	Marichal (8–4)	40–18	–½
59	June 9	@St. Louis	4–8	Sadecki	Sanford (6–5)	40–19	–½
60	June 10	@St. Louis (1)	5–6	Shantz	O'Dell (7–4)	40–20	
61	June 10	@St. Louis (2)	3–13	Washburn	Duffalo (1–2)	40–21	–2½
62	June 12	@Cincy (1)	2–1	Marichal (9–4)	O'Toole	41–21	
63	June 12	@Cincy (2)	7–5	McCormick (3–2)	Drabowsky	42–21	–1
64	June 13	@Cincinnati	0–5	Purkey	Sanford (6–6)	42–22	–2
65	June 14	@Cincinnati	0–8	Jay	Pierce (8–2)	42–23	–2
66	June 15	St. Louis	2–5	Sadecki	O'Dell (7–5)	42–24	–2
67	June 16	St. Louis	5–0	Marichal (10–4)	Jackson	43–24	–1
68	June 17	St. Louis	6–3	Sanford (7–6)	Washburn	44–24	–1
69	June 19	Houston	4–6	Giusti	O'Dell (7–6)	44–25	–2½
70	June 20	Houston	5–9	Stone	Miller (3–2)	44–26	–2½
71	June 22	Milwaukee	9–11	Fischer	Miller (3–3)	44–27	–2½
72	June 23	Milwaukee	4–2	McCormick (4–2)	Shaw	45–27	–2½
73	June 24	Milwaukee	3–1	Marichal (11–4)	Spahn	46–27	–1½
74	June 25	Cincinnati	3–1	O'Dell (8–6)	Maloney	47–27	–½
75	June 26	Cincinnati	*6–5	Miller (4–3)	Sisler	48–27	+½

76	June 27	Cincinnati	6-3	Bolin (1-0)	Wills	49-27	+ ½
77	June 28	Philadelphia	2-7	Smith	Marichal (11-5)	49-28	– ½
78	June 29	Philadelphia	*4-3	O'Dell ((9-6)	Baldschun	50-28	+ ½
79	June 30	Philadelphia	8-3	Bolin (2-0)	McLish	51-28	+ ½

JULY (16–11)

Game	Date	Opponent	Score	Winner	Loser	W–L	GB/GA
80	July 1	Philadelphia	5-4	Larsen (4-1)	Mahaffey	52-28	+ ½
81	July 2	New York	5-8	MacKenzie	Miller (4-4)	52-29	– 1
82	July 3	New York	10-1	Sanford (8-6)	Jackson	53-29	– ½
83	July 4	New York (1)	11-4	Bolin (3-0)	Miller	54-29	
84	July 4	New York (2)	10-3	O'Dell (10-6)	Hunter	55-29	– ½
85	July 5	Los Angeles	3-11	Drysdale	McCormick (4-3)	55-30	– 1½
86	July 6	Los Angeles	12-3	Marichal (12-5)	Williams	56-30	– ½
87	July 7	Los Angeles	10-3	Sanford (9-6)	Podres	57-30	+ ½
88	July 8	Los Angeles	0-2	Koufax	O'Dell (10-7)	57-31	– ½
89	July 12	@Philadelphia	5-3	Sanford (10-6)	Hamilton	58-31	– ½
90	July 13	@Philadelphia	2-3	Bennett	O'Dell (10-8)	58-32	– 1½
91	July 14	@Philadelphia	*5-6	Baldschun	Miller (4-5)	58-33	– 2½
92	July 15	@New York (1)	3-5	Hook	Pierce (8-3)	58-34	
93	July 15	@New York (2)	9-8	Bolin (4-0)	Hunter	59-34	– 2½
94	July 16	New York	3-2	Sanford (11-6)	Craig	60-34	– 2
95	July 17	@Milwaukee	4-3	O'Dell (11-8)	Raymond	61-34	– 1
96	July 18	@Milwaukee	0-6	Shaw	Marichal (12-6)	61-35	– 2
97	July 19	@Milwaukee	7-3	Bolin (5-0)	Willey	62-35	– 1
98	July 20	@Pittsburgh	6-3	Sanford (12-6)	Law	63-35	– 1
99	July 21	@Pittsburgh	*6-7	Face	Larsen (4-2)	63-36	– 2
100	July 22	@Pittsburgh	5-4	Marichal (13-6)	Haddix	64-36	– 2
101	July 23	@Houston	5-1	Bolin (6-0)	Woodeshick	65-36	– 2
102	July 24	@Houston	3-1	Sanford (13-6)	Farrell	66-36	– 1
103	July 25	@Houston	3-2	O'Dell (12-8)	Golden	67-36	– 1
104	July 27	@Los Angeles	1-3	Podres	Marichal (13-7)	67-37	– 2
105	July 28	@Los Angeles	6-8	Roebuck	Bolin (6-1)	67-38	– 3
106	July 29	@Los Angeles	1-11	Drysdale	O'Dell (12-9)	67-39	– 4

AUGUST (18–10)

Game	Date	Opponent	Score	Winner	Loser	W–L	GB/GA
107	Aug. 1	Chicago	*2-3	Buhl	O'Dell (12-10)	67-40	– 4
108	Aug. 2	Chicago	4-3	Pierce (9-3)	Ellsworth	68-40	– 4
109	Aug. 3	Pittsburgh	2-5	McBean	Marichal (13-8)	68-41	– 5
110	Aug. 4	Pittsburgh	6-5	Sanford (14-6)	Olivo	69-41	– 5
111	Aug. 5	Pittsburgh	2-1	O'Dell (13-10)	Friend	70-40	– 4½
112	Aug. 6	Philadelphia	9-2	Pierce (10-3)	Green	71-41	– 4½
113	Aug. 7	Philadelphia	4-2	Marichal (14-8)	Mahaffey	72-41	– 4½
114	Aug. 8	New York	2-5	Craig	Bolin (6-2)	72-42	– 5½
115	Aug. 9	New York	7-1	Sanford (15-6)	Miller	73-42	– 5½
116	Aug. 10	Los Angeles	11-2	O'Dell (14-10)	Podres	74-42	– 4½
117	Aug. 11	Los Angeles	5-4	Pierce (11-3)	Drysdale	75-42	– 3½
118	Aug. 12	Los Angeles	5-1	Marichal (15-8)	Williams	76-42	– 2½
119	Aug. 14	@Chicago	9-2	Sanford (16-6)	Hobbie	77-42	– 1½
120	Aug. 15	@Chicago	5-7	Anderson	Miller (4-6)	77-43	– 1½
121	Aug. 16	@Chicago	0-6	Cardwell	Pierce (11-4)	77-44	– 2½
122	Aug. 17	@Milwaukee	4-6	Shaw	Marichal (15-9)	77-45	– 3½
123	Aug. 18	@Milwaukee	6-4	Sanford (17-6)	Hendley	78-45	– 2½
124	Aug. 19	@Milwaukee	8-13	Cloninger	O'Dell (14-11)	78-46	– 3½
125	Aug. 20	@Milwaukee	4-9	Spahn	Larsen (4-3)	78-47	– 3½
126	Aug. 22	@New York	4-5	MacKenzie	Larsen (4-4)	78-48	– 3½
127	Aug. 23	@New York	*2-1	Marichal (16-9)	Jackson	79-48	– 3½
128	Aug. 24	@Philadelphia	6-0	O'Dell (15-11)	McLish	80-48	– 2½

129	Aug. 25	@Philadelphia	6-1	Pierce (12-4)	Green	81-48	-2½
130	Aug. 26	@Philadelphia	7-4	Sanford (18-6)	Mahaffey	82-48	-2½
131	Aug. 28	Milwaukee	4-3	Marichal (17-9)	Willey	83-48	-2½
132	Aug. 29	Milwaukee	3-10	Hendley	O'Dell (15-12)	83-49	-3½
133	Aug. 30	Milwaukee	3-2	Sanford (19-6)	Spahn	84-49	-2½
134	Aug. 31	Cincinnati	10-2	Pierce (13-4)	Maloney	85-49	-2½

SEPTEMBER (16-12)

Game	Date	Opponent	Score	Winner	Loser	W-L	GB/GA
135	Sept. 1	Cincinnati	5-10	Nuxhall	Marichal (17-10)	85-50	-3½
136	Sept. 2	Cincinnati	6-4	O'Dell (16-12)	Brosnan	86-50	-3½
137	Sept. 3	@Los Angeles	7-3	Sanford (20-6)	Williams	87-50	-2½
138	Sept. 4	@Los Angeles	4-5	Perranoski	Pierce (13-5)	87-51	-3½
139	Sept. 5	@Los Angeles	3-0	Marichal (18-10)	Podres	88-51	-2½
140	Sept. 6	@Los Angeles	9-6	Bolin (7-2)	Perranoski	89-51	-1½
141	Sept. 7	Chicago	6-5	Sanford (21-6)	Buhl	90-51	-½
142	Sept. 8	Chicago	7-2	Pierce (14-5)	Cardwell	91-51	-½
143	Sept. 9	Chicago	5-4	McCormick (5-3)	Hobbie	92-51	-½
144	Sept. 10	Pittsburgh	4-1	O'Dell (17-12)	Haddix	93-51	-½
145	Sept. 11	Pittsburgh	2-0	Sanford (22-6)	Sturdivant	94-51	-½
146	Sept. 12	@Cincinnati	1-4	Maloney	Pierce (14-6)	94-52	-1½
147	Sept. 13	@Cincinnati	2-7	O'Toole	McCormick (5-4)	94-53	-2
148	Sept. 14	@Pittsburgh	1-5	Francis	O'Dell (17-13)	94-54	-3
149	Sept. 15	@Pittsburgh	1-5	Friend	Sanford (22-7)	94-55	-4
150	Sept. 16	@Pittsburgh	4-6	Gibbon	Miller (4-7)	94-56	-4
151	Sept. 17	@Pittsburgh	2-5	Sturdivant	McCormick (5-5)	94-57	-4
152	Sept. 19	@St. Louis	7-4	O'Dell (18-13)	Jackson	95-57	-3½
153	Sept. 20	@St. Louis	4-5	Duliba	LeMay (0-1)	95-58	-4
154	Sept. 21	@Houston	11-5	Perry (3-1)	Brunet	96-58	-3
155	Sept. 22	@Houston	5-6	Umbricht	Miller (4-8)	96-59	-4
156	Sept. 23	@Houston	10-3	O'Dell (19-13)	Bruce	97-59	-3
157	Sept. 25	St. Louis	4-2	Sanford (23-7)	Broglio	98-59	-2
158	Sept. 26	St. Louis	6-3	Pierce (15-6)	Simmons	99-59	-2
159	Sept. 27	St. Louis	4-7	Washburn	O'Dell (19-14)	99-60	-2
160	Sept. 29	Houston (1)	11-5	Sanford (24-7)	Johnson	100-60	
161	Sept. 29	Houston (2)	2-4	Bruce	Marichal (18-11)	100-61	-1
162	Sept. 30	Houston	2-1	Miller (5-8)	Farrell	101-61	Tie

OCTOBER PLAYOFF (2-1)

Game	Date	Opponent	Score	Winner	Loser	W-L	GB/GA
163	Oct. 1	Los Angeles	8-0	Pierce (16-6)	Koufax	102-61	+1
164	Oct. 2	@Los Angeles	7-8	Williams	Bolin (7-3)	102-62	Tie
165	Oct. 3	@Los Angeles	6-4	Larsen (5-4)	Roebuck	103-62	+1

*Indicates extra innings; GB/GA of Dodgers

With Billy Pierce pitching a three-hit shutout and Willie Mays hitting two home runs, the Giants drubbed the Dodgers, 8–0, in the first game of the best-of-three playoffs. The scene shifted to Los Angeles for Game 2, and the Dodgers stayed alive with an 8–7 victory. The Giants captured their only pennant for San Francisco in dramatic fashion in Game 3, scoring four times in the ninth for a 6–4 victory before heading home for a tumultuous airport welcome.

1962 PLAYOFF BOXES

GAME 1 — Oct. 1 at Candlestick Park

LOS ANGELES	AB	R	H	RBI	SAN FRANCISCO	AB	R	H	RBI
Wills, ss	4	0	0	0	Kuenn, lf	5	0	0	0
Gilliam, 2b	3	0	0	0	Hiller, 2b	4	0	1	0
T. Davis, lf	4	0	0	0	F. Alou, rf	4	1	1	0
Howard, rf	4	0	0	0	Mays, cf	3	3	3	3
Walls, 1b	3	0	0	0	Cepeda, 1b	4	1	1	1
Roseboro, c	3	0	0	0	Davenport, 3b	3	2	2	1
Carey, 3b	3	0	1	0	Bailey, c	2	1	1	0
W. Davis, cf	3	0	0	0	Pagan, ss	3	0	1	2
Koufax, p	0	0	0	0	Pierce, p	4	0	0	0
Roebuck, p	1	0	0	0					
McMullen, ph	1	0	1	0					
Tracewski, pr	0	0	0	0					
L. Sherry, p	0	0	0	0					
Smith, p	0	0	0	0					
Camilli, ph	1	0	1	0					
Ortega, p	0	0	0	0					
Perranoski, p	0	0	0	0					
TOTALS	30	0	3	0	TOTALS	32	8	10	7

	R	H	E
Los Angeles.... 0 0 0 0 0 0 0 0 0 —	0	3	1
San Francisco .. 2 1 0 0 0 2 0 3 x —	8	10	0

E—Howard. DP—Los Angeles 1. LOB—Los Angeles 4, San Francisco 5. 2B—F. Alou, Camilli, Pagan. HR—Mays 2, Davenport, Cepeda. SB—Mays. Sac—Pagan.

PITCHING SUMMARY

Los Angeles	IP	H	R	ER	BB	SO
Koufax (L, 14-7)	1	4	3	3	0	0
Roebuck	4	1	0	0	0	2
L. Sherry	0.3	3	2	2	1	0
Smith	1.7	1	0	0	0	0
Ortega	0.3	0	2	2	2	0
Perranoski	0.7	1	1	0	1	0
San Francisco						
Pierce (W, 16-6)	9	3	0	0	1	6

Umpires—Conlan, Boggess, Donatelli and Landes. Time—2:39. Attendance—32,660.

GAME 2 — Oct. 2 at Dodger Stadium

SAN FRANCISCO	AB	R	H	RBI	LOS ANGELES	AB	R	H	RBI
Hiller, 2b	3	1	1	1	Wills, ss	4	1	0	0
Nieman, ph	1	0	0	0	Gilliam, 2b-3b	3	1	0	0
Bowman, 2b	1	0	0	0	Snider, lf	3	1	1	0
Davenport, 3b	6	1	2	1	Spencer, ph	0	0	0	0
Mays, cf	5	0	1	0	T. Davis, 3b-cf3	0	1	1	0
McCovey, lf	2	0	1	1	Moon, lf	2	1	1	0
Miller, p	0	0	0	0	Fairly, 1b	1	0	1	1
O'Dell, p	0	0	0	0	Howard, rf	3	1	1	1
Larsen, p	0	0	0	0	Roseboro, c	2	0	0	0
Bailey, ph	1	0	1	1	Camilli, ph-c	2	1	1	0
Boles, pr	0	1	0	0	W. Davis, cf	2	0	0	0
Bolin, p	0	0	0	0	Carey, ph	0	0	0	1
LeMay, p	0	0	0	0	Burright, pr	0	1	0	0
Perry, p	0	0	0	0	Drysdale, p	2	0	0	0
McCormick, p	0	0	0	0	Roebuck, p	0	0	0	0
Cepeda, 1b	5	1	1	0	Walls, ph	1	1	1	3
F. Alou, rf	4	0	2	1	Perranoski, p	0	0	0	0
Haller, c	1	1	0	0	Smith, p	0	0	0	0
Orsino, c	1	0	1	1	Williams, p	1	0	0	0
Pagan, ss	5	1	3	0					
Sanford, p	3	1	0	0					
M. Alou, lf	0	0	0	0					
Kuenn, ph-lf	2	0	0	0					
TOTALS	40	7	13	6	TOTALS	29	8	7	7

	R	H	E
San Francisco .. 0 1 0 0 0 4 0 2 0 —	7	13	1
Los Angeles.... 0 0 0 0 0 7 0 0 1 —	8	7	2

E—Drysdale, Haller, Howard. DP—none. LOB—San Francisco 13, Los Angeles 7. 2B—F. Alou, Pagan, Snider, Walls. SB—Wills. Sac—Spencer. SF—T. Davis, Orsino, Fairly.

GAME 3 — Oct. 3 at Dodger Stadium

SAN FRANCISCO	AB	R	H	RBI	LOS ANGELES	AB	R	H	RBI
Kuenn, lf	5	1	2	1	Wills, ss	5	1	4	0
Hiller, 2b	3	0	1	0	Gilliam, 2b-3b	5	0	0	0
McCovey, ph	0	0	0	0	Snider, lf	3	2	2	0
Bowman, pr-2b	0	1	0	0	Burright, 2b	1	0	0	0
F. Alou, rf	4	1	1	0	Walls, rf	1	0	0	0
Mays, cf	3	1	1	1	T. Davis, 3b-lf	3	1	2	2
Cepeda, 1b	4	0	1	1	Moon, 1b	3	0	0	0
Bailey, c	4	0	2	0	Fairly, 1b-rf	0	0	0	0
Davenport, 3b	4	0	1	1	Howard, rf	4	0	0	1
Pagan, ss	5	1	2	0	Harkness, 1b	0	0	0	0
Marichal, p	2	1	1	0	Roseboro, c	3	0	0	0
Larsen, p	0	0	0	0	W. Davis, cf	3	0	0	0
M. Alou, ph	1	0	1	0	Podres, p	2	0	0	0
Nieman, ph	1	0	0	0	Roebuck, p	2	0	0	0
Pierce, p	0	0	0	0	Williams, p	0	0	0	0
					Perranoski, p	0	0	0	0
TOTALS	36	6	13	4	TOTALS	35	4	8	3

	R	H	E
San Francisco .. 0 0 2 0 0 0 0 0 4 —	6	13	3
Los Angeles.... 0 0 0 1 0 2 1 0 0 —	4	8	4

E—Marichal, Podres, Roseboro, Gilliam, Pagan Bailey, Burright. DP—Los Angeles 3. LOB—San Francisco 12, Los Angles 8. 2B—Snider, Hiller. HR—T. Davis. SB—Wills 3, T. Davis. Sac—Hiller, Marichal, Fairly. SF—Cepeda.

PITCHING SUMMARY

San Francisco	IP	H	R	ER	BB	SO
Marichal	7	8	4	3	1	2
Larsen (W, 5-4)	1	0	0	0	2	1
Pierce (save)	1	0	0	0	0	0
Los Angeles						
Podres	5	9	2	1	1	0
Roebuck (L, 10-2)...	3.3	4	4	3	3	0
Williams	0.3	0	0	0	2	0
Perranoski	0.3	0	0	0	0	1

WP—Williams. Umpires—Boggess, Donatelli, Conlan and Barlick. Time—3:00. Attendance—45,693.

PITCHING SUMMARY

San Francisco	IP	H	R	ER	BB	SO
Sanford	5	2	1	1	3	4
Miller	0.3	2	3	3	1	0
O'Dell	0	2	3	2	0	0
Larsen	1.7	1	0	0	0	1
Bolin (L, 7-3).......	1	0	1	1	2	2
LeMay	0	0	0	0	1	0
Perry	0.3	0	0	0	0	0
McCormick	0.3	0	0	0	1	0
Los Angeles						
Drysdale...........	5.3	7	5	3	4	4
Roebuck	0.7	1	0	0	0	0
Perranoski	1	4	1	1	0	0
Smith	0.3	1	1	0	0	0
Williams (W, 14-12) .	1.7	0	0	0	1	2

HB—Hiller (Drysdale), Carey (O'Dell). Umpires—Barlick, Boggess, Donatelli and Conlan. Time—4:18. Attendance—25,321.

1962 WORLD SERIES

The Giants and the Yankees met in a World Series for the seventh time, forging one of the most dramatic clashes in history. Neither powerhouse could win more than one game in a row, and the pitchers stole the show from heralded sluggers such as Willie Mays, Orlando Cepeda, Willie McCovey, Mickey Mantle and Roger Maris. Jack Sanford was brilliant for the Giants, firing a shutout in Game 2, but the Yankees' Ralph Terry was even better, pitching a 1–0 victory over Sanford in the decisive Game 7.

Game 1: October 4 at Candlestick Park

Yankee great lefty Whitey Ford scattered ten Giant hits en route to a 6-2 victory over Billy O'Dell. Outfielder Roger Maris doubled in two runs for a first-inning 2-0 Yankee lead, but the Giants tied the game with single runs in the second and third innings. Third baseman Clete Boyer put the Yanks ahead with a solo homer in the seventh and the Bronx Bombers iced the game with two more runs in the eighth.

Yankees   200 000 121   6 11   0
Giants   011 000 000   2 10   0
Pitchers: **Ford** vs. **O'Dell**, Larsen (8), Miller (9)
Home Run: Boyer   Att: 43,852

Game 2: October 5 at Candlestick Park

Giant right-hander Jack Sanford shut out the Yanks 2-0 to defeat Ralph Terry. The Giants scored in the first inning on second baseman Chuck Hiller's double and Matty Alou's groundout. Willie McCovey's long home run provided the other Giant run in the seventh inning.

Yankees   000 000 000   0   3   1
Giants   100 000 10#   2   6   0
Pitchers: **Sanford** vs. **Terry**, Daley (8)
Home Run: McCovey   Att: 43,910

Game 3: October 7 at Yankee Stadium

Starters Billy Pierce and Bill Stafford pitched shutout ball for six innings. Then the New Yorkers broke the deadlock with three runs in the bottom of the seventh on Maris' two-run single and Boyer's run-scoring ground ball.   The Giants rallied with two runs on Mays' double and catcher Ed Bailey's home run, but Stafford retired Jim Davenport to end the game.

Giants   000 000 002   2   4   3
Yankees   000 000 30#   3   5   1
Pitchers: **Stafford** vs. **Pierce**, Larsen (7), Bolin (8)
Home Run: Bailey   Att: 71,434

Game 4: October 8 at Yankee Stadium

Juan Marichal outpitched Whitey Ford for four innings, but the Dominican Dandy had to leave the game after the fourth inning because he injured his hand while batting. At the time the Giants led 2-0 on Tom Haller's two-run homer. The Yanks tied the game in the sixth on run-scoring hits by Bill Skowron and Clete Boyer. But the Giants put the game away in the top of the seventh when Chuck Hiller hit a grand-slam home run off Yankee right-hander Tom Coates. Billy O'Dell held on in relief for a 7-3 win, tying the Series at two games apiece.

Giants   020 000 401   7   9   1
Yankees   000 002 001   3   9   1
Pitchers: Marichal, Bolin (5), **Larsen** (6), O'Dell (7) SV vs. Ford, **Coates** (7), Bridges (7)
Home Runs: Haller, Hiller   Att: 66,607

Game 5: October 10 at Yankee Stadium

Ralph Terry and Jack Sanford dueled to a 2-2 tie after seven innings. Yankee left fielder Mike Tresh hit a three-run homer in the bottom of the eighth to power the Yankees to a 5-3 win.

Giants   001 010 001   3   8   2
Yankees   000 101 03#   5   6   0
Pitchers: **Terry** vs. **Sanford**, Miller (8)
Home Runs: Pagan, Tresh   Att: 63,165

Game 6: October 15 at Candlestick Park

The Giants tied the Series at three-all with a 5-2 win in San Francisco. Bill Pierce bested Whitey Ford by pitching a steady game, allowing only three hits, including a home run by Roger Maris. Orlando Cepeda led the Giant attack with three hits and two RBI.

Yankees   000 010 010   2   3   2
Giants   000 320 00#   5 10   1
Pitchers: **Pierce** vs. **Ford**, Coates (5), Bridges (8)
Home Run: Maris   Att: 43,948

Game 7: October 16 at Candlestick Park

Ralph Terry outpitched Jack Sanford as the Yanks won 1-0 to win the Series. The only run of the game was scored in the fifth inning on Tony Kubek's double-play grounder. The Giants threatened to score in the bottom of the ninth, but with men on second and third and two

out, Yankee second baseman Bobby Richardson reached up and
pulled down Willie McCovey's liner to right.

Yankees	000	010	000	1	7	0
Giants	000	000	000	0	4	1

Pitchers: **Terry** vs. **Sanford**, O'Dell (8)   Att: 43,948

Total Attendance: 376,864
Winning Player's Share: $9,883
Losing Player's Share: $7,291

1962 WORLD SERIES BOXES

GAME 1 — Oct. 4 at Candlestick Park

NEW YORK	AB	R	H	RBI	SAN FRANCISCO	AB	R	H	RBI
Kubek, ss	5	0	2	0	Kuenn, lf	5	0	0	0
Richardson, 2b	5	1	1	0	Hiller, 2b	4	1	1	0
Tresh, lf	5	2	2	0	F. Alou, rf	4	0	1	0
Mantle, cf	4	0	0	0	Mays, cf	4	1	3	1
Maris, rf	4	1	2	2	Cepeda, 1b	4	0	0	0
Howard, c	3	1	2	1	Davenport, 3b	2	0	1	0
Skowron, 1b	2	0	0	0	Bailey, c	4	0	0	0
Long, 1b	2	0	1	1	Miller, p	0	0	0	0
Boyer, 3b	3	1	1	2	Pagan, ss	4	0	3	1
Ford, p	3	0	0	0	O'Dell, p	3	0	1	0
					Larsen, p	0	0	0	0
					Orsino, c	1	0	0	0
TOTALS	36	6	11	6	TOTALS	35	2	10	2

		R	H	E
New York	200 000 121 —	6	11	0
San Francisco	011 000 000 —	2	10	0

E—none. DP—New York 2, San Francisco 1. LOB—New York 10, San Francisco 8. 2B—Maris, Hiller. HR—Boyer. SB—Mantle, Tresh. SF—Boyer.

PITCHING SUMMARY

New York	IP	H	R	ER	BB	SO
Ford (W)	9	10	2	2	2	6
San Francisco						
O'Dell (L)	7.3	9	5	5	3	8
Larsen	1	1	1	1	1	0
Miller	0.7	1	0	0	1	0

HB—Howard (O'Dell). Umpires—Barlick, Berry, Landes, Honochick, Burkhart and Soar. Time—2:43. Attendance—43,852.

GAME 2 — Oct. 5 at Candlestick Park

NEW YORK	AB	R	H	RBI	SAN FRANCISCO	AB	R	H	RBI
Kubek, ss	4	0	0	0	Hiller, 2b	3	1	1	0
Richardson, 2b	4	0	0	0	F. Alou, rf	2	0	1	0
Tresh, lf	3	0	1	0	M. Alou, lf	4	0	1	1
Mantle, cf	4	0	1	0	Mays, cf	4	0	0	0
Maris, rf	3	0	0	0	McCovey, 1b	4	1	1	1
Berrra, c	2	0	0	0	Haller, c	3	0	1	0
Long, 1b	3	0	0	0	Davenport, 3b	3	0	0	0
Boyer, 3b	3	0	1	0	Pagan, ss	1	0	0	0
Terry, p	2	0	0	0	Sanford, p	3	0	1	0
Blanchard, ph	1	0	0	0					
Daley, p	0	0	0	0					
TOTALS	29	0	3	0	TOTALS	27	2	6	2

		R	H	E
New York	000 000 000 —	0	3	1
San Francisco	100 000 10x —	2	6	0

E—Kubek. DP—San Francisco 1. LOB—New York 4, San Francisco 6. 2B—Haller, Mantle. HR—McCovey. SB—Tresh. Sac—F. Alou, Pagan.

PITCHING SUMMARY

New York	IP	H	R	ER	BB	SO
Terry (L)	7	5	2	2	1	5
Daley	1	1	0	0	1	0
San Francisco						
Sanford (W)	9	3	0	0	3	6

HB—Pagan (Terry). Umpires—Berry, Landes, Honochick, Barlick, Burkhart and Soar. Time—2:11. Attendance—43,910.

GAME 3 — Oct. 7 at Yankee Stadium

SAN FRANCISCO	AB	R	H	RBI	NEW YORK	AB	R	H	RBI
F. Alou, lf	4	0	0	0	Kubek, ss	4	0	1	0
Hiller, 2b	3	0	0	0	Richardson, 2b	4	0	0	0
Mays, cf	4	1	1	0	Tresh, lf	4	1	1	0
McCovey, rf	3	0	0	0	Mantle, cf	3	1	1	0
Cepeda, 1b	4	0	0	0	Maris, rf	3	1	1	2
Bailey, c	4	1	1	2	Howard, c	3	0	1	0
Davenport, ss	3	0	1	0	Skowron, 1b	2	0	0	0
Pagan, ss	3	0	1	0	Boyer, 3b	3	0	0	1
Pierce, p	2	0	0	0	Stafford, p	3	0	0	0
Larsen, p	0	0	0	0					
Bolin, p	0	0	0	0					
M. Alou, ph	1	0	0	0					
TOTALS	32	2	4	2	TOTALS	29	3	5	3

		R	H	E
San Francisco	000 000 000 —	2	4	3
New York	000 000 30x —	3	5	1

E—F. Alou, McCovey, Davenport, Boyer. DP—San Francisco 1. LOB—San Francisco 5, New York 3. 2B—Davenport, Kubek, Howard, Mays. HR— Bailey.

PITCHING SUMMARY

San Francisco	IP	H	R	ER	BB	SO
Pierce (L)	6	5	3	2	0	3
Larsen	1	0	0	0	0	0
Bolin	1	0	0	0	0	1
New York						
Stafford (W)	9	4	2	2	2	5

HB—Skowron (Larsen). Umpires—Landes, Honochick, Barlick, Berry, Soar and Burkhart. Time—2:06. Attendance—71,434.

GAME 4 — Oct. 8 at Yankee Stadium

SAN FRANCISCO	AB	R	H	RBI	NEW YORK	AB	R	H	RBI
Kuenn, rf	3	0	0	0	Kubek, ss	4	1	1	0
O'Dell, p	0	0	0	0	Richardson, 2b	4	0	1	0
Hiller, 2b	5	1	2	4	Tresh, lf	5	0	2	1
Mays, cf	5	0	1	0	Mantle, cf	4	1	0	0
F. Alou, lf	4	1	1	0	Maris, rf	3	1	0	0
Cepeda, 1b	4	0	0	0	Howard, c	4	0	0	0
Davenport, 3b	2	1	0	0	Skowron, 1b	4	0	3	1
Haller, c	4	1	2	2	Boyer, 3b	4	0	2	1
Pagan, ss	2	0	1	0	Ford, p	2	0	0	0
M. Alou, ph-rf	2	2	2	0	Berra, ph	0	0	0	0
Marichal, p	2	0	0	0	Coates, p	0	0	0	0
Bolin, p	0	0	0	0	Bridges, p	0	0	0	0
Larsen, p	0	0	0	0	Lopez, ph	1	0	0	0
Bailey, ph	0	0	0	0					
Nieman, ph	0	0	0	0					
Bowman, pr-ss	1	1	0	0					
TOTALS	34	7	9	6	TOTALS	35	3	9	3

		R	H	E
San Francisco	020 000 401 —	7	9	1
New York	000 002 001 —	3	9	1

E—Davenport, Richardson. DP—San Francisco 2, New York 1. LOB—San Francisco 5, New York 10. 2B—F. Alou, M. Alou. 3B—Skowron. HR—Haller, Hiller. Sac—O'Dell.

PITCHING SUMMARY

San Francisco	IP	H	R	ER	BB	SO
Marichal	4	2	0	0	2	4
Bolin	1.7	4	2	2	2	1
Larsen (W)	0.3	0	0	0	1	0
O'Dell (save)	3	3	1	1	0	0
New York						
Ford	6	5	2	2	1	3
Coates (L)	0.3	1	2	2	1	1
Bridges	2.7	3	3	2	2	3

Umpires—Honochick, Barlikc, Berry, Landes, Soar and Burkhart. Time—2:55. Attendance—66,607.

GAME 5 — Oct. 10 at Yankee Stadium

SAN FRANCISCO	AB	R	H	RBI	NEW YORK	AB	R	H	RBI
Hiller, 2b	3	0	1	1	Kubek, ss	4	1	2	0
Davenport, 3b	4	0	0	0	Richardson, 2b	4	2	2	0
M. Alou, rf	4	0	0	0	Tresh, lf	3	2	2	3
Mays, cf	4	0	0	0	Mantle, cf	3	0	0	0
McCovey, 1b	4	1	1	0	Maris, rf	3	0	0	0
F. Alou, c	4	0	1	1	Howard, c	4	0	0	0
Haller, c	4	0	1	1	Skowron, 1b	3	0	0	0
Pagan, ss	4	2	2	1	Boyer, 3b	3	0	0	0
Sanford, p	2	0	1	0	Terry, p	3	0	0	0
Miller, p	0	0	0	0					
Bailey, ph	1	0	0	0					
TOTALS	34	3	8	3	TOTALS	30	5	6	3

	R	H	E
San Francisco ..	001 010 001 —	3	8	2
New York	000 101 03x —	5	6	0

E—Hiller, McCovey. DP—San Francisco 1. LOB—San Francisco 6, New York 4. 2B—Hiller, Tresh, Haller. 3B—F. Alou. HR—Pagan, Tresh. SB—Mantle. Sac—Sanford, Tresh.

PITCHING SUMMARY

San Francisco	IP	H	R	ER	BB	SO
Sanford (L)	7.3	6	5	4	1	10
Miller	0.7	0	0	0	1	0
New York						
Terry (W)	9	8	3	3	1	7

WP—Sanford. PB—Haller. Umpires—Barlick, Berry, Landes, Honochick, Soar and Burkhart. Time—2:42. Attendance—63,165.

GAME 6 — Oct. 15 at Candlestick Park

NEW YORK	AB	R	H	RBI	SAN FRANCISCO	AB	R	H	RBI
Kubek, ss	4	0	1	1	Kuenn, lf	4	1	1	0
Richardson, 2b	4	0	0	0	M. Alou, lf	0	0	0	0
Tresh, lf	4	0	0	0	Hiller, 2b	4	1	2	0
Mantle, cf	4	0	0	0	F. Alou, rf	4	1	2	1
Maris, rf	3	1	1	1	Mays, cf	3	1	1	0
Howard, c	3	0	0	0	Cepeda, 1b	4	1	3	2
Skowron, 1b	3	0	0	0	Davenport, 3b	4	0	1	1
Boyer, 3b	2	1	1	0	Bailey, c	4	0	0	0
Ford, p	2	0	0	0	Pagan, ss	3	0	0	0
Coates, p	0	0	0	0	Pierce, p	3	0	0	0
Lopez, ph	1	0	0	0					
Bridges, p	0	0	0	0					
TOTALS	30	2	3	2	TOTALS	33	5	10	4

	R	H	E
New York	000 010 010 —	2	3	2
San Francisco ..	000 320 00x —	5	10	1

E—Boyer, Ford, Davenport. DP—New York 2, San Francisco 1. LOB—New York 3, San Francisco 5. 2B—Cepeda, Boyer. HR—Maris. SB—Mays.

PITCHING SUMMARY

New York	IP	H	R	ER	BB	SO
Ford (L)	4.7	9	5	5	1	3
Coates	2.3	0	0	0	0	2
Bridges	1	1	0	0	0	0
San Francisco						
Pierce (W)	9	3	2	2	2	2

Umpires—Berry, Landes, Honochick, Barlick, Burkhart and Soar. Time—2:00. Attendance—43,948.

GAME 7 — Oct. 16 at Candlestick Park

NEW YORK	AB	R	H	RBI	SAN FRANCISCO	AB	R	H	RBI
Kubek, ss	4	0	1	0	F. Alou, rf	4	0	0	0
Richardson, 2b	2	0	0	0	Hiller, 2b	4	0	0	0
Tresh, lf	4	0	1	0	Mays, cf	4	0	1	0
Mantle, cf	3	0	1	0	McCovey, lf	4	0	1	0
Maris, rf	4	0	0	0	Cepeda, 1b	3	0	0	0
Howard, c	4	0	0	0	Haller, c	3	0	0	0
Skowron, 1b	4	1	1	0	Davenport, 3b	3	0	0	0
Boyer, 3b	4	0	2	0	Pagan, ss	2	0	0	0
Terry, p	3	0	1	0	Bailey, ph	1	0	0	0
					Bowman, ss	0	0	0	0
					Sanford, p	2	0	1	0
					O'Dell, p	0	0	0	0
					M. Alou, ph	1	0	1	0
TOTALS	32	1	7	0	TOTALS	31	0	4	0

	R	H	E
New York	000 010 000 —	1	7	0
San Francisco ..	000 000 000 —	0	4	1

E—Pagan. DP—San Francisco 2. LOB—New York 8, San Francisco 4. 2B—Mays, 3B—McCovey.

PITCHING SUMMARY

New York	IP	H	R	ER	BB	SO
Terry (W)	9	4	0	0	0	4
San Francisco						
Sanford (L)........	7	7	1	1	4	3
O'Dell	2	0	0	0	0	1

Umpires—Landes, Honochick, Barlick, Berry, Burkhart and Soar. Time—2:29. Attendance—43,948.

1962 WORLD SERIES STATISTICS

YANKEES BATTING

Name	POS	AVG	G	AB	R	H	2B	3B	HR	RBI
Kubek	SS	.276	7	29	2	8	1	0	0	1
Tresh	OF	.321	7	28	5	9	1	0	1	4
Richardson	2B	.148	7	27	3	4	0	0	0	0
Mantle	OF	.120	7	25	2	3	1	0	0	0
Maris	OF	.174	7	23	4	4	1	0	1	5
Boyer	3B	.318	7	22	2	7	1	0	1	4
Howard	C	.143	6	21	1	3	1	0	0	1
Skowron	1B	.222	6	18	1	4	0	1	0	1
Terry	P	.125	3	8	0	1	0	0	0	0
Ford	P	.000	3	7	0	0	0	0	0	0
Long	1B	.200	2	5	0	1	0	0	0	1
Stafford	P	.000	1	3	0	0	0	0	0	0
Berra	C	.000	2	2	0	0	0	0	0	0
Lopez	PH	.000	2	2	0	0	0	0	0	0
Blanchard	PH	.000	1	1	0	0	0	0	0	0
Coates	P	.000	2	0	0	0	0	0	0	0
Bridges	P	.000	2	0	0	0	0	0	0	0
Daley	P	.000	1	0	0	0	0	0	0	0
New York Totals		.199	7	221	20	44	6	1	3	17

GIANTS BATTING

Name	POS	AVG	G	AB	R	H	2B	3B	HR	RBI
Mays	OF	.250	7	28	3	7	2	0	0	1
Hiller	2B	.269	7	26	4	7	3	0	1	5
F. Alou	OF	.269	7	26	2	7	1	1	0	1
Davenport	3B	.136	7	22	1	3	1	0	0	1
Pagan	SS	.368	7	19	2	7	0	0	1	2
Cepeda	1B	.158	5	19	1	3	1	0	0	2
McCovey	1B–OF	.200	4	15	2	3	0	1	1	1
Haller	C	.286	4	14	1	4	1	0	1	3
Bailey	C	.071	6	14	1	1	0	0	1	2
M. Alou	OF	.333	6	12	2	4	1	0	0	1
Kuenn	OF	.083	3	12	1	1	0	0	0	0
Sanford	P	.429	3	7	0	3	0	0	0	0
Pierce	P	.000	2	5	0	0	0	0	0	0
O'Dell	P	.333	3	3	0	1	0	0	0	0
Marichal	P	.000	1	2	0	0	0	0	0	0
Bowman	SS	.000	2	1	1	0	0	0	0	0
Orsino	C	.000	1	1	0	0	0	0	0	0
Larsen	P	.000	3	0	0	0	0	0	0	0
Miller	P	.000	2	0	0	0	0	0	0	0
Bolin	P	.000	2	0	0	0	0	0	0	0
Nieman	PH	.000	1	0	0	0	0	0	0	0
San Francisco Totals		.226	7	226	21	51	10	2	5	19

YANKEES PITCHING

Name	W	L	ERA	G	IP	H	BB	SO
Terry	2	1	1.80	3	25	17	2	16
Ford	1	1	4.12	3	19.2	24	4	12
Stafford	1	0	2.00	1	9	4	2	5
Bridges	0	0	4.91	2	3.2	4	2	3
Coates	0	1	6.75	2	2.2	1	1	3
Daley	0	0	0.00	1	1	1	1	0
New York Totals	4	3	2.95	7	61	51	12	39

GIANTS PITCHING

Name	W	L	ERA	G	IP	H	BB	SO
Sanford	1	2	1.93	3	23.1	16	8	19
Pierce	1	1	2.40	2	15	8	2	5
O'Dell	0	1	4.38	2	12.1	12	3	9
Marichal	0	0	0.00	1	4	2	2	4
Bolin	0	0	6.75	2	2.2	4	2	2
Larsen	1	0	3.86	3	2.1	1	2	0
Miller	0	0	0.00	2	1.1	1	2	0
San Francisco Totals	3	4	2.66	7	61	44	21	39

6

ALL-STAR GAMES

Perhaps no team has meant more to the National League's success in the All-Star Game than the Giants, who have used the midsummer classic as a showcase for the talent. Their feats abound in the first fifty years of the spectacle.

King Carl Hubbell's magnificent strikeout achievement in 1934 is regarded as the finest pitching performance in the game's history, and Larry Jansen, Juan Marichal, Stu Miller, and Vida Blue have had their moments. Willie Mays has no peers as an All-Star Game hitter, holding many of the game's records. But Bill Terry was dynamite in the early classics and Willie McCovey and Bobby Bonds were MVPs of modern All-Star Games.

Hubbell's accomplishment, before 48,363 at the Polo Grounds, deserves special mention. The American League won the game 9-7, but that didn't diminish what Hub achieved against five Hall of Fame hitters.

"I never had any more control and stuff in my life than for that All-Star Game," recalled Hubbell, who made history by striking out Babe Ruth, Lou Gehrig, Jimmy Foxx, Al Simmons, and Joe Cronin in succession. "It was as big a surprise for me to strike out those fellows as it probably was to them. When I went over the hitters with Gabby Hartnett, my catcher, he told me to waste everything but the screwball."

It didn't start out like a superior performance by Hubbell. Leadoff batter Charley Gehringer singled, and Heinie Manush walked on a 3-2 pitch in the very first inning. The infielders converged around the mound to settle down the Giants ace. "I could imagine how they felt with two on, nobody out, and Ruth at bat," Hubbell said. "To strike him out was the last thing on my mind. The thing was to make him hit on the ground. He wasn't too fast and he'd be a cinch to double up. Babe never took the bat off his shoulder. You could have pushed me over with your little finger. I fed him three straight screwballs, all over the plate, after wasting a fastball, and he just stood there. Hartnett was laughing when he threw the ball back.

"Up came Gehrig," Hub continued. "Striking out Ruth and Gehrig in succession was too big an order. By golly, he fanned on four pitches. He swung at the last screwball, and you should have heard that crowd. I felt a lot easier then, even though Gehringer and Manush pulled a double steal.

"We were really trying to strike Foxx out, so Gabby didn't bother to waste any pitches. I threw three more screwballs and he went down swinging. We had set down the side on twelve pitches.

"The second inning was easier because Simmons and Cronin both struck out with nobody on base" said Hubbell, who then yielded a single to Bill Dickey before fanning Lefty Gomez.

Hubbell retired the side in the third inning and finished with six strikeouts in three frames, throwing twenty-seven strikes among forty-eight pitches to thirteen American League batters. He allowed two hits and then left the game winning 4-0.

When it comes to all-around All-Star play, nobody did it better than the incomparable Mays, who hit safely in twelve of his first fourteen games, belting twenty hits in forty-eight at bats (.417), and scoring fifteen runs through 1963.

The games that stick out in Mays' memory were played in Cleveland in 1954 and 1963. The first was his All-Star Game debut and the second had him batting cleanup following several stints as the lead-off hitter.

"You can't imagine how nervous I was in the 1954 game," said Mays, whose All-Star Game records include twenty-four appearances, twenty-three hits, and twenty runs. "I was in the service in '52 and '53, so it was like being a rookie again. I was more nervous in that game than in any other I've been in. I was so young, and here I was in the same clubhouse with guys like Duke Snider, Roy Campanella, and Stan Musial, and around the batting cage with guys like Ted Williams and Larry Doby. These were players I had idolized, and there I was, playing with them.

"I had my best game in Cleveland, too," Mays added. "That was in 1963, when I hit fourth for one of the few times. I drove in two runs, stole two bases, scored a couple of times, and made a catch to save a run."

Mays was the MVP of the 1973 affair, repeating in 1968 when he replaced injured Pete Rose in the starting lineup at Houston and came through in typical Mays fashion. Wondrous Willie led off the first with a single off Luis Tiant, advanced to second on Tiant's wild pickoff throw, reached third on a wild pitch, and scored the game's only run on McCovey's double-play grounder.

Like Mays, Marichal was in a class of his own as an All-Star game performer. Whereas Hubbell registered the game's greatest pitching moment, no hurler in either league was as consistently superb as the Dominican Dandy. Marichal pitched in eight games from 1962 to 1971, yielding but seven hits and one earned run in eighteen stingy innings. He struck out twelve, walked two, and posted an incredible 0.50 ERA. He was the winner in '62 and '64, and was named the game's MVP in '65.

A capsule summary of significant Giants' contributions in the All-Star Game follows.

1933—Hubbell set the stage for his 1934 heroics by working two scoreless innings in the first All-Star Game at Comiskey Park. Terry belted two hits in four trips, and the last National League player to hit .400 appropriately went on to collect four hits in ten All-Star trips.

1934—Terry had one of eight National League hits, but Hubbell stole the show by striking out the aforementioned five Hall of Famers in succession.

1935—Hal Schumacher struck out five in four innings and Terry had another hit, but the Americans won their third straight, posting a 4-1 victory at Cleveland.

1936 — The Nationals finally won a game, 4-3, at Braves Field, and Hubbell helped with three scoreless innings. Mel Ott singled as a pinch hitter for his first All-Star Game safety.

1938 — Ott tripled and scored a run in the Nationals' 4-1 triumph at Cincinnati.

1940—Harry (The Horse) Danning contributed a run-scoring single, Ott scored, and Hubbell worked a scoreless ninth to help the Nationals to a 4-0 victory at St. Louis.

1947 — Johnny Mize's fourth-inning homer off Spec Shea accounted for the only National League run in a 2-1 defeat at Wrigley Field.

1950—Jansen was the outstanding pitcher in a game won on Red Schoendienst's fourteenth-inning homer, 4-3 at Comiskey. With the Nationals trailing 3-2, Larry entered the game in the seventh inning and pitched a one-hitter for five innings, striking out six.

1951 — Sal Maglie, though not pitching particularly well, was the winner of the Nationals' 8-3 romp at Detroit. Alvin Dark singled.

1954—Mays singled and scored in his All-Star Game debut, Marv Grissom hurled scoreless relief, and Don Mueller ripped a run-scoring, pinch double, but the Americans won 11-9 at Cleveland.

1955—Mays had two singles, scored twice, and started the National League back from a 5-0 deficit to a 6-5 victory earned on Musial's twelfth-inning homer at Milwaukee.

1956—Mays belted a two-run, pinch homer off Whitey Ford, and Johnny Antonelli worked four scoreless innings during the Nationals' 7-3 romp at Washington.

1959—Mays' run-scoring triple in the bottom of the eighth capped a two-run rally and made the Nationals a 5-4 winner in the first All-Star Game that year. Antonelli pitched one-third of an inning and got the decision at Pittsburgh.

1960—The National League posted a 5-3, 6-0 sweep at Kansas City and Yankee Stadium. Mays was at his magnificent best. Willie, in the two games, was a combined six for eight with a double, a triple, and a homer. Mays led off with a triple and scored the first run in the opener, then made a triumphant return to New York in the second game, rapping a homer off Ford.

1961—Mays doubled and scored the winning run on Roberto Clemente's single as the National League scored twice in the tenth for a windy, 5-4 decision at Candlestick Park in the first game that year. Stu Miller worked a total of 4 2/3 innings in the two games, yielding one hit and no earned runs while striking out nine. He was the winner of the Candlestick clash, though victimized by the wind while throwing a costly balk in the Americans' game-tying, two-run ninth.

1962—Marichal made his All-Star Game debut and was the winner with two scoreless innings as the National League posted a 3-1 victory at Washington. Jim Davenport contributed a single and Felipe Alou a sacrifice fly in the eighth for an insurance run.

1963—The All-Star Game returned to a single-game format. Mays was the hero of a 5-3 victory at Cleveland that pulled the Nationals to within one game of the American League, which once had a 12-4 advantage in the series. Willie walked in the second, stole second, and scored on Dick Groat's single. Mays and Giants teammate Ed Bailey added run-scoring singles in the third, and Willie knocked in the winning run with a grounder in the fifth.

1964—Marichal was the winner when the National League erupted with four runs in the bottom of the ninth for a 7-4 victory at Shea Stadium. Mays walked and Orlando Cepeda singled in the winning rally.

1965—Marichal and Mays were the heroes as the National League posted a 6-5 victory at Minnesota to take a lead in the All-Star Game series for the first time. Juan was the MVP, facing a minimum of nine batters in a one-hit starting stint. Mays led off the game with a 415-foot homer off Milt Pappas and scored the winning run in the seventh. He walked, raced to third on Hank

Aaron's single, and scored on Ron Santo's grounder to short.

1966—Marichal and Gaylord Perry blanked the American League over the last five innings in a 2-1 victory at St. Louis. Juan worked three frames and Gaylord was the winner. Mays scored the first National League run in the fourth on Santo's infield hit.

1968—Mays scored the only run on McCovey's double-play grounder in the first, and Marichal pitched two hitless innings during a 1-0 National League decision at Houston.

1969—McCovey became the fourth All-Star Game performer to wallop two home runs in one game, connecting off Blue Moon Odom and Denny McLain to power a 9-3 runaway at Washington. MVP McCovey finished with three RBI.

1970—Dick Dietz and McCovey had big hits in the Nationals' 5-4, twelfth-inning victory at Cincinnati. The American League entered the bottom of the ninth leading 4-1, but Dietz triggered a three-run rally with a homer off Catfish Hunter. McCovey added a run-scoring single in the rally.

1971 — Marichal pitched two hitless innings, but two future Giants combined to give the American League its last victory in the series through 1982. Frank Robinson belted a two-run homer and was the MVP, while Blue was the winner in a 6-4 decision at Detroit.

1973—Bonds didn't enter the game at Kansas City until he replaced Billy Williams in the fourth. Bobby belted a homer off Bill Singer in the fifth and stretched a single into a double in the seventh to earn MVP honors in the Nationals' 7-1 rout.

1976—John Montefusco pitched two hitless innings to help the Nationals crush the Americans 7-1 at Philadelphia.

1981—Blue worked one hitless inning and was the winner of the Nationals' 5-4 decision at Cleveland following the strike layoff. That made Vida the only pitcher to win games for each league in the All-Star Game Series.

1986 — Chris Brown doubled in his All-Star game batting debut, then grounded into a double play to kill a ninth-inning rally as the N.L. lost at Houston. Mike Krukow pitched a perfect ninth inning.

7

HOME BALL PARKS

Ball Park	Years Used	First Game	Last Game
First Polo Grounds (110th St. and Sixth Ave.)	1883-1888	N.Y. 7, Boston 5 May 1, 1883	Indianapolis 6, N.Y. 4 Oct. 13, 1888
Oakland Park (Jersey City)	1889 (2 games)	Boston 8, N.Y. 7 April 24, 1889	N.Y. 11, Bost. 10 April 25, 1889
St. George Grounds (Staten Island)	1889 (25 games)	N.Y. 4, Washington 2 April 29, 1889	N.Y. 14, Philadelphia 4 June 14, 1889
Second Polo Grounds (155th St. and 8th Ave.)	1889-1890	N.Y. 7, Pittsburgh 5 July 8, 1889	Boston 8, N.Y. 5 Sept. 10, 1890
Third Polo Grounds (157th St. and 8th Ave.)	1891-1957	Boston 4, N.Y. 3 April 22, 1891	Pittsburgh 9, N.Y. 1 Sept. 29, 1957
Seals Stadium (San Francisco)	1958-1959	S.F. 8, L.A. 0 April 15, 1958	L.A. 8, S.F. 2 Sept. 20, 1959
Candlestick Park (San Francisco)	1960-present	S.F. 3, St. Louis 1 April 12, 1960	

The original Polo Grounds, the Giants' home park from 1883 through 1888, was located at 110th Street and Sixth Avenue in Manhattan. The Giants shared the park with Giant owner John B. Day's other club, the New York Metropolitans, from 1883 until 1885. The champion Giants of 1889 were forced abruptly to vacate their first home park in February 1889 when New York City took over the site for inclusion in the Douglass Circle development.

Day hastily arranged for the Giants to move to Manhattan Field, which was situated at 155th Street and Eighth Avenue in Manhattan. Work began immediately on the construction of a wooden grandstand structure. But the new stadium was not sufficiently completed for the Giants' use on Opening Day. As a result, the Giants opened the 1889 season at Oakland Park in Jersey City. They played their second game at the same park, then moved to St. George Grounds in Staten Island for their next twenty-five home games. They played their first home game at the new Polo Grounds on July 8, 1889.

Day's club played in the second Polo Grounds for two seasons, 1889 and 1890. When the Players League folded after the 1890 season, the Giants purchased the larger Brotherhood Park (the home of the Players League New York entrant), which adjoined the second Polo Grounds to the north. Renamed the "New Polo Grounds," this would be the Giants' home park in New York for the next sixty-seven years.

The (third) Polo Grounds was destroyed by fire on April 14, 1911. The Giants used the Yankees' Hilltop Park at 168th Street and Broadway as a temporary home park until they returned to the partially rebuilt Polo Grounds on June 28, 1911. Their completely rebuilt home, which was dedicated on April 19, 1912, had double-decked, reinforced concrete and steel-supported stands that increased the park's seating capacity greatly, raising the pre-fire capacity of 17,300 to 34,000.

The Giants shared the Polo Grounds with the Yankees during the 1913-1922 period. The two clubs co-existed without noticeable hostility until the Yanks purchased Babe Ruth from the Red Sox before the 1920 season. The Yanks' resulting improvement on the field and at the box office led to increased friction between the two clubs, which culminated in an eviction notice issued to the Yankees by the Giants on May 14, 1920. Although the eviction action was rescinded shortly thereafter, Yankee owner Jacob Ruppert began to look for a location for his own park, finally selecting the Yankee Stadium site at River Avenue and 161st Street in the Bronx, just across the Harlem River from the Polo Grounds.

In 1924 the Polo Grounds playing field was completely enclosed by stands with the construction of double-decked, covered grandstands extending into the outfield, leaving only 4,600 uncovered bleacher seats (long, wooden planks rather than individual seats). This brought the capacity of the Polo Grounds to its eventual fifty-six thousand.

The only other significant modification to the Polo Grounds came in 1940, when the stadium was equipped for night baseball.

The San Francisco-bound Giants played their last game at the Polo Grounds on September 29, 1957, losing to Pittsburgh, 9-1.

The Polo Grounds, built in the 1890s and torn down in 1963 to make way for a housing development, was something special. Like many of the older parks, it had a unique charm and atmosphere that the newer stadiums are not likely to match.

The rectangular park was situated in a hollow overlooked by a mini-cliff known as Coogan's Bluff. It was bound on its home-plate side by Coogan's Bluff and the "Speedway" (now the Harlem River Drive), a road running along the Harlem River from 155th Street to 200th Street in upper Manhattan. Outside its first-base and right-field stands was an enormous lot used extensively by local cricket teams. The third-base and left-field stands were bound by subway yards, and the street bordering the park's center-field area was sun-sheltered by an IRT elevated station.

The green, double-decked, horseshoe-shaped stands seated 56,000. The unusual layout included high fences 257 feet down the right-field line and 279 feet down the left-field line, and a center field that terminated 483 feet from the plate at the base of the clubhouse wall. Right- and left-field bleachers, fronted by large, green "batters' background" screens 460 feet from the plate, were separated by 25 feet of open space extending from the screens back to the clubhouse. Each inner bleacher side had a flight of stairs leading to the separated clubhouses (the Giants' on the right-field side and their opponents' on the left-field side). The bullpens were in the outfield corners of the playing field. Owner Charles A. Stoneham's office, later used by his son Horace, was located above the clubhouses along with two ancient, iron loudspeakers and a large clock.

The Polo Grounds was ideal for hitters capable of pulling the ball directly down the line. However, the distances from the plate to the fences increased sharply from the foul lines out, and many long drives that were not hit close to the foul lines were converted into easy outs. The narrowness of the park also permitted outfielders to play relatively close to each other, thereby reducing the chances of hitting extra-base drives between the outfielders.

The outfield walls were probably the most difficult to play of any major league park, and not only because of their sharp angles. The right-field wall presented a solid stretch of concrete where most drives struck. Accordingly, a hard drive off the wall was likely to rebound back toward the infield. Balls hit not quite so hard usually caromed off toward center field, and softer drives, particularly those that just reached the wall, usually bounced off toward right center field or continued bouncing along the base of the wall.

The left-field wall was even more difficult to play. Compounding the problems of playing the carom, the left-field wall had a corrugated iron door on its gate that caused particularly unpredictable rebounds. Judgment of fly balls was complicated further because this was the sun field. In addition, the upper-deck facing extended well beyond the lower deck. This meant that, in cases where fly balls just missed the upper deck, there was a split second during which the fielder lost sight of the ball.

The outfield walls, as in all the older parks, were covered by advertisements (GEM razor blades, Stahl-Meyer frankfurters, Botany clothes, etc.) until 1948. After that the walls were painted a restful green to conform with the rest of the park, which may not have pleased the outfielders, who had used the letters in the advertisements as reference points for judging rebounds.

There was only one point outside the park from which any field action could be seen. High above Coogan's Bluff was an area from which the second-base area and a small part of the outfield was visible. An experienced viewer could have a good idea of what was taking place on the field simply by watching this sector and listening to the changing crowd noises. This was before the day of the portable radio and, for that matter, before the Giant games were on radio.

When the Giants shifted to San Francisco they played in the smallest major league park (23,741 capacity), but Seals Stadium was recognized among the most beautiful ballparks in the minors and certainly was major league in terms of beauty, location, and playing dimensions.

Seals was a cozy stadium, but home runs were not easy to come by because it was 365 feet down the left-field line, 355 to right, 410 to dead center, and 375 in the alleys. There were painted stars on the outfield walls, honoring some of the longest pokes. Names like Al Lyons, Joe Brovia, and Jerry Casale are recalled, the latter a pitcher in the Red Sox system who cleared the center-field wall with a mammoth blow in the mid-fifties.

Seals Stadium was built at a cost of $600,000 by three men who owned the Pacific Coast League's San Francisco Seals: Charles Graham, George Putnam, and Charles (Doc) Strub. The property at 16th and Bryant Streets once was the site of a mine, which by coincidence was listed as Home Plate Mine on the original deed.

The stadium was opened in April of 1931, and 14,235 attended an exhibition between the Seals and the Detroit Tigers. Former Yankees star Frankie Crosetti, a native San Franciscan, belted three hits, and the Seals stomped the Tigers, 5-2. That was the first in a series of eleven exhibitions in the new park, games that attracted close to one-hundred-thousand.

It wasn't until the fifth game, a spring skirmish between the Cubs and the Pirates, that a player was able to clear the wall with a homer; Gabby Hartnett connected for a 370-foot drive to left field that had to be at least 20 feet high to soar out of the park. One day later, Cubs manager Rogers Hornsby became the second man to turn the trick.

Jerry Donovan, a future Seals president and a Giants executive, hit the first home run that counted at Seals Stadium, blasting one for the Seals in the 1931 opener off Portland's Curt Fullerton. At the time, it took a clout of 385-plus feet for a home run to right. None of the big leaguers could do it in the exhibitions, but veteran outfielder Red Wingo of the Seals gained the distinction in the second Pacific Coast League series of the season against the crosstown arch-rival Mission Reds.

The Seals and the Missions shared Seals Stadium until 1938, when the Missions became the Hollywood Stars. Seals Stadium ranked as the largest uncovered park in organized baseball until the Dodgers moved into the Los Angeles Coliseum in 1958. Also, a minor league attendance record was established at Seals Stadium in 1946, when future Giants star Larry Jansen's thirty victories paced Lefty O'Doul's club to a pennant.

As much as Northern California fans craved major league baseball, they always had a soft spot for the Seals, who gave their followers a Pacific Coast League flag in 1957, a fitting going-away present. The Red Sox supplied the talent in those days, and Joe Gordon was the manager. There weren't many dry eyes at the final Pacific Coast League game in Seals Stadium because the club's fans knew the famed S.F. Seals were dead.

But enthusiasm abounded for the start of the city's first major league season (on April 15, 1958), and 23,449 were on hand for the Giants' 8-0 whipping of the Dodgers. After years of annual major league exhibitions, including visits by the Giants (who provided talent for the Oakland Oaks), the fans were eager for the real thing.

They watched Daryl Spencer of the Giants belt the first official major league homer at Seals Stadium. One day later, Duke Snider of the Dodgers cleared the right-field wall with one of the longest home runs in the park's history. More tears flowed when the Dodgers downed the Giants 8-2 on September 20, 1959, because the faithful fans realized it was the last game to be played at Seals Stadium, which was demolished by a wrecking crew a few months later.

Seals Stadium was the perfect location for a major league facility. It was five minutes from downtown, and there was talk of adding a deck to the park to bring it up to major league attendance standards. Unfortunately the plan was doomed because of inadequate parking. Too bad, because it wasn't nearly as windy at 16th and Bryant as it is at Candlestick Cove.

Moreover, expansion of Seals Stadium would have raised the capacity to only thirty-three-thousand, and the Giants insisted on a facility with a minimum of forty-thousand seats and plenty of parking when they elected to move from the Polo Grounds. The prospects for a new stadium were outstanding long before Horace Stoneham took Horace Greeley's advice.

In 1954, S.F. voters approved a $5 million bond issue to finance a stadium, but there was a catch. The funds would not be released unless a major league franchise was obtained within five years. The search was on and Supervisor Francis McCarty, author of the bond measure, discussed with Bill Veeck the possibility of moving the Browns to San Francisco. There also were talks with Calvin Griffith about shifting the Senators.

When George Christopher became mayor in 1956, his top priority was landing a major league baseball team. The Giants were considering a move to Minneapolis, so Christopher realized that a new ballpark was imperative to lure an established franchise. A site selection committee was appointed and Candlestick Point became the most feasible because downtown merchants opposed a stadium in their area.

Candlestick Park was a convenient alternative. A minimum of 75 acres were needed for a forty-thousand-capacity stadium with twelve-thousand parking spaces, and construction magnate Charles Harney happened to own 67 acres at Candlestick Point. Financially, it seemed like a sound move. Harney sold the city his property for $2.7 million, and Christopher later pointed out that it would have cost $33 million to purchase land downtown.

Construction on the new stadium began in September of 1958. Stoneham was anxious to have it completed by the 1959 World Series because the Giants were threatening to go all the way that year. As it was, the Giants folded down the stretch, and Candlestick Park, after a multitude of snags, wasn't opened until April 12, 1960.

Parts of Bay View Hill had to be cut to provide fill for the new park and its surroundings, so wind was a problem from the start. There were other problems, too, because it was the first stadium erected since the Depression, thus there were no standards by which to compare. The final announced cost was $14,855,990, less than $6 million of which went into the stadium itself.

For all its faults, Candlestick Park was attractive. It had 42,500 seats for the historic opener, and the playing dimensions were symmetrical: 335 feet down each foul line, 420 to dead center, and 390 in the alleys. An $850,000 lighting system was regarded as the finest in the nation at the time, and the curved seats were comfortable. A radiant heating system was designed to combat the cold for night games, but it didn't perform as promised.

A paid attendance of 42,269 for the opener shattered the S.F. record of 23,192 paid for the 1958 inaugural at Seals Stadium. The Giants downed the Cardinals 3-1, with Leon Wagner of St. Louis belting the initial home run in the new stadium, which had a deck but no stands beyond the fence in right and center. The open areas made hitting homers much easier for left-handed batters and worked against those who swung from the right side.

As a possible remedy, the Giants drastically moved in the fences for the 1961 season, dissatisfied that only eighty home runs were walloped in seventy-seven games at Candlestick in its maiden season. The distance in left-center was reduced to 365 feet and the new distances in center and right center were 410 and 375. A 45-foot backdrop was installed behind the center-field fence to reduce glare for batters.

After Stu Miller was blown off the mound in the 1961 All-Star Game, the park's capricious winds gained national attention. The City hired a firm to do a wind study in March of 1962. At a cost of $55,000, the Palo Alto firm released its findings in September of 1963, recommending a cut through the south end of Bay View Hill and a partial dome over the stadium. Those efforts to reduce wind would have cost an estimated $3 million, the firm pointed out.

Heels dragged and nothing was done at City Hall until Joseph Alioto became mayor and urged the demolition of Candlestick Park. "Why should we perpetuate mediocrity?" asked Alioto, whose joint committee recommended the construction of a fifty-five-thousand-seat stadium in downtown San Francisco. The report noted that it would cost $874,000 annually to improve Candlestick and $1.5 million annually to build a downtown stadium, but the committee stated it would be more advantageous to follow the latter plan because of the revenue that would be generated downtown.

Alioto's dream didn't gain much support, so steps were taken to improve Candlestick for the Giants and for its new tenants, the NFL's 49ers. Artificial turf was installed, as recommended by the Recreation and Parks Department in 1967, and the park was enclosed in an effort to reduce the wind and increase the capacity (to sixty-two-thousand) for football through use of movable stands. The work was completed in January of 1972.

The 49ers pushed for the synthetic surface, but numerous knee injuries made them change their mind and natural grass was planted in time for the 1979 baseball season. But that didn't calm the winds, which often make the game a nightmare for players and a nuisance for well-bundled fans. As a result, another study was launched and there was continuing talk of a dome for Candlestick or a downtown stadium as the Giants headed into the mid-eighties.

The much-maligned ballpark again was the focus of controversy following the 1984 season. Owner Bob Lurie's patience was running thin after attendance barely exceeded one million, so he vowed not to play at Candlestick Park beyond 1985.

Flames were fueled when the city of San Francisco announced major renovations at the stadium, most of them geared to appease the NFL's 49ers. Lurie and Giants brass deemed Candlestick unacceptable for baseball and their efforts to move to a new stadium increased after attendance dipped below one million in 1985.

When the 100-loss season concluded, it generally was felt the Giants had played at Candlestick for the last time. But plans to play temporarily at Oakland and Denver never got off the ground, parallelling the lack of success in obtaining a firm commitment for a new stadium in downtown San Francisco or elsewhere in the Bay Area.

There was moderate interest by San Jose officials but they backed off when S.F. Mayor Dianne Feinstein warned of tampering. Downtown stadium sites were mentioned, but those plans fell through. On Jan. 29, 1986, Lurie announced the club was to remain at Candlestick in 1986.

During the season, the club financed a feasibility study which discouraged downtown stadium plans because of the money involved in such a project. Lurie would not commit to Candlestick Park beyond 1987, hopeful that a stadium would be built somewhere in the Bay Area, perhaps as far away as Sacramento.

There was one notable change last year. Because of the club's success during the summer months, there was a reduction in grumbling about the ballpark by fans and players alike. The final attendance of 1,528,748 was the club's second highest in 20 years, representing an 87 percent increase over 1985.

Lurie, however, wasn't gushing. The businessman boss of the Giants noted that 1.8 million was the break-even figure for the club. He renewed his intentions of keeping the club in the Bay Area, but as of the end of the year there were no concrete plans for a new stadium west of Sacramento.

8

STATS AND FACTS

WILLIE MAYS AND
THE NEW GIANTS—1958

Baseball excitement was at a fever pitch in the Bay Area in 1958 because long-anticipated major league baseball had come to the West Coast. The fans were especially fond of the new Giants who didn't have a link with the past, yet Willie Mays won them over with one of his finest seasons. He'd won a batting title with a .345 average for New York in 1954, but he never batted higher in his illustrious career than he had with his .347 in 1958, barely losing the championship to Richie Ashburn of the Phillies. Mays' 208 hits in 1958 also were a career best. A day-by-day glance at the incomparable Mays and the 1958 Giants:

Date	Opponent	Score	AB	H	HR	R	RBI	AVG.
4/15	Los Angeles	8–0	5	2	0	0	2	.400
4/16	Los Angeles	1–13	4	2	0	0	1	.444
4/17	Los Angeles	7–4	3	0	0	1	0	.333
4/18	@Los Angeles	5–6	4	2	0	0	0	.375
4/19	@Los Angeles	11–4	5	3	0	2	1	.429
4/20	@Los Angeles	12–2	5	3	0	2	0	.462
4/22	St. Louis	5–7	5	3	0	0	0	.484
4/23	St. Louis	8–7	5	0	0	1	0	.417
4/24	St. Louis	6–5	4	1	0	1	1	.400
4/25	Chicago	2–0	3	1	0	1	0	.395
4/26	Chicago	3–1	4	3	1	3	1	.426
4/27	Chicago	4–5	4	1	0	0	1	.412
4/29	Philadelphia	4–7	3	2	0	2	0	.426
4/30	Philadelphia	10–1	4	0	0	0	0	.397
April Totals:			58	23	1	13	7	.397
5/1	Philadelphia	0–7	4	2	0	0	0	.403
5/2	Philadelphia	4–2	2	1	0	1	0	.406
5/3	Philadelphia	2–4	4	1	0	1	0	.397
5/4 (1)	Pittsburgh	2–6	4	1	0	0	0	.389

Date	Opponent	Score	AB	H	HR	R	RBI	AVG.
5/4 (2)	Pittsburgh	4–3	5	1	0	0	0	.377
5/5	Pittsburgh	10–11	3	1	0	0	1	.375
5/6	Pittsburgh	7–0	3	2	0	1	1	.386
5/7	Pittsburgh	8–6	3	0	0	0	0	.372
5/9	Los Angeles	11–3	4	3	2	3	5	.389
5/10	Los Angeles	3–2	3	1	1	1	1	.387
5/12	@Los Angeles	12–3	5	3	2	2	5	.398
5/13	@Los Angeles	16–9	5	5	2	4	4	.427
5/14	@St. Louis	2–3	4	0	0	1	0	.411
5/15	@St. Louis	4–2	4	2	1	1	1	.414
5/16	@Chicago	5–6	4	1	1	1	3	.409
5/17	@Chicago	9–4	4	2	1	2	1	.412
5/18 (1)	@Chicago	7–3	4	1	0	0	0	.407
5/18 (2)	@Chicago	4–0	5	2	0	0	0	.406
5/20	@Cincinnati	4–2	4	2	0	0	0	.409
5/21	@Cincinnati	5–4	4	3	1	1	2	.419
5/22	@Milwaukee	3–9	4	1	0	0	0	.414
5/23	@Milwaukee	5–3	4	2	1	2	2	.417
5/24	@Milwaukee	3–6	4	0	0	0	0	.405
5/25 (1)	@Pittsburgh	5–2	5	2	0	0	0	.405
5/25 (2)	@Pittsburgh	6–1	4	1	0	1	0	.401
5/27	@Philadelphia	1–5	4	1	0	0	0	.398
5/28	@Philadelphia	7–6	5	2	0	1	0	.398
5/30 (1)	@St. Louis	6–7	5	4	0	1	2	.409
5/30 (2)	@St. Louis	1–8	3	0	0	0	0	.400
5/31	@St. Louis	9–10	5	2	0	0	1	.402
May Totals:			121	49	12	26	29	.405
6/1	@St. Louis	7–2	3	2	0	2	1	.407
6/2	Milwaukee	6–7	5	2	0	3	1	.406
6/4	Milwaukee	9–10	6	4	0	1	1	.415
6/5	Milwaukee	5–4	5	4	0	2	0	.424
6/6	Cincinnati	4–5	3	3	1	2	1	.433
6/7	Cincinnati	7–3	4	0	0	0	2	.424
6/8	Cincinnati	3–6	4	0	0	0	0	.416
6/9	Cincinnati	3–0	4	0	0	0	0	.408
6/10	Pittsburgh	4–5	4	1	0	1	1	.406
6/11	Pittsburgh	6–14	3	0	0	1	0	.400
6/12	Pittsburgh	1–2	4	0	0	0	0	.393
6/13	Philadelphia	6–1	3	1	0	1	0	.392
6/14	Philadelphia	2–3	4	2	0	0	0	.394
6/15	Philadelphia	3–1	4	0	0	0	0	.387
6/17	@Pittsburgh	1–6	4	1	0	0	0	.385
6/18	@Pittsburgh	2–1	2	0	0	0	0	.382
6/19	@Pittsburgh	5–6			DID NOT PLAY			
6/20	@Philadelphia	4–5			DID NOT PLAY			
6/22 (1)	@Philadelphia	5–4	6	1	0	1	0	.377
6/22 (2)	@Philadelphia	2–3	5	3	0	0	0	.381
6/23	@Milwaukee	0–7	4	2	0	0	0	.383

Date	Opponent	Score	AB	H	HR	R	RBI	AVG.
6/24	@Milwaukee	1-2	4	0	0	0	0	.377
6/25	@Milwaukee	10-2	5	1	0	2	0	.374
6/26	@Cincinnati	5-1	3	1	0	1	0	.373
6/27	@Cincinnati	5-6	5	2	0	1	0	.374
6/28	@Cincinnati	2-8	3	0	0	1	0	.370
6/29	@Cincinnati	2-0	5	2	0	0	1	.370
June Totals:			102	32	1	19	8	.314
7/1	@Chicago	5-9	3	1	1	1	1	.370
7/2	@Chicago	5-2	4	1	1	1	1	.368
7/3	Chicago	3-4	4	1	0	1	1	.366
7/4 (1)	Chicago	6-5	4	1	0	0	2	.365
7/4 (2)	Chicago	1-6	4	0	0	0	0	.360
7/5	St. Louis	5-4	4	1	0	2	0	.359
7/6	St. Louis	5-4	3	1	0	0	0	.358
7/10	Cincinnati	0-4	4	0	0	0	0	.354
7/11	Cincinnati	7-4	4	0	0	2	0	.350
7/12	Milwaukee	5-3	2	0	0	0	1	.347
7/13	Milwaukee	6-5	4	0	0	1	0	.343
7/14	Milwaukee	3-12	4	1	0	0	0	.342
7/15	Philadelphia	1-0	3	1	0	0	0	.341
7/16	Philadelphia	9-2	5	3	0	1	2	.345
7/17	Philadelphia	8-7	3	1	0	1	1	.345
7/18	Pittsburgh	3-4	3	1	0	1	2	.345
7/19	Pittsburgh	5-4	2	0	0	0	0	.343
7/20	Pittsburgh	7-3	4	2	0	1	0	.345
7/23	@Philadelphia	0-2	4	1	0	0	0	.344
7/25	@Pittsburgh	0-10	2	2	0	0	0	.348
7/26	@Pittsburgh	1-0	4	0	0	0	0	.344
7/27 (1)	@Pittsburgh	1-2	4	1	0	0	0	.343
7/27 (2)	@Pittsburgh	3-4	4	3	0	0	0	.349
7/28 (1)	@Philadelphia	3-2	4	1	0	0	0	.346
7/28 (2)	@Philadelphia	2-1	4	1	0	0	0	.345
7/29	@Cincinnati	4-3	4	1	0	1	0	.344
7/30	@Cincinnati	1-5	4	1	0	1	0	.344
7/31	@Cincinnati	9-10	5	1	0	0	0	.341
July Totals:			103	27	2	13	11	.262
8/1	@Milwaukee	2-4	5	1	0	0	0	.339
8/2	@Milwaukee	0-10	4	1	0	0	0	.338
8/3 (1)	@Milwaukee	3-4	3	0	0	1	0	.336
8/3 (2)	@Milwaukee	0-6	4	1	0	0	0	.335
8/4	@Chicago	6-4	5	3	1	2	1	.338
8/5	@Chicago	9-10	5	3	0	2	1	.341
8/6	@St. Louis	7-8	4	1	0	1	0	.340
8/7	@St. Louis	1-12	4	0	0	0	0	.339
8/8	@Los Angeles	3-6	4	2	0	0	1	.340
8/9	@Los Angeles	6-3	4	0	0	0	0	.335
8/10	@Los Angeles	12-8	5	2	0	1	1	.336

Date	Opponent	Score	AB	H	HR	R	RBI	AVG.
8/12	St. Louis	3–7	3	0	0	1	0	.334
8/13	St. Louis	11–2	5	1	1	1	3	.332
8/14	St. Louis	4–3	4	2	1	1	1	.334
8/15	Chicago	1–3	4	0	0	0	0	.331
8/16	Chicago	7–4	4	1	1	1	2	.330
8/17	Chicago	8–6	3	1	1	2	3	.330
8/19	Cincinnati	4–3	4	1	0	1	0	.330
8/20	Cincinnati	4–3	3	0	0	0	0	.328
8/21	Cincinnati	1–8	3	1	0	0	0	.328
8/22	Cincinnati	3–7	3	0	0	1	0	.325
8/23	Cincinnati	5–2	4	2	1	1	2	.327
8/24	Milwaukee	5–8	3	1	0	2	0	.327
8/25	Milwaukee	1–6	4	1	0	0	1	.326
8/26	Milwaukee	3–7	4	2	1	1	2	.328
8/27	Milwaukee	3–2	4	1	0	0	0	.327
8/28	Milwaukee	0–3	3	1	0	0	0	.329
8/29	Los Angeles	1–4	1	0	0	0	0	.327
8/30 (1)	Los Angeles	3–2	4	1	0	1	0	.326
8/30 (2)	Los Angeles	3–1	3	1	1	1	3	.326
8/31	Los Angeles	14–2	4	3	1	3	2	.329
August Totals:			117	34	9	24	23	.291
9/1 (2)	Los Angeles	8–6	5	5	1	3	2	.336
9/1 (2)	Los Angeles	6–5	4	1	1	1	2	.335
9/2	@Los Angeles	0–4	4	1	0	0	0	.335
9/3	@Los Angeles	3–5	3	0	0	0	0	.333
9/4	@Los Angeles	13–3	5	3	1	2	2	.335
9/6	@Chicago	3–6	2	0	0	1	0	.334
9/7 (1)	@Chicago	4–6	3	0	0	1	0	.332
9/7 (2)	@Chicago	1–4	4	0	0	0	0	.330
9/9	@Pittsburgh	1–2	3	0	0	1	0	.328
9/10	@Pittsburgh	4–6	5	2	0	0	0	.328
9/12 (1)	@Philadelphia	5–2	5	3	0	0	2	.331
9/12 (2)	@Philadelphia	19–2	4	3	0	4	2	.334
9/13	@Philadelphia	6–5	4	1	0	1	2	.333
9/14 (1)	@Cincinnati	3–4	5	0	0	0	0	.330
9/14 (2)	@Cincinnati	6–4	5	4	0	2	1	.335
9/16	@Milwaukee	1–4	4	2	0	0	0	.336
9/19	@St. Louis	8–1	5	3	0	1	2	.338
9/20	@St. Louis	5–1	5	3	0	1	1	.340
9/21	@St. Louis	7–4	3	2	0	2	0	.342
9/23	Chicago	2–3	5	3	0	1	0	.344
9/24	Chicago	3–10	3	2	0	0	0	.346
9/26	St. Louis	4–3	3	0	0	0	0	.344
9/27	St. Louis	7–11	5	2	0	1	1	.345
9/28	St. Louis	7–2	5	3	1	3	1	.347
September Totals:			99	43	4	26	18	.434
Totals:			600	208	29	121	96	.347

Source: The Sporting News

WILLIE McCOVEY'S
ROOKIE SEASON—1959

Willie McCovey used a sensational major league debut, July 30, as a springboard toward National League Rookie of the Year honors in 1959. McCovey broke in with two singles and two triples in a perfect day against Robin Roberts of the Phillies at Seals Stadium. He only played 52 major league games, but his .354 average was impressive enough to earn him freshman honors in one-third of a season. McCovey's 1959 day-by-day:

Date	Opponent	Score	AB	H	2B	3B	HR	R	RBI
7/30	Philadelphia	7-2	4	4	0	2	0	3	2
7/31	Pittsburgh	4-3	4	1	0	0	0	0	1
8/1	Pittsburgh	9-5	5	3	2	0	0	3	0
8/2	Pittsburgh	5-3	5	1	0	0	1	1	2
8/4	Milwaukee	1-6	4	1	0	0	0	0	0
8/5	Milwaukee	4-1	4	2	0	0	2	2	3
8/6	Milwaukee	7-1	4	2	0	0	0	0	1
8/7	Cincinnati	3-2	2	0	0	0	0	0	0
8/8	Cincinnati	6-9	4	1	0	0	1	1	1
8/9	Cincinnati	4-3	4	0	0	0	0	1	0
8/10	@St. Louis	3-2	3	1	0	0	0	0	1
8/11	@St. Louis	5-4	DID NOT PLAY						
8/13	@Chicago	9-20	1	1	0	0	0	0	0
8/14	@Chicago	5-7	4	3	0	0	1	1	3
8/15	@Chicago	6-4	4	2	0	0	1	1	1
8/16	@Chicago	4-5	5	0	0	0	0	0	0
8/17	@Cincinnati	6-3	1	1	0	0	0	0	1
8/18	@Cincinnati	0-7	DID NOT PLAY						
8/10	@Milwaukee	2-5	4	2	0	0	0	0	0
8/20	@Milwaukee	5-3	5	3	0	0	1	1	3
8/21 (1)	@Philadelphia	6-0	4	1	0	0	0	1	0
8/21 (2)	@Philadelphia	10-6	5	1	0	1	0	1	2
8/22	@Philadelphia	8-1	5	2	0	0	0	0	1
8/24	@Pittsburgh	0-6	5	1	0	0	0	0	0
8/25	@Pittsburgh	12-5	4	1	0	0	0	0	0
8/26	@Pittsburgh	4-5	4	2	0	1	0	0	1
8/27 (1)	@Philadelphia	2-7	3	1	0	0	0	0	0
8/27 (2)	@Philadelphia	1-2	3	2	0	0	0	0	0
8/29	@Los Angeles	5-0	3	2	1	0	0	1	1
8/30	@Los Angeles	6-7	3	1	0	0	0	0	0
8/31	@Los Angeles	2-5	4	1	0	0	1	1	1
9/2	Chicago	4-3	4	1	0	0	1	1	1
9/3	Chicago	8-5	4	1	0	0	1	1	1
9/4	Chicago	1-2	4	1	0	1	0	1	0
9/5	St. Louis	3-2	4	1	0	0	1	1	1
9/6	St. Louis	0-1	4	1	0	0	0	0	0
9/7	St. Louis	4-2	4	1	0	0	0	0	0
9/9	Pittsburgh	7-2	1	1	0	0	0	1	0

Date	Opponent	Score	AB	H	2B	3B	HR	R	RBI
9/10	Pittsburgh	3–5	4	3	0	0	0	0	0
9/11	Philadelphia	0–1	3	0	0	0	0	0	0
9/12	Philadelphia	9–1	3	0	0	0	0	0	1
9/13	Philadelphia	1–0	4	1	0	0	0	0	0
9/14	Cincinnati	1–4	4	0	0	0	0	0	0
9/15	Cincinnati	13–6	5	3	1	0	1	2	2
9/16	Milwaukee	0–2	4	0	0	0	0	0	0
9/17	Milwaukee	13–6	3	1	1	0	0	2	2
9/19 (1)	Los Angeles	1–4	2	1	0	0	0	0	0
9/19 (2)	Los Angeles	3–5	3	1	0	0	0	0	1
9/20	Los Angeles	2–8	4	1	0	0	0	1	0
9/22	@Chicago	4–5	4	3	2	0	0	1	0
9/23	@Chicago	8–9	5	2	2	0	0	1	2
9/26	@St. Louis	4–0	4	2	0	0	1	2	2
9/27 (1)	@St. Louis	1–2	4	0	0	0	0	0	0
9/27 (2)	@St. Louis	8–14	1	0	0	0	0	0	0
Totals:	52 games	28–26	192	68	9	5	13	32	38

Source: The Sporting News

THE REAL M&M BOYS

Because they were centered in New York and created quite a stir chasing Babe Ruth in 1961, Roger Maris and Mickey Mantle of the Yankees became known as the M&M Boys. The fact of the matter is that the Giants' version of M&M, Willies Mays and McCovey, were a much more productive power pair. As teammates on the Yankees from 1960 through 1966, Maris and Mantle combined for 419 home runs and 1,107 RBI, averaging 59.9 homers and 158.1 RBI for each of those seven seasons. In the same 1960–66 span, even though McCovey hardly had reached his prime, the Giants' M&M Boys totaled 480 home runs and 1,295 RBI, averaging 68.6 and 185.0. For the 13-year period (1959–71) they appeared in the S.F. lineup, Mays and McCovey combined for 800 home runs and 2,306 RBI, averaging 61.5 homers and 177.4 RBI. You can look it up. The Giants' Hall of Famers had their best single season in 1965, erupting for 91 homers and 204 RBI. The Yankees exploded for 115 homers and 270 RBI in 1961, the year Maris' 61 homers surpassed Ruth.

JACK SANFORD'S S.F. RECORD
16-GAME WINNING STREAK OF 1962

Date	Opponent	Score	Record	IP	H	R	ER	BB	SO	Loser
June 17	St. Louis	6–3	7–6	9	5	3	3	5	5	Washburn
June 22	Milwaukee	9–11	ND	4	6	5	4	0	2	
June 26	Cincinnati	6–5	ND	7	8	4	4	4	5	
July 3	New York	10–1	8–6	9	9	1	1	1	0	Jackson
July 7	Los Angeles	10–3	9–6	6	3	2	2	1	6	Podres
July 12	@Philadelphia	5–3	10–6	7.7	8	2	2	1	3	Hamilton
July 16	@New York	3–2	11–6	6	6	1	1	1	6	Craig
July 20	@Pittsburgh	6–3	12–6	6.3	7	3	3	4	5	Law
July 24	@Houston	3–1	13–6	6.7	5	1	1	2	4	Farrell
July 28	@Los Angeles	6–8	ND	3.3	6	3	3	0	2	
Aug. 4	Pittsburgh	6–5	14–6	7	10	5	5	1	4	Olivo
Aug. 9	New York	7–1	15–6	9	3	1	0	3	3	Miller
Aug. 14	@Chicago	9–2	16–6	9	8	2	2	3	9	Hobbie
Aug. 18	@Milwaukee	6–4	17–6	5.3	8	3	3	3	5	Hendley
Aug. 22	@New York	4–5	ND	7	6	4	4	0	5	
Aug. 26	@Philadelphia	7–4	18–6	6.7	9	4	4	2	2	Mahaffey
Aug. 30	Milwaukee	3–2	19–6	6.7	4	2	2	4	3	Spahn
Sep. 3	@Los Angeles	7–3	20–6	9	8	3	3	0	5	Williams
Sep. 7	Chicago	6–5	21–6	7.3	7	5	3	1	4	Buhl
Sep. 11	Pittsburgh	2–0	22–6	9	8	0	0	1	3	Sturdivant
TOTALS		121–71	16–0	141	134	54	50	37	81	3.19 ERA

JUANDERFUL JUAN

Juan Marichal, arguably the greatest righthander in Giants' history, was the dominant hurler of the pitching-rich Sixties, but one would never know it when awards were being distributed. Incredibly, Marichal never won a Cy Young Award despite winning 27 more games in the Sixties than his greatest contemporary, Bob Gibson of the Cardinals. It was Marichal's ill fortune to play on only one pennant-winner, and to be overshadowed in his finest years. When he went 25–8 in 1963, for instance, Sandy Koufax was 25–5. When Marichal was 25–6 in 1966, Koufax went 27–9 prior to retirement. And in 1968, when Juan posted 26 victories, Gibson set a record with a 1.12 earned run average. The winningest pitchers, 1960–69:

	Won-Lost	Pct.	20 Wins
Juan Marichal. . . .	191–88	.685	6
Bob Gibson	164–105	.610	4
Don Drysdale	158–126	.556	2
Jim Bunning	147–117	.557	0
Sandy Koufax	137–60	.695	3

WILLIE MAY'S
52 HOME RUNS IN 1965

No.	Date	Inning	MOB	Opponent	Stadium	Pitcher
1	April 13	8	1	Pittsburgh	Forbes	Friend
2	April 14	3	1	Philadelphia	Connie Mack	Bunning
3	April 20	2	0	Pittsburgh	Candlestick	Friend
4	April 25 (2)	9	0	New York	Candlestick	Spahn
5	April 28	1	0	Philadelphia	Candlestick	Culp
6	May 3	9	0	St. Louis	Busch	Simmons
7	May 4	1	1	St. Louis	Busch	Sadecki
8	May 5	8	0	St. Louis	Busch	Schultz
9	May 7	2	0	Los Angeles	Candlestick	Osteen
10	May 7	4	0	Los Angeles	Candlestick	Osteen
11	May 13	3	0	Chicago	Candlestick	Broglio
12	May 15	1	0	Houston	Candlestick	Dierker
13	May 16 (1)	2	0	Houston	Candlestick	MacKenzie
14	May 18	1	2	Chicago	Wrigley	McDaniel
15	May 20	7	0	Chicago	Wrigley	L. Jackson
16	May 22 (1)	1	1	Houston	Astrodome	Bruce
17	May 22 (2)	1	1	Houston	Astrodome	Farrell
18	June 9	1	1	New York	Shea	Fisher
19	June 11	3	2	Pittsburgh	Forbes	Cardwell
20	June 12	1	1	Pittsburgh	Forbes	Friend
21	June 18	4	1	New York	Candlestick	Cisco
22	June 23	2	0	Pittsburgh	Candlestick	Veale
23	July 8 (2)	7	0	Philadelphia	Connie Mack	Herbert
24	July 30	5	0	Milwaukee	County	Sadowski
25	August 2	6	0	Milwaukee	County	Johnson
26	August 5	1	2	Cincinnati	Crosley	Tsitouris
27	August 5	2	0	Cincinnati	Crosley	Locke
28	August 7	5	1	St. Louis	Busch	Stallard
29	August 7	7	1	St. Louis	Busch	Briles
30	August 8	6	0	St. Louis	Busch	Purkey
31	Aug. 12 (1)	6	0	Pittsburgh	Candlestick	Friend
32	Aug. 12 (2)	6	0	Pittsburgh	Candlestick	Law
33	August 16	14	0	New York	Candlestick	Parsons
34	August 18	1	0	New York	Candlestick	B. Miller
35	August 19	1	1	Los Angeles	Candlestick	Drysdale
36	August 20	3	1	Los Angeles	Candlestick	Reed
37	August 21	8	0	Los Angeles	Candlestick	B. Miller
38	August 22	3	2	Los Angeles	Candlestick	Koufax
39	Aug. 26 (2)	9	0	Pittsburgh	Forbes	McBean
40	August 27	8	1	New York	Shea	Parsons
41	August 29	3	2	New York	Shea	Fisher
42	Sept. 4	6	1	Chicago	Wrigley	Broglio
43	Sept. 5	4	1	Chicago	Wrigley	Ellsworth
44	Sept. 8	2	2	Houston	Candlestick	Nottebart
45	Sept. 8	8	1	Houston	Candlestick	Taylor
46	Sept. 12 (2)	8	1	Chicago	Candlestick	Abernathy
47*	Sept. 13	4	0	Houston	Astrodome	Nottebart
48	Sept. 14	9	1	Houston	Astrodome	Raymond

No.	Date	Inning	MOB	Opponent	Stadium	Pitcher
49	Sept. 19	1	0	Milwaukee	County	Cloninger
50	Sept. 25	4	1	Milwaukee	Candlestick	Sadowski
51	Sept. 28	8	0	St. Louis	Candlestick	Jaster
52	Oct. 3	4	0	Cincinnati	Candlestick	McCool

*Career Homer Run No. 500.

WILLIE McCOVEY'S
CAREER GRAND-SLAM HOMERS

No.	Date	Inning	Opponent	Ballpark	Pitcher
1	June 12, 1960	*7th	Milwaukee	Candlestick	Willey
2	June 22, 1964	6th	Cincinnati	Crosley	Tsitouris
3	Sept. 10, 1965	*6th	Chicago	Candlestick	Abernathy
4	April 27, 1966	5th	Cincinnati	Candlestick	Pappas
5	April 22, 1967	8th	Atlanta	Candlestick	Hernandez
6	Sept. 23, 1967	8th	Pittsburgh	Candlestick	Pizarro
7	Sept. 27, 1967	3rd	New York	Candelstick	McGraw
8	May 4, 1968	3rd	St. Louis	Candlestick	Jaster
9	June 28, 1969	1st	Cincinnati	Crosley	Fisher
10	Aug. 26, 1969	3rd	Philadelphia	Candlestick	J. Johnson
11	April 26, 1970	1st	Montreal	Candlestick	Stoneman
12	May 10, 1970	4th	New York	Shea	McGraw
13	July 21, 1971	9th	Pittsburgh	Three Rivers	Giusti
14	July 2, 1972	7th	Los Angeles	Candlestick	Sutton
15	May 19, 1974	5th	San Francisco	Candlestick	Bradley
16	May 30, 1975	*8th	New York	Shea	Apodaca
17	June 27, 1977	6th	Cincinnati	Riverfront	Hoerner
18	Aug. 1, 1977	3rd	Montreal	Olympic	Twitchell

JACK CLARK'S 26-GAME HITTING STREAK—1978

Jack Clark, playing only his second full season, established the all-time Giants' record with a 26-game hitting streak, June 30 to July 25, 1978. During the streak, which included a successful pinch-hitting appearance in the second game of a July 16 doubleheader to make it 17 in a row, Clark batted .368. He hit 10 doubles and 8 home runs for a .689 slugging percentage, and added 19 runs and 29 RBI. What isn't as well known is the fact he hit safely in 19 consecutive games earlier in the season, May 9–29, and was even hotter. In the mini-streak, Clark batted .459 with 34 hits in 74 trips. By hitting in 26 straight, Clark surpassed the previous Giants' mark of 24 shared by Freddie Lindstrom, Don Mueller and Willie McCovey. The torrid 26:

Date	Opponent	Score	AB	H	2B	3B	HR	R	RBI
6/30 (1)	@Atlanta	9–10	5	2	0	0	2	2	3
6/30 (2)	@Atlanta	5–10	4	1	0	0	1	1	1
7/1	@Atlanta	15–4	5	2	0	0	1	2	4
7/2	@Atlanta	7–9	4	1	0	0	1	1	3
7/3	San Diego	3–4	3	2	0	0	1	1	1
7/4	San Diego	5–7	4	1	0	0	0	0	1
7/5	San Diego	5–4	5	2	1	0	0	2	1
7/6	San Diego	5–4	4	1	0	0	0	0	0
7/7 (1)	@Cincinnati	7–6	5	2	0	0	0	1	0
7/7 (2)	@Cincinnati	1–2	5	2	1	0	0	0	0
7/8	@Cincinnati	4–2	4	1	0	0	0	1	0
7/9	@Cincinnati	2–8	5	1	0	0	0	0	0
7/11	ALL-STAR GAME								
7/13	@Pittsburgh	4–0	4	1	0	0	0	0	0
7/14	@Pittsburgh	2–5	5	3	1	0	0	0	0
7/15	@Pittsburgh	6–5	5	1	0	0	0	1	0
7/16 (1)	@St. Louis	4–9	5	2	0	0	1	1	2
7/16 (2)	@St. Louis	6–0	1	1	1	0	0	0	2
7/17	@St. Louis	9–7	4	2	1	0	0	1	2
7/18	@Chicago	6–7	5	2	1	0	0	0	4
7/19 (1)	@Chicago	7–4	5	2	1	0	0	2	0
7/19 (2)	@Chicago	5–7	3	1	0	0	0	1	1
7/20	@Chicago	9–8	4	2	0	0	1	2	3
7/21	Pittsburgh	0–3	4	1	1	0	0	0	0
7/22	Pittsburgh	3–2	2	1	1	0	0	0	0
7/23	Pittsburgh	3–1	4	1	0	0	0	0	1
7/25	St. Louis	3–2	2	1	1	0	0	0	0
Totals:		14–12	106	39	10	0	8	19	29

GIANTS NO-HITTERS

JUAN MARICHAL
June 15, 1963, at Candlestick Park

HOUSTON	AB	R	H	RBI	SAN FRANCISCO	AB	R	H	RBI
Fazio, 2b	3	0	0	0	Hiller, 2b	3	0	1	1
Runnels, ph	1	0	0	0	F. Alou, rf	4	0	0	0
Davis, cf	4	0	0	0	Mays, cf	3	0	1	0
Aspromonte, 3b	2	0	0	0	McCovey, lf	2	0	0	0
Warwick, rf	3	0	0	0	Cepeda, 1b	3	0	0	0
Staub, 1b	3	0	0	0	Bailey, c	3	0	0	0
Spangler, lf	2	0	0	0	Davenport, 3b	3	1	1	0
Lillis, ss	3	0	0	0	Pagan, ss	1	0	0	0
Bateman, c	3	0	0	0	M. Alou, ph	1	0	0	0
Drott, p	2	0	0	0	Bowman, ss	0	0	0	0
Temple, ph	1	0	0	0	Marichal, p	3	0	0	0
TOTALS	27	0	0	0	TOTALS	26	1	3	1

						R	H	E
Houston	0 0 0	0 0 0	0 0 0	—	0	0	0
San Francisco . .	0 0 0	0 0 0	0 1 x	—	1	3	0

E—none. DP—Houston 1. LOB—Houston 2, San Francisco 4. 2B—Davenport, Hiller.

PITCHING SUMMARY
Houston	IP	H	R	ER	BB	SO
Drott (L, 2-4)	8	3	1	1	3	7
San Francisco						
Marichal (W, 10-3) . .	9	0	0	0	2	5

Umpires—Sudol, Forman, Gorman and Landes. Time—1:41. Attendance—18,869.

GAYLORD PERRY
Sept. 17, 1968, at Candlestick Park

ST. LOUIS	AB	R	H	RBI	SAN FRANCISCO	AB	R	H	RBI
Tolan, lf	4	0	0	0	Bonds, cf-rf	3	0	1	0
Flood, cf	4	0	0	0	Hunt, 2b	3	1	1	1
Maris, rf	3	0	0	0	Cline, lf	3	0	1	0
Cepeda, 1b	3	0	0	0	McCovey, 1b	3	0	0	0
McCarver, c	3	0	0	0	Hart, 3b	3	0	0	0
Shannon, 3b	2	0	0	0	Davenport, 3b	0	0	0	0
Gagliano, 2b	2	0	0	0	Marshall, rf	2	0	0	0
Maxvill, ss	2	0	0	0	Mays, cf	1	0	0	0
Edwards, ph	1	0	0	0	Dietz, c	2	0	0	0
Schofield, ss	0	0	0	0	Lanier, ss	3	0	1	0
Gibson, p	2	0	0	0	Perry, p	3	0	0	0
Brock, ph	1	0	0	0					
TOTALS	27	0	0	0	TOTALS	26	1	4	1

						R	H	E
St. Louis	0 0 0	0 0 0	0 0 0	—	0	0	0
San Francisco . .	1 0 0	0 0 0	0 0 x	—	1	4	1

E—None. DP—St. Louis 1. LOB—St. Louis 2, San Francisco 4. 2B—Lanier, Bonds. HR—Hunt. SB—Bonds. Sac—Hunt.

PITCHING SUMMARY
St. Louis	IP	H	R	ER	BB	SO
Gibson (L, 21-8)	8	4	1	1	2	10
San Francisco						
Perry (W, 15-14)	9	0	0	0	2	9

Umpires—Wendelstedt, Jackowski, Secory and Burkhart. Time—1:40. Attendance—9,546.

ED HALICKI
Aug. 24, 1975, at Candlestick Park

NEW YORK	AB	R	H	RBI	SAN FRANCISCO	AB	R	H	RBI
Unser, cf	3	0	0	0	Thomas, 2b	2	2	0	0
Millan, 2b	4	0	0	0	Rader, c	3	2	1	0
Garrett, 3b	4	0	0	0	Thomasson, cf	4	2	3	2
Staub, rf	3	0	0	0	Matthews, lf	3	0	0	0
Kingman, 1b	3	0	0	0	Montanez, 1b	4	0	2	2
Milner, lf	3	0	0	0	Speier, ss	4	0	1	0
Phillips, ss	3	0	0	0	Ontiveros, rf	4	0	1	0
Stearns, c	3	0	0	0	Miller, 3b	3	0	0	0
Swan, p	1	0	0	0	Halicki, p	4	0	0	0
Vail, ph	0	0	0	0					
Baldwin, p	0	0	0	0					
J. Alou, ph	1	0	0	0					
TOTALS	28	0	0	0	TOTALS	31	6	8	4

						R	H	E
New York	0 0 0	0 0 0	0 0 0	—	0	0	0
San Francisco . .	2 0 0	0 2 0	2 0 x	—	6	8	1

E—Thomas. DP—New York 1. LOB—New York 3, San Francisco 6. 2B—Speier. 3B—Thomasson. SB—Thomas 3, Rader, Thomasson.

PITCHING SUMMARY
New York	IP	H	R	ER	BB	SO
Swan (L, 1-1)	5	4	4	4	3	5
Baldwin	3	4	2	2	2	1
San Francisco						
Halicki (W, 8-10) . . .	9	0	0	0	2	10

WP—Baldwin. Umpires—Froemming, A. Williams, Runge and Vargo. Time—2:15. Attendance—24,132.

JOHN MONTEFUSCO
Sept. 29, 1976, at Atlanta

SAN FRANCISCO	AB	R	H	RBI	ATLANTA	AB	R	H	RBI
Herndon, cf	5	0	2	1	Royster, 3b	3	0	0	0
Perez, 2b	5	0	0	0	Gilbreath, 2b	3	0	0	0
Matthews, lf	5	2	2	0	Montanez, 1b	3	0	0	0
Murcer, rf	4	2	2	1	May, lf	3	0	0	0
Alexander, c	4	2	1	0	Asselstine, cf	3	0	0	0
Thomasson, 1b	4	0	2	2	Paciorek, rf	3	0	0	0
Thomas, 3b	4	1	1	1	Murphy, c	3	0	0	0
LeMaster, ss	3	2	2	3	Chaney, ss	2	0	0	0
					Capra, p	0	0	0	0
					Wynn, ph	1	0	0	0
					Easterly, p	0	0	0	0
					Hanna, p	0	0	0	0
					Camp, p	0	0	0	0
					Rockett, ph-ss	1	0	0	0
					Gaston, ph	1	0	0	0
TOTALS	38	9	12	9	TOTALS	27	0	0	0

						R	H	E
San Francisco . .	0 4 0	1 3 0	0 0 1	—	9	12	0
Atlanta	0 0 0	0 0 0	0 0 0	—	0	0	2

E—Royster, Murphy. DP—Atlanta 1. LOB—San Francisco 5, Atlanta 1. 2B—LeMaster, Matthews, Murcer. 3B—LeMaster. SF—LeMaster.

PITCHING SUMMARY
San Francisco	IP	H	R	ER	BB	SO
Montefusco (W, 16-14)	9	0	0	0	1	4
Atlanta						
Easterly (L, 1-1)	1.7	6	4	4	0	1
Hanna	2.3	4	4	3	2	0
Camp	2	0	0	0	0	1
Capra	3	2	1	1	0	2

Umpires—Davidson, Colosi, Olsen and Weyer. Time—1:59. Attendance—1,369.

UNUSUAL GAMES

GIANTS' S.F. OPENER
April 15, 1958, at Seals Stadium

LOS ANGELES	AB	R	H	RBI	SAN FRANCISCO	AB	R	H	RBI
Cimoli, cf	5	0	1	0	Davenport, 3b	4	1	2	1
Reese, ss	3	0	0	0	King, lf	3	1	2	1
Snider, lf	2	0	0	0	Mays, cf	5	0	2	2
Hodges, 1b	4	0	0	0	Kirkland, rf	5	0	1	1
Neal, 2b	4	0	2	0	Cepeda, 1b	5	1	1	1
Gray, 3b	4	0	2	0	Spencer, ss	4	1	1	1
Furillo, rf	3	0	0	0	O'Connell, 2b	2	1	0	0
Walker, c	3	0	1	0	Thomas, c	1	2	0	0
Roseboro, pr-c	1	0	0	0	Gomez, p	4	1	2	1
Drysdale, p	1	0	0	0					
Bessent, p	0	0	0	0					
Larker, ph	1	0	0	0					
Negray, p	0	0	0	0					
Gilliam, ph	0	0	0	0					
TOTALS	**31**	**0**	**6**	**0**	**TOTALS**	**33**	**8**	**11**	**8**

										R	H	E
Los Angeles....	0 0 0	0 0 0	0 0 0	—						0	6	1
San Francisco ..	0 0 2	4 1 0	0 1 x	—						8	11	0

E—Hodges. DP—San Francisco 1. LOB—Los Angeles 10, San Francisco 9. HR—Spencer, Cepeda. SF—Davenport.

PITCHING SUMMARY

Los Angeles	IP	H	R	ER	BB	SO
Drysdale (L, 0-1)....	3.7	5	6	6	3	1
Bessent	2.3	4	1	1	1	0
Negray	2	2	1	1	3	1
San Francisco						
Gomez (W, 1-10) ...	9	6	0	0	6	6

Balk—Negray. PB—Walker. Umpires—Conlan, Secory, Dixon and Venzon. Time—2:29. Attendance—23,448.

WILLIE MAYS' FOUR-HOMER GAME
April 30, 1961, at County Stadium

SAN FRANCISCO	AB	R	H	RBI	MILWAUKEE	AB	R	H	RBI
Hiller, 2b	6	2	3	1	McMillan, ss	4	1	1	0
Davenport, 3b	4	3	1	1	Bolling, 2b	4	1	2	0
Mays, cf	5	4	4	8	Matthews, 3b	4	0	1	0
McCovey, 1b	3	0	0	0	Aaron, cf	4	2	2	4
Marshall, 1b	0	0	0	0	Roach, lf	4	0	1	0
Cepeda, lf	5	1	1	1	Adcock, 1b	4	0	0	0
M. Alou, lf	0	0	0	0	Lau, c	3	0	1	0
F. Alou, rf	4	1	1	1	McMahon, p	0	0	0	0
Bailey, c	4	0	0	0	Brunet, p	0	0	0	0
Pagan, ss	5	3	4	2	Maye, ph	1	0	0	0
Loes, p	3	0	0	0	DeMerit, rf	4	0	0	0
					Burdette, p	1	0	0	0
					Willey, p	0	0	0	0
					Drabowsky, p	0	0	0	0
					Martin, p	1	0	0	0
					Morehead, p	0	0	0	0
					MacKenzie, p	0	0	0	0
					Logan, ph	1	0	0	0
					Taylor, c	0	0	0	0
TOTALS	**39**	**14**	**14**	**14**	**TOTALS**	**34**	**4**	**8**	**4**

						R	H	E
San Francisco ..	1 0 3	3 0 4	0 3 0	—		14	14	0
Milwaukee	3 0 0	0 0 1	0 0 0	—		4	8	1

E—Mathews. DP—San Francisco 1, Milwaukee 2. LOB—San Francisco 6, Milwaukee 4. 2B—Hiller 2. 3B—Davenport. HR—Mays 4, Pagan, Cepeda, F. Alou, Aaron 2. Sac—Loes 2.

PITCHING SUMMARY

San Francisco	IP	H	R	ER	BB	SO
Loes (W, 2-1)	9	8	4	4	1	3
Milwaukee						
Burdette (L, 1-1)....	3	5	5	5	0	0
Willey	1	3	2	2	0	0
Drabowsky.........	1	0	0	0	1	0
Morehead	1	2	4	4	1	1
MacKenzie.........	1	0	0	0	0	1
McMahon..........	1	3	3	3	2	0

HB—Burdette (Davenport), MacKenzie (Bailey). Umpires—Pelekoudas, Forman, Conlan, Donatelli and Burkhart. Time—2:40. Attendance—13,114.

THE MARICHAL-SPAHN CLASSIC
July 2, 1963, at Candlestick Park

MILWAUKEE	AB	R	H	RBI	SAN FRANCISCO	AB	R	H	RBI
Maye, lf	6	0	0	0	Kuenn, 3b	7	0	1	0
Bolling, 2b	7	0	2	0	Mays, cf	6	1	1	1
Aaron, rf	6	0	0	0	McCovey, lf	6	0	1	0
Mathews, 3b	2	0	0	0	F. Alou, rf	6	0	1	0
Menke, 3b	5	0	2	0	Cepeda, 1b	6	0	2	0
Larker, 1b	5	0	0	0	Bailey, c	6	0	1	0
Jones, cf	5	0	1	0	Pagan, ss	2	0	0	0
Dillard, cf	1	0	0	0	Hiller, 2b	6	0	0	0
Crandall, c	6	0	2	0	Marichal, p	6	0	0	0
McMillan, ss	6	0	0	0	Davenport, ph	1	0	0	0
Spahn, p	6	0	1	0	Bowman, ss	3	0	2	0
TOTALS	**55**	**0**	**8**	**0**	**TOTALS**	**55**	**1**	**9**	**1**

						R	H	E
Milwaukee	0 0 0	0 0 0	0 0 0	—		0	8	1
San Francisco ..	0 0 0	0 0 0	0 0 1	—		1	9	1

E—Kuenn, Menke. DP—none. LOB—Milwaukee 11, San Francisco 9. 2B—Spahn, Kuenn. HR—Mays. SB—Cepeda, Maye, Menke.

PITCHING SUMMARY

Milwaukee	IP	H	R	ER	BB	SO
Spahn (L, 11-4) ...	15.3	9	1	1	1	2
San Francisco						
Marichal (W, 13-3)	16	8	0	0	4	11

Umpires—Burkhart, Pelekoudas, Walsh and Conlan. Time—4:10. Attendance—15,921.

THE LONGEST DAY—May 31, 1964
at Shea Stadium
Second Game

SAN FRANCISCO	AB	R	H	RBI	NEW YORK	AB	R	H	RBI
Kuenn, lf	5	1	0	0	Kanehl, 2b	1	0	0	0
Perry, p	3	0	0	0	Gonder, ph	1	0	0	0
Crandall, ph	1	0	1	1	Samuel, 2b	7	0	2	0
Hendley, p	0	0	0	0	McMillan, ss	10	1	2	0
J. Alou, rf	10	1	4	2	Thomas, lf	10	1	2	0
Mays, cf-ss	10	1	1	1	Christopher, rf	10	2	4	3
Cepeda, 1b	9	1	3	0	Kranepool, 1b	11	1	3	1
Haller, c	10	1	4	1	Hickman, cf	10	1	2	0
Hiller, 2b	8	1	1	1	C. Smith, 3b	9	0	4	1
Hart, 3b	4	0	1	1	Cannizzaro, c	7	0	1	1
M. Alou, ph-cf	6	0	0	0	Wakefield, p	0	0	0	0
Garrido, ss	3	0	0	0	Altman, ph	0	0	0	0
McCovey, ph	1	0	0	0	Jackson, pr	0	0	0	0
Davenport, ss-3b	4	1	1	1	Anderson, p	0	0	0	0
Bolin, p	2	0	1	0	Sturdivant, p	0	0	0	0
MacKenzie, p	0	0	0	0	D. Smith, ph	1	0	0	0
Shaw, p	0	0	0	0	Lary, ph	1	0	0	0
Snider, ph	1	0	0	0	Taylor, ph	1	0	0	0
Herbel, p	0	0	0	0	Bearnarth, p	3	0	0	0
Peterson, ph-3b	4	1	0	0	Cisco, p	2	0	0	0
					Stephenson, ph	1	0	0	0
TOTALS	**81**	**8**	**17**	**8**	**TOTALS**	**83**	**6**	**20**	**6**

			R	H	E
S.F...	204 000 000 000 000 000 000 02	—	8	17	3
N.Y. .	010 002 300 000 000 000 000 00	—	6	20	1

E—Garrido, Haller, Cepeda, Cisco. DP—San Francisco 2, New York 1. TP—New York 1. LOB—San Francisco 16, New York 14. 2B—J. Alou, Kranepool, Cepeda, Crandall. 3B—Kranepool, Haller, Davenport. HR—Christopher. Sac—Herbel, Hiller, C. Smith, Cisco.

PITCHING SUMMARY

San Francisco	IP	H	R	ER	BB	SO
Bolin..............	6.7	8	6	5	2	7
MacKenzie.........	0	1	0	0	0	0
Shaw	1.3	1	0	0	0	1
Herbel	4	3	0	0	0	3
Perry (W, 3-1)	10	7	0	0	1	9
Hendley (save)	1	0	0	0	0	2
New York						
Wakefield	2	2	2	2	2	1
Anderson	0.3	4	4	4	0	0
Sturdivant	2.7	3	0	0	1	2
Lary	2	0	0	0	0	2
Bearnarth	7	3	0	0	4	4
Cisco (L, 2-5)	9	5	2	2	2	5

HB—Samuel (Shaw), Cepeda (Cisco). PB—Cannizzaro. Umpires—Sudol, Pryor, Secory, Burkhart. Time—7:23. Attendance—57,037.

S.F. HALL OF FAMERS

JUAN MARICHAL'S RECORD

Year	Club	W–L	ERA	G	GS	CG	IP	H	R	ER	BB	SO
1958	Michigan City	21–8	1.87	35	28	24	245	200	69	51	50	246
1959	Springfield	18–13	2.39	37	32	23	271	238	85	72	47	208
1960	Tacoma	11 5	3.11	18	18	12	139	116	52	48	34	121
	San Francisco	6–2	2.67	11	11	6	81	59	29	24	28	58
1961	San Francisco	13–10	3.89	29	27	9	185	183	8	80	48	124
1962	San Francisco	18–11	3.35	37	36	18	263	233	112	98	90	153
1963	San Francisco	25–8	2.41	41	40	18	321	259	102	86	61	248
1964	San Francisco	21–8	2.48	33	33	22	269	241	89	74	52	206
1965	San Francisco	22–13	2.14	39	37	24	295	224	78	70	46	240
1966	San Francisco	25–6	2.23	37	36	25	307	228	88	76	36	222
1967	San Francisco	14–10	2.76	26	26	18	202	195	79	62	42	166
1968	San Francisco	26–9	2.43	38	38	30	326	295	106	88	46	218
1969	San Francisco	21–11	2.10	37	36	27	300	244	90	70	54	205
1970	San Francisco	12–10	4.11	34	33	14	243	269	128	111	48	123
1971	San Francisco	18–11	2.94	37	37	18	279	244	113	91	56	159
1972	San Francisco	6–16	3.71	25	24	6	165	176	82	68	46	72
1973	San Francisco	11–15	3.79	34	32	9	207	231	104	88	37	87
1974	Boston	0–1	4.89	11	9	0	57	61	32	31	14	21
1975	Los Angeles	0–1	13.50	2	2	0	6	11	9	9	5	1
N.L.	Totals	238–141	2.86	460	448	244	3449	3092	1297	1095	695	2282
A.L.	Totals	5–1	4.89	11	9	0	57	61	32	31	14	21
M.L.	Totals	243–142	2.89	471	457	244	3506	3153	1329	1126	709	2303

WILLIE MAYS' RECORD

Year	Club	AVG	G	AB	R	H	2B	3B	HR	RBI	BB	SO	SB
1950	Trenton	.353	81	306	50	108	20	8	4	55	42	34	7
1951	Minneapolis	.477	35	149	38	71	18	3	8	30	14	10	5
	New York	.274	121	464	59	127	22	5	20	68	56	60	7
1952	New York	.236	34	127	17	30	2	4	4	23	16	17	4
1952			(In Military Service)										
1953			(In Military Service)										
1954	New York	.345	151	565	119	195	33	13	41	110	66	57	8
1955	New York	.319	152	580	123	185	18	13	51	127	79	60	24
1956	New York	.296	152	578	101	171	27	8	36	84	68	65	40
1957	New York	.333	152	585	112	195	26	20	35	97	76	62	38
1958	San Francisco	.347	152	600	121	208	33	11	29	96	78	56	31
1959	San Francisco	.313	151	575	125	180	43	5	34	104	65	58	27
1960	San Francisco	.319	153	595	107	190	29	12	29	103	61	70	25
1961	San Francisco	.308	154	572	129	176	32	3	40	123	81	77	18
1962	San Francisco	.304	162	621	130	189	36	5	49	141	78	85	18
1963	San Francisco	.314	157	596	115	187	32	7	38	103	66	83	8
1964	San Francisco	.296	157	578	121	171	21	9	47	111	82	72	19
1965	San Francisco	.317	157	558	118	177	21	3	52	112	76	71	9
1966	San Francisco	.288	152	552	99	159	29	4	37	103	70	81	5
1967	San Francisco	.263	141	486	83	128	22	2	22	70	51	92	6
1968	San Francisco	.289	148	498	84	144	20	5	23	79	67	81	12
1969	San Francisco	.283	117	403	64	114	17	3	13	58	49	71	6
1970	San Francisco	.291	139	478	94	139	15	2	28	83	79	90	5
1971	San Francisco	.271	136	417	82	113	24	5	18	61	112	123	23
1972	San Francisco	.184	19	49	8	9	2	0	0	3	17	5	3
	New York	.267	69	195	27	52	9	1	8	19	43	43	1
1973	New York	.211	66	209	24	44	10	0	6	25	27	47	1
M.L.	Totals	.302	2992	10881	2062	3283	523	140	660	1903	1463	1526	338

WILLIE McCOVEY'S RECORD

Year	Club	AVG	G	AB	R	H	2B	3B	HR	RBI	BB	SO	SB
1955	Sandersville	.305	107	410	82	125	24	1	19	113	56	89	15
1956	Danville	.310	152	519	119	161	38	8	29	89	90	113	10
1957	Dallas	.281	115	395	63	111	21	9	11	65	52	52	11
1958	Phoenix	.319	146	527	91	168	37	10	14	89	52	83	4
1959	Phoenix	.372	95	349	84	130	26	11	29	92	51	48	0
	San Francisco	.354	52	192	32	68	9	5	13	38	22	35	2
1960	San Francisco	.238	101	260	37	62	15	5	13	51	45	53	1
	Tacoma	.286	17	63	14	18	1	3	3	16	11	6	1
1961	San Francisco	.271	106	328	59	89	12	3	18	50	37	60	1
1962	San Francisco	.293	91	229	41	67	6	1	20	54	29	35	3
1963	San Francisco	.280	152	564	103	158	19	5	44	102	50	119	1
1964	San Francisco	.220	130	364	55	80	14	1	18	54	61	73	2
1965	San Francisco	.276	160	540	93	149	17	4	39	92	88	118	0
1966	San Francisco	.295	150	502	85	148	26	6	36	96	76	100	2
1967	San Francisco	.276	135	456	73	126	17	4	31	91	71	110	3
1968	San Francisco	.293	148	523	81	153	16	4	36	105	72	71	4
1969	San Francisco	.320	149	491	101	157	26	2	45	126	121	66	0
1970	San Francisco	.289	152	495	98	143	39	2	39	126	137	75	0
1971	San Francisco	.277	105	329	45	91	13	9	18	70	64	57	0
1972	San Francisco	.213	81	263	30	56	8	0	14	35	38	45	0
1973	San Francisco	.266	130	383	52	102	14	3	29	75	105	78	1
1974	San Diego	.253	128	344	53	87	19	1	22	63	96	76	1
1975	San Diego	.252	122	413	43	104	17	0	23	68	57	80	1
1976	San Diego	.203	71	202	20	41	9	0	7	36	21	39	0
	Oakland	.208	11	24	0	5	0	0	0	0	3	4	0
1977	San Francisco	.280	141	478	54	134	21	0	28	86	67	106	3
1978	San Francisco	.228	108	351	32	80	19	2	12	64	36	57	1
1979	San Francisco	.249	117	353	34	88	9	0	15	57	36	70	0
1980	San Francisco	.204	48	113	8	23	8	0	1	16	13	23	0
N.L.	Totals	.270	2577	8173	1229	2206	353	46	521	1555	1342	1546	26
A.L.	Totals	.208	11	24	0	5	0	0	0	0	3	4	0
M.L.	Totals	.270	2588	8197	1229	2211	353	46	521	1555	1345	1550	26

THE JUNE SWOON

Is the so-called June Swoon fact or fiction for the Giants? The legend originated during the club's early years in San Francisco, and there seems to be a grain of truth to it. In their 30-year West Coast history, for instance, the Giants have suffered through 16 losing Junes and have posted a winning record only 10 times that month. Four other years, the record was .500 in June.

The only other weak month for the Giants has been April, which has produced 15 losing records. In fact, until the 1986 and 1987 clubs posted winning Aprils, it hadn't happened since the 1973 team went 18–6 the opening month. Overall, the Giants are 401–435 in June through 1987, a .480 percentage.

Even the championship S.F. teams have had their difficulties in June. The pennant-winners of 1962 won more than 100 games, yet were a mere 16–13 in June after entering the month 35–15. The only two division champs had losing Junes, swooning to 13–15 in 1971 after going 37–14 the first two months and plunging to 11–15 in 1987 following a 27–22 start.

The June Swoon was apparent from the start. The 1958 Giants carried a 27–17 record into the month before dropping to 10–16 in June. In 1960, they were 26–16 in April-May and 11–16 in June. Following the pennant in 1962, the Giants started 1963 with a 30–18 record before going 13–15 in June. Those early failures, more than anything, started the June Swoon legacy.

Following is the Giants' 30-year record in June, their cruelest month:

1958: 10–16	1968: 14–16	1978: 17–13
1959: 17–14	1969: 15–14	1979: 13–13
1960: 11–16	1970: 12–12	1980: 15–13
1961: 15–15 ˙	1971: 13–15	1981: 2–7
1962: 16–13	1972: 13–15	1982: 14–13
1963: 13–15	1973: 13–14	1983: 12–16
1964: 19–11	1974: 7–20	1984: 14–16
1965: 14–13	1975: 14–17	1985: 10–20
1966: 18–12	1976: 13–17	1986: 16–12
1967: 16–16	1977: 14–16	1987: 11–15

ALL-TIME TEAMS

Former National League President Chub Feeney's all-time Giants among the players he's seen perform:

New York
Bill Terry (1B), Eddie Stanky (2B), Travis Jackson (3B), Alvin Dark (SS), Monte Irvin (LF), Willie Mays (CF), Mel Ott (RF), Gus Mancuso and Wes Westrum (tie-C), Carl Hubbell (left-hander), Sal Maglie (right-hander), Hoyt Wilhelm (reliever), Sid Gordon (utility), Bill Terry (mgr).

San Francisco
Willie MCovey (1B), Tito Fuentes (2B), Jim Davenport (3B), Jose Pagan (SS), Bobby Bonds (LF), Willie Mays (CF), Felipe Alou (RF), Tom Haller (C), Mike McCormick (left-hander), Juan Marichal (right-hander), Frank Linzy (reliever), Orlando Cepeda (utility), Bill Rigney (mgr).

Long-time Giants front office man Eddie Brannick's all-time Giants (from 1905 through the 1960s):
Bill Terry (1B), Frankie Frisch (2B), Dave Bancroft (SS), Fred Lindstrom (3B), Joe Moore (LF), Willie Mays (CF), Ross Youngs (RF), Pancho Snyder and Chief Meyers (tie-C), Christy Mathewson (right-hander), Carl Hubbell (left-hander), Mel Ott and Heinie Groh (utility), and John McGraw (mgr).

The 25th Anniversary San Francisco dream team, as selected by the club's fans at the conclusion of the 1981 season:

Willie McCovey (1B), Tito Fuentes (2B), Jim Davenport (3B), Johnnie LeMaster (SS), Gary Matthews (LF), Willie Mays (CF), Jack Clark (RF), Tom Haller (C), Orlando Cepeda (Utility), Juan Marichal (RHP), Vida Blue (LHP), Stu Miller (RH reliever), Al Holland (LH reliever) and Frank Robinson (mgr).

The 30-year S.F. all-star squad as selected by the author in 1988: Willie McCovey (1B), Joe Morgan (2B), Jim Davenport (3B), Jose Uribe (SS), Orlando Cepeda (LF), Willie Mays (CF), Bobby Bonds (RF), Tom Haller (C), Jack Clark (RHPH), Will Clark (LHPH), Juan Marichal and Gaylord Perry (RHP), Mike McCormick and Vida Blue (LHP), Stu Miller and Don McMahon (RH relief), Gary Lavelle and Billy Pierce (LH relief) and Roger Craig (mgr).

AWARDS AND HONORS

Retired Giant Uniform Numbers

Player	Uniform Number
Bill Terry	3
Mel Ott	4
Carl Hubbell	11
Willie Mays	24
Juan Marichal	27
Willie McCovey	44

Giant MVP Award Winners

Player	Year
Chalmers Award:	
Larry Doyle	1912
Baseball Writers	
Association of America:	
Carl Hubbell	1933
Carl Hubbell	1936
Willie Mays	1954
Willie Mays	1965
Willie McCovey	1969

Rookie of the Year Awards

	Year
Baseball Writers	
Association of America:	
Willie Mays	1951
Orlando Cepeda	1958
Willie McCovey	1959
Gary Matthews	1973
John Montefusco	1975
The Sporting News:	
Orlando Cepeda	1958
Willie McCovey	1959
Frank Linzy	1965
Dave Rader	1972
Gary Matthews	1973
John D'Acquisto	1974
John Montefusco	1975
Larry Herndon	1976
Robby Thompson	1986

Cy Young Award

Pitcher	Year
Mike McCormick	1967

9

RECORDS

GIANTS' CAREER LEADERS 1958–87
BATTING TOP 10

Games		At Bats		Hits		Doubles	
Player	**Total**	**Player**	**Total**	**Player**	**Total**	**Player**	**Total**
McCovey	2,256	Mays	7,578	Mays	2,284	Mays	376
Mays	2,095	McCovey	7,214	McCovey	1,974	McCovey	308
Davenport	1,501	Davenport	4,427	Cepeda	1,286	Cepeda	226
Cepeda	1,114	Cepeda	4,178	Davenport	1,142	J. Clark	197
Lanier	1,101	Bonds	4,047	Bonds	1,116	Bonds	188
Evans	1,094	Fuentes	3,823	J. Clark	1,034	Davenport	177
Fuentes	1,054	J. Clark	3,731	Fuentes	1,000	Evans	159
J. Clark	1,044	Evans	3,728	Hart	965	Fuentes	152
Bonds	1,014	Speier	3,522	Evans	952	Davis	144
Speier	1,004	Lanier	3,514	Speier	878	Speier	140

Triples		Home Runs		Runs		RBI	
Mays	76	McCovey	469	Mays	1,480	McCovey	1,388
McCovey	45	Mays	459	McCovey	1,113	Mays	1,350
Bonds	42	Cepeda	226	Bonds	765	Cepeda	767
Herndon	39	Bonds	186	Cepeda	652	J. Clark	595
Davenport	37	J. Clark	163	J. Clark	597	Bonds	552
Fuentes	33	Hart	157	Davenport	552	Hart	526
J. Clark	30	Evans	142	Evans	534	Evans	525
Hart	27	Haller	107	Hart	528	Davenport	456
Matthews	24	Davis	101	Davis	432	Davis	418
Speier	23	Leonard	97	Fuentes	417	Leonard	415
Leonard	23						

Stolen Bases		Batting Average		Total Bases		Slugging Percentage	
Bonds	263	Cepeda	.308	Mays	4,199	Mays	.554
Mays	211	Mays	.301	McCovey	3,729	Cepeda	.535
North	129	Madlock	.296	Cepeda	2,234	McCovey	.517
Leonard	108	Maddox	.292	Bonds	1,946	Bonds	.481
Davis	95	Whitfield	.289	J. Clark	1,780	J. Clark	.477
LeMaster	93	Matthews	.287	Hart	1,625	Hart	.474
Fuentes	63	F. Alou	.286	Davenport	1,624	Kingman	.469
Herndon	60	J. Alou	.283	Evans	1,565	F. Alou	.466
J. Clark	60	Hart	.282	Davis	1,327	Ivie	.466
Maddox	58	Kuenn	.282	Leonard	1,238	Leonard	.444

Extra-Base Hits

Mays	911
McCovey	822
Cepeda	474
Bonds	416
J. Clark	390
Evans	320
Hart	319
Davenport	291
Davis	265
Leonard	253

PITCHING TOP 10

Games		Innings		Strikeouts		Shutouts	
Player	Total	Player	Total	Player	Total	Player	Total
Lavelle	647	Marichal	3,443	Marichal	2,281	Marichal	52
Minton	552	Perry	2,295	Perry	1,606	Perry	21
Moffitt	459	Barr	1,800	Bolin	977	Barr	20
Marichal	458	McCormick	1,741	McCormick	976	McCormick	19
Barr	394	Sanford	1,404	Montefusco	869	Montefusco	12
Perry	367	Bolin	1,282	Sanford	781	Knepper	11
McCormick	357	Montegusco	1,182	Krukow	709	Bolin	10
Bolin	345	Blue	1,132	Blue	704	Sanford	9
Linzy	308	Krukow	987	Lavelle	696	Blue	7
Miller	269	Lavelle	981	Barr	650	Jones	7

Wins		Won–Lost Percentage		Earned Run Average		Saves	
Marichal	238	McMahon	.659	Linzy	2.71	Lavelle	127
Perry	134	Marichal	.630	Marichal	2.84	Minton	125
McCormick	104	Garrelts	.578	Lavelle	2.82	Moffitt	83
Barr	90	Antonelli	.577	Perry	2.96	Linzy	79
Sanford	89	Sanford	.571	Miller	3.07	Miller	46
Bolin	73	Bolin	.566	Henry	3.07	McMahon	36
Lavelle	73	Jones	.560	Shaw	3.25	Garrelts	35
Blue	72	Shaw	.558	Bolin	3.26	Johnson	29
Montefusco	59	Blue	.554	Antonelli	3.28	Sosa	26
Bryant	57	Perry	.551	McMahon	3.28	Bolin	21

GIANTS' SINGLE-SEASON LEADERS 1958-87

BATTING TOP 10

Games

Player	Total
Pagan—1962	164
Cepeda—1962	162
Mays—1962	162
Hiller—1962	161
McCovey—1965	160
Fuentes—1973	160
Evans—1979	160
Evans—1978	159
Bonds—1969	158
Five with	157

At Bats

Player	Total
Bonds—1970	663
Fuentes—1973	656
Bonds—1973	643
Davis—1982	641
Fuentes—1971	630
Bonds—1972	626
Cepeda—1962	625
Bonds—1969	622
Mays—1962	621
Bonds—1971	619

Hits

Player	Total
Mays—1958	208
Bonds—1970	200
Cepeda—1959	192
Cepeda—1962	191
Mays—1960	190
Mays—1962	189
Cepeda—1958	188
Mays—1963	187
Maddox—1973	187
Three with	182

Doubles

J. Clark—1978	46
Mays—1959	43
McCovey—1970	39
Cepeda—1958	38
Cepeda—1960	36
Mays—1962	36
Bonds—1970	36
Dietz—1970	36
Cepeda—1959	35
Henderson—1970	35

Triples

Mays—1960	12
Mays—1958	11
Bonds—1970	10
Matthews—1973	10
Maddox—1973	10
Joshua—1975	10
Thomas—1977	10
F. Alou—1963	9
Mays—1964	9
Lanier—1965	9
Thomas—1975	9
Herndon—1978	9

Home Runs

Mays—1965	52
Mays—1962	49
Mays—1964	47
Cepeda—1961	46
McCovey—1969	45
McCovey—1963	44
Mays—1961	40
McCovey—1965	39
McCovey—1970	39
Bonds—1973	39

Runs

Bonds—1970	134
Bonds—1973	131
Mays—1962	130
Mays—1961	129
Mays—1964	121
Bonds—1969	120
Mays—1965	118
Bonds—1972	118
Mays—1963	115
Bonds—1971	110

RBI

Cepeda—1961	142
Mays—1962	141
McCovey—1969	126
McCovey—1970	126
Mays—1961	123
Cepeda—1962	114
Mays—1965	112
Mays—1964	111
Dietz—1970	107
Cepeda—1959	105
McCovey—1968	105

Stolen Bases

North—1979	58
Bonds—1970	48
Bonds—1969	45
North—1980	45
Bonds—1972	44
Bonds—1973	43
Bonds—1974	41
LeMaster—1983	39
Leonard—1983	36
Gladden—1985	32

Batting Average

Mays—1958	.347
McCovey—1969	.320
J. Clark—1984	.320
Mays—1960	.319
Maddox—1973	.319
Joshua—1975	.318
Cepeda—1959	.317
Mays—1965	.317
Brown—1986	.317
F. Alou—1962	.316
Cepeda—1963	.316

Walks

McCovey—1970	137
McCovey—1969	121
Mays—1971	112
McCovey—1973	105
Evans—1978	105
North—1979	96
Bonds—1974	95
Murcer—1975	91
Evans—1979	91
J. Clark—1982	90

Total Bases

Mays—1962	382
Mays—1965	360
Cepeda—1961	356
Mays—1964	351
Mays—1958	350
Mays—1963	347
Bonds—1973	341
Mays—1959	335
Mays—1961	334
Bonds—1970	334

Slugging Percentage

McCovey—1969	.656
Mays—1965	.645
Mays—1962	.615
McCovey—1970	.612
Cepeda—1961	.609
Mays—1964	.607
McCovey—1966	.586
Mays—1961	.584
Mays—1958	.583
Mays—1959	.583

Extra-Base Hits

Mays—1962	90
Mays—1959	82
McCovey—1970	80
J. Clark—1978	79
Cepeda—1961	78
Mays—1963	77
Mays—1964	77
Bonds—1973	77
Mays—1965	76
Mays—1961	75

PITCHING TOP 10

Games

Player	Total
Lavelle—1984	77
Davis—1985	77
Minton—1984	74
Garrelts—1985	74
Minton—1963	73
Lavelle—1979	70
Minton—1980	68
Lavelle—1982	68
Minton—1985	68
Johnson—1971	67
Davis—1986	67

Complete Games

Player	Total
Marichal—1968	30
Marichal—1969	27
Perry—1969	26
Marichal—1966	25
Marichal—1965	24
Perry—1970	23
Marichal—1964	22
O'Dell—1962	20
Perry—1968	19
Four with	18

Innings

Player	Total
Perry—1970	329
Marichal—1968	326
Perry—1969	325
Marichal—1963	321
Marichal—1966	307
Marichal—1969	300
Marichal—1965	295
Perry—1967	293
Perry—1968	291
Sanford—1963	284

Wins

Marichal—1968	26
Marichal—1963	25
Marichal—1966	25
Sanford—1962	24
Bryant—1973	24
Perry—1970	23
Marichal—1965	22
McCormick—1967	22
Jones—1959	21
Marichal—1964	21
Perry—1966	21
Marichal—1969	21

W-L Percentage

Marichal—1966	.806
Sanford—1962	.774
MArichal—1963	.758
Linzy—1965	.750
Marichal—1968	.743
Miller—1961	.737
Caldwell—1974	.737
Pierce—1962	.727
Marichal—1964	.724
Perry—1966	.724

Strikeouts

Marichal—1963	248
Marichal—1965	240
Perry—1969	233
Perry—1967	230
Marichal—1966	222
Marichal—1968	218
Montefusco—1975	215
Perry—1970	214
Marichal—1964	206
Sadecki—1968	206

ERA (Starters)

Bolin—1968	1.98
Marichal—1969	2.10
Marichal—1965	2.14
Marichal—1966	2.23
Hammaker—1983	2.25
Marichal—1963	2.41
Marichal—1968	2.43
Perry—1968	2.44
Miller—1958	2.47
Blue—1981	2.45

ERA (Relievers)

F. Williams—1986	1.20
Linzy—1965	1.43
Linzy—1967	1.50
McMahon—1971	1.50
Holland—1980	1.76
Henry—1967	2.05
Linzy—1968	2.08
Pierce—1964	2.20
Willoughby—1972	2.35
Holland—1981	2.41

Saves

Minton—1982	30
Minton—1983	22
Linzy—1965	21
Minton—1981	21
Lavelle—1977	20
Lavelle—1979	20
Lavelle—1983	20
Miller—1962	19
McMahon—1970	19
Minton—1980	19
Minton—1984	19

Shutouts

Marichal—1965	10
Marichal—1969	8
Sanford—1960	6
Montefusco—1976	6
Knepper—1978	6
Marichal—1963	5
Marichal—1968	5
Barr—1974	5
Perry—1970	5

BATTING RECORDS

GIANTS WHO LED THE NATIONAL LEAGUE IN VARIOUS CATEGORIES

1883–1987

Walks

Year	Player	Total
1888	Roger Connor	73
1889	Mike Tiernan	96
1908	Roger Bresnahan	83
1917	George Burns	75
1919	George Burns	82
1920	George Burns	76
1921	George Burns	80
1927	Rogers Hornsby	86
1929	Mel Ott	113
1931	Mel Ott	80
1932	Mel Ott	100
1933	Mel Ott	75
1937	Mel Ott	102
1942	Mel Ott	109
1950	Eddie Stanky	144
1970	Willie McCovey	137
1971	Willie Mays	112

Runs

Year	Player	Total
1889	Mike Tiernan	147
1904	George Browne	99
1905	Mike Donlin	124
1907	Spike Shannon	104
1908	Fred Tenney	101
1914	George Burns	100
1916	George Burns	105
1917	George Burns	103
1919	George Burns	86
1920	George Burns	115
1923	Ross Youngs	121
1927	Rogers Hornsby	133
1938	Mel Ott	116
1942	Mel Ott	118
1961	Willie Mays	129
1969	Bobby Bonds	120
1973	Bobby Bonds	131

Slugging Percentage

Year	Player	Pct
1889	Roger Connor	.528
1890	Mike Tiernan	.495
1891	Mike Tiernan	.500
1938	Mel Ott	.588
1954	Willie Mays	.667
1955	Willie Mays	.659
1957	Willie Mays	.626
1964	Willie Mays	.607
1965	Willie Mays	.645
1968	Willie McCovey	.545
1969	Willie McCovey	.656
1970	Willie McCovey	.612

Stolen Bases

Year	Player	Total
1887	Monte Ward	111
1905	Art Devlin	59
1914	George Burns	62
1921	Frankie Frisch	49
1956	Willie Mays	40
1957	Willie Mays	38
1958	Willie Mays	31
1959	Willie Mays	27

Hits

Year	Player	Total
1885	Roger Connor	169
1890	Jack Glasscock	172
1909	Larry Doyle	172
1915	Larry Doyle	189
1923	Frankie Frisch	223
1928	Freddie Lindstrom	231
1930	Bill Terry	254
1954	Don Mueller	212
1957	Red Schoendienst	200
1960	Willie Mays	190

Triples

Year	Player	Total
1884	Bill Ewing	20
1885	Jim O'Rourke	16
1886	Roger Connor	20
1896	George Van Haltren	21
1911	Larry Doyle	25
1931	Bill Terry	20
1952	Bobby Thomson	14
1954	Willie Mays	13
1955	Willie Mays	13
1957	Willie Mays	20

Doubles

Year	Player	Total
1903	Sam Mertes	32
1915	Larry Doyle	40
1919	Ross Youngs	31
1951	Alvin Dark	41

LEADING GIANT HITTERS*

1883-1987

Year	Player	BA	Year	Player	BA
1883	R. Connor	.357	1929	B. Terry	.372
1884	R. Connor	.317	1930	B. Terry	.401*
1885	R. Connor	.371*	1931	B. Terry	.349
1886	R. Connor	.355	1932	B. Terry	.350
1887	M. Ward	.338	1933	B. Terry	.322
1888	B. Ewing	.306	1934	B. Terry	.354
1889	M. Tiernan	.335	1935	B. Terry	.341
1890	J. Glasscock	.336*	1936	M. Ott	.328
1891	M. Tiernan	.306	1937	J. Ripple	.317
1892	B. Ewing	.310	1938	M. Ott	.311
1893	G. Davis	.362	1939	Z. Bonura	.321
1894	J. Doyle	.369	1940	F. Demaree	.302
1895	M. Tiernan	.347	1941	D. Bartell	.303
1896	M. Tiernan	.369	1942	J. Mize	.305
1897	G. Davis	.358	1943	M. Witek	.314
1898	G. Van Haltren	.312	1944	J. Medwick	.337
1889	G. Davis	.346	1945	M. Ott	.308
1900	K. Selbach	.337	1946	J. Mize	.337
1901	G. Van Haltren	.335	1947	W. Cooper	.305
1902	D. McGann	.300	1948	S. Gordon	.299
1903	R. Bresnahan	.350	1949	B. Thomson	.309
1904	D. McGann	.286	1950	E. Stanky	.300
1905	M. Donlin	.356	1951	M. Irvin	.312
1906	C. Seymour	.320	1952	A. Dark	.301
1907	D. McGann	.298	1953	D. Mueller	.333
1908	M. Donlin	.334	1954	W. Mays	.345*
1909	L. Doyle	.302	1955	W. Mays	.319
1910	F. Snodgrass	.321	1956	J. Brandt	.299
1911	C. Meyers	.332	1957	W. Mays	.333
1912	C. Meyers	.358	1958	W. Mays	.347
1913	C. Meyers	.312	1959	O. Cepeda	.317
1914	G. Burns	.303	1960	W. Mays	.319
1915	L. Doyle	.320*	1961	O. Cepeda	.311
1916	D. Robertson	.307	1962	F. Alou	.316
1917	B. Kauff	.308	1962	O. Cepeda	.316
1918	R. Youngs	.302	1964	O. Cepeda	.304
1919	R. Youngs	.311	1965	W. Mays	.317
1920	R. Youngs	.351	1966	W. Mays	.317
1921	F. Frisch	.341	1966	W. Mays	.288
1922	F. Snyder	.343	1967	J. Alou	.292
1923	F. Frisch	.348	1968	W. McCovey	.293
1924	R. Youngs	.356	1969	W. McCovey	.320
1925	F. Frisch	.331	1970	B. Bonds	.302
1926	T. Jackson	.327	1971	B. Bonds	.288
1927	R. Hornsby	.361	1972	C. Speier	.269
1928	F. Lindstrom	.358	1973	G. Maddox	.319

*Led National League

Year	Player	BA	Year	Player	BA
1974	D. Rader	.291	1981	M. May	.310
1975	V. Joshua	.318	1982	J. Morgan	.289
1976	L. Herndon	.288	1983	J. Younghlood	.292
1977	B. Madlock	.302	1984	D. Gladden	.351
1978	B. Madlock	.309	1985	C. Brown	.271
1979	M. Ivie	.286	1986	C. Brown	.317
1980	T. Whitfield	.296	1987	W. Clark	.308

GIANT HOME-RUN LEADERS

1883–1986

Year	Player	Home Runs	Year	Player	Home Runs
1883	B. Ewing	10*	1904	D. McGann	6
1884	A. McKinnon	4	1905	B. Dahlen	7
	R. Connor		1906	C. Seymour	4
1885	B. Ewing	6		S. Strang	4
1886	R. Connor	7	1907	G. Browne	5
1887	R. Connor	17	1908	M. Donlin	6
1888	R. Connor	14	1909	R. Murray	7*
1889	R. Connor	13	1910	L. Doyle	8
1890	M. Tiernan	13	1911	L. Doyle	13
1891	M. Tiernan	17*	1912	F. Merkle	11
1892	D. Lyons	8	1913	L. Doyle	5
1893	M. Tiernan	15		T. Shafer	5
1894	G. Davis	9	1914	F. Merkle	7
1895	G. Van Haltren	8	1915	F. Merkle	4
1896	M. Tiernan	7		L. Doyle	
1897	G. Davis	9	1916	D. Robertson	12*
1898	B. Joyce	10	1917	D. Robertson	12*
1899	T. O'Brien	6	1918	G. Burns	4
1900	P. Hickman	9	1919	B. Kauff	10
1901	G. Davis	7	1920	G. Kelly	11
1902	S. Brodie	3	1921	G. Kelly	23
1903	S. Mertes	7	1922	G. Kelly	17

GIANT HOME-RUN LEADERS

1883-1987

Year	Player	Home Runs	Year	Player	Home Runs
1923	E. Meusel	19	1956	W. Mays	36
1924	G. Kelly	21	1957	W. Mays	35
1925	E. Meusel	21	1958	W. Mays	29
1926	G. Kelly	13	1959	W. Mays	34
1927	R. Hornsby	26	1960	W. Mays	29
1928	M. Ott	18	1961	O. Cepeda	46
1929	M. Ott	42	1962	W. Mays	49*
1930	M. Ott	25	1963	W. McCovey	44**
1931	M. Ott	29	1964	W. Mays	47*
1932	M. Ott	38**	1965	W. Mays	52*
1933	M. Ott	23	1966	W. Mays	37
1934	M. Ott	35*	1967	W. McCovey	31
1935	M. Ott	31**	1968	W. McCovey	36*
1936	M. Ott	33*	1969	W. McCovey	45*
1937	M. Ott	31**	1970	W. McCovey	39
1938	M. Ott	36*	1971	B. Bonds	33
1939	M. Ott	27	1972	D. Kingman	29
1940	M. Ott	19	1973	B. Bonds	39
1941	M. Ott	27	1974	B. Bonds	21
1942	M. Ott	30*	1975	G. Matthews	12
1943	M. Ott	18	1976	B. Murcer	23
1944	M. Ott	26	1977	W. McCovey	28
1945	M. Ott	21	1978	J. Clark	25
1946	J. Mize	22	1979	M. Ivie	27
1947	J. Mize	51**	1980	J. Clark	22
1948	J. Mize	40**	1981	J. Clark	17
1949	B. Thomson	27	1982	J. Clark	27
1950	B. Thomson	25	1983	D. Evans	30
1951	B. Thomson	32	1984	J. Leonard	21
1952	B. Thomson	24		C. Davis	
1953	B. Thomson	26	1985	B. Brenly	19
1954	W. Mays	41	1986	C. Maldonado	18
1955	W. Mays	51*	1987	W. Clark	35

*Led National League
**Tied for National League Lead

GIANTS WITH 100 OR MORE RBI IN A SEASON

1883-1987

Year	Player	RBI	Year	Player	RBI
1889	H. Connor	130*	1933	M. Ott	103
	D. Richardson	100	1934	M. Ott	135*
1893	G. Davis	119		T. Jackson	101
	R. Connor	105	1935	M. Ott	114
	M. Tiernan	102		H. Leiber	107
1984	G. Van Haltren	104	1936	M. Ott	135
	J. Doyle	100	1938	M. Ott	116
1895	G. Van Haltren	103	1940	B. Young	101
	G. Davis	101	1941	B. Young	104
1897	G. Davis	134	1942	J. Mize	110*
	K. Gleason	106	1947	J. Mize	138*
1903	S. Mertes	104*		W. Cooper	122
1905	S. Mertes	108		W. Marshall	107
1908	M. Donlin	106	1948	J. Mize	125
1917	H. Zimmerman	102*		S. Gordon	107
1921	G. Kelly	122	1949	B. Thomson	109
	R. Youngs	102	1951	M. Irvin	121*
	F. Frisch	100	1952	B. Thomson	108
1922	E. Meusel	132	1953	B. Thomson	106
	G. Kelly	107	1954	W. Mays	110
1923	E. Meusel	125*	1955	W. Mays	127
	F. Frisch	111	1959	O. Cepeda	105
	G. Kelly	103		W. Mays	104
1924	G. Kelly	136*	1960	W. Mays	103
	E. Meusel	102	1961	O. Cepeda	142*
1925	E. Meusel	111		W. Mays	123
1927	R. Hornsby	125	1962	W. Mays	141
	B. Terry	121		O. Cepeda	114
1928	F. Lindstrom	107	1963	W. Mays	103
	B. Terry	101		W. McCovey	102
1929	M. Ott	151	1964	W. Mays	111
	B. Terry	117	1965	W. Mays	112
1930	B. Terry	129	1966	W. Mays	103
	M. Ott	119	1968	W. McCovey	105*
	F. Lindstrom	106	1969	W. McCovey	126*
1931	M. Ott	115	1970	W. McCovey	126
	B. Terry	112		D. Dietz	107
1932	M. Ott	123	1971	B. Bonds	102
	B. Terry	117	1982	J. Clark	103

*Led National League

GIANTS WITH THREE- AND FOUR-HOME-RUN GAMES

Player	HR/Game	Date	Opponent	Consecutive	Home/Away
Willie Mays	4	4/30/61	Milwaukee	no	away
Roger Connor	3	5/9/88	Indianapolis	no	away
George Kelly	3	9/17/23	Chicago	yes	away
George Kelly	3	6/14/24	Cincinnati	no	home
Mel Ott	3	8/31/30	Boston	yes	home
Bill Terry	3	8/13/32	Brooklyn	no	home
Johnny Mize	3	4/24/47	Boston	yes	away
Wes Westrum	3	6/24/50	Cincinnati	no	home
Don Mueller	3	9/1/51	Brooklyn	no	home
Dusty Rhodes	3	8/26/53	St. Louis	yes	home
Dusty Rhodes	3	7/28/54	St. Louis	yes	home
Willie Mays	3	6/29/61	Milwaukee	no	away
Willie Mays	3	6/2/63	Philadelphia	no	away
Willie McCovey	3	9/22/63	New York	yes	home
Willie McCovey	3	4/22/64	Milwaukee	yes	away
Willie McCovey	3	9/17/66	New York	no	home
Gary Matthews	3	9/25/76	Houston	no	home
Darrell Evans	3	6/15/83	Houston	no	home

PLAYERS WITH MOST GRAND-SLAM HOME RUNS DURING GIANT CAREERS

1883–1987

Player	Number of Grand Slams
Willie McCovey	16*
Willie Mays	8
Mel Ott	7
George Kelly	5
Babe Young	5
Wes Westrum	5
Travis Jackson	4
Bill Terry	4
Bobby Thomson	4
Bobby Bonds	4
Hank Thompson	4
Jack Clark	4
Dave Robertson	3
Ernie Lombardi	3
Walker Cooper	3
Sid Gordon	3
Monte Irvin	3
Alvin Dark	3
Orlando Cepeda	3
Jim Davenport	3
Jim Hart	3
Dick Dietz	3
Dave Kingman	3
Chris Speier	3

*All-time National League leader with 18

CAREER RECORDS OF TOP
SAN FRANCISCO GIANTS HITTERS, 1958–1987*

Hitter	Games	BA	Hits	Doubles	Triples	HR	RBI	Runs	Walks	SO	SB
W. Mays	2,992	.302	3,283	523	140	660	1,903	2,062	1,463	1,526	338
O. Cepeda	2,124	.297	2,351	417	27	379	1,365	1,131	588	1,169	142
F. Alou	2,082	.286	2,101	359	49	206	852	985	423	706	107
G. Matthews	1,944	.282	1,972	315	52	231	983	1,070	921	1,092	180
T. Whitfield	732	.281	537	93	12	33	179	233	138	288	18
J. Alou	1,380	.280	1,216	170	26	32	377	448	138	267	31
J. Hart	1,125	.278	1,052	148	29	170	578	518	380	573	17
J. Clark	1,235	.275	1,213	235	35	194	705	702	535	717	62
J. Leonard	862	.273	808	127	31	81	428	379	228	628	120
W. McCovey	2,588	.270	2,211	353	46	521	1,555	1,229	1,345	1,550	26
C. Davis	725	.270	715	122	19	77	342	352	289	469	79
B. Bonds	1,849	.268	1,886	302	66	332	1,024	1,258	914	1,757	461

*Includes overall major league totals
All players listed played at least 500 games as Giants

PITCHING RECORDS

GIANT PITCHERS WHO LED THE NATIONAL LEAGUE IN VARIOUS CATEGORIES

1883–1987

Strikeouts

Year	Pitcher	Total
1888	Tim Keefe	333
1890	Amos Rusie	345
1891	Amos Rusie	337
1893	Amos Rusie	208
1894	Amos Rusie	195
1895	Amos Rusie	201
1903	Christy Mathewson	267
1904	Christy Mathewson	212
1905	Christy Mathewson	206
1907	Christy Mathewson	178
1908	Christy Mathewson	259
1910	Christy Mathewson	190
1911	Rube Marquard	237
1937	Carl Hubbell	159
1944	Bill Voiselle	161

Innings Pitched

Year	Pitcher	Total
1885	Tim Keefe	540
1893	Amos Rusie	482
1903	Christy Mathewson	434
1904	Joe McGinnity	408
1908	Christy Mathewson	391
1912	Christy Mathewson	310
1933	Carl Hubbell	309
1944	Bill Voiselle	313
1963	Juan Marichal	321
1968	Juan Marichal	326
1969	Gaylord Perry	325
1970	Gaylord Perry	329

ERA

Year	Pitcher	Total
1885	Tim Keefe	1.58
1888	Tim Keefe	1.74
1891	John Ewing	2.27
1894	Amos Rusie	2.78
1897	Amos Rusie	2.54
1904	Joe McGinnity	1.61
1905	Christy Mathewson	1.27
1908	Christy Mathewson	1.43
1909	Christy Mathewson	1.14
1911	Christy Mathewson	1.99
1912	Jeff Tesreau	1.96
1913	C. Mathewson	2.06
1922	Rosy Ryan	3.01
1929	Bill Walker	3.09
1931	Bill Walker	2.26
1933	Carl Hubbell	1.66
1934	Carl Hubbell	2.30
1936	Carl Hubbell	2.31
1949	Dave Koslo	2.50
1950	Jim Hearn	2.49
1952	Hoyt Wilhelm	2.43
1954	Johnny Antonelli	2.30
1958	Stu Miller	2.47
1959	Sam Jones	2.83
1960	Mike McCormick	2.70
1969	Juan Marichal	2.10
1983	Atlee Hammaker	2.25

Saves

Year	Pitcher	Total
1889	Mickey Welch	2
1904	Joe McGinnity	5
1905	Claude Elliott	6
1906	George Ferguson	6
1907	Joe McGinnity	4
1908	Christy Mathewson	5
1917	Slim Sallee	4
1918	Fred Anderson	3
1922	Claude Jonnard	5
1923	Claude Jonnard	5
1926	Chick Davies	6
1934	Carl Hubbell	8
1937	Cliff Melton	7
1938	Dick Coffman	12
1940	Jumbo Brown	7
1941	Jumbo Brown	8
1944	Ace Adams	13
1945	Ace Adams	15
1961	Stu Miller	17

GIANTS 20-GAME WINNERS

1883–1987

Year	Pitcher	W	L	Year	Pitcher	W	L
1883	Mickey Welch	27	21	1917	Ferdie Schupp	21	7
1887	Mickey Welch	23	15	1919	Jesse Barnes	25*	9
1888	Mickey Welch	26	19	1920	Jesse Barnes	20	15
1889	Mickey Welch	27	12		Art Nehf	21	12
	Tim Keefe	28	13		Fred Toney	21	11
1890	Amos Rusie	29	30	1921	Art Nehf	20	10
1891	John Ewing	21	8	1928	Larry Benton	25*	9
1892	Silver King	22	24		Freddy Fitzsimmons	20	9
1893	Amos Rusie	29	18	1933	Carl Hubbell	23*	12
1895	Amos Rusie	22	21	1934	Hal Schumacher	23	10
1896	Jouett Meekin	26	14		Carl Hubbell	21	12
1897	Amos Rusie	29	8	1935	Carl Hubbell	23	12
	Jouett Meekin	20	11	1936	Carl Hubbell	26*	6
1898	Cy Seymour	25	17	1937	Carl Hubbell	22*	8
	Amos Rusie	20	11		Cliff Melton	20	9
1901	Christy Mathewson	20	17	1944	Bill Voiselle	21	16
1904	Dummy Taylor	21	15	1947	Larry Jansen	21	5
1905	Joe McGinnity	21	15	1951	Larry Jansen	23*	11
	Red Ames	22	8		Sal Maglie	23*	6
1906	Joe McGinnity	27*	12	1954	Johnny Antonelli	21	7
	Christy Mathewson	22	12	1956	Johnny Antonelli	20	13
1907	Christy Mathewson	24*	13	1959	Sam Jones	21*	15
1908	Hooks Wiltse	23	14	1962	Jack Sanford	24	7
1909	Christy Mathewson	25	6	1963	Juan Marichal	25*	8
	Hooks Wiltse	20	11	1964	Juan Marichal	21	8
1910	Christy Mathewson	27*	9	1965	Juan Marichal	22	13
1911	Christy Mathewson	26	13	1966	Juan Marichal	25	6
	Rube Marquard	24	7	1967	Mike McCormick	22*	10
1912	Rube Marquard	26*	11	1968	Juan Marichal	26*	9
	Christy Mathewson	23	12	1969	Juan Marichal	21	11
1913	Rube Marquard	23	10	1970	Gaylord Perry	23*	13
	Christy Mathewson	25	11	1973	Ron Bryant	24*	12
1914	Jeff Tesreau	26	10	1986	Mike Krukow	20	9
	Christy Mathewson	24	13				

*League leader

GIANTS 30- AND 40-GAME WINNERS

1883-1987

Year	Pitchers	W	L
1884	Mickey Welch	39	21
1885	Mickey Welch	44	11
	Tim Keefe	32	13
1886	Tim Keefe	42*	20
	Mickey Welch	33	22
1887	Tim Keefe	35	19
1888	Tim Keefe	35*	12
1891	Amos Rusie	33	20
1892	Amos Rusie	32	28
1894	Amos Rusie	36*	13
	Jouett Meekin	36*	10
1903	Joe McGinnity	31*	20
	Christy Mathewson	30	13
1904	Joe McGinnity	35*	8
	Christy Mathewson	33	12
1905	Christy Mathewson	31*	8
1908	Christy Mathewson	37*	11

*League leader

GIANT PITCHERS' NO-HITTERS

1883-1987

Date	Pitcher	Score	Walks	Strikeouts	Opponent
July 31, 1891	Amos Rusie	6-0	8	4	Brooklyn
July 15, 1901	Christy Mathewson	5-0	4	4	St. Louis
June 13, 1905	Christy Mathewson	1-0	0	2	Chicago
July 4, 1908	Hooks Wiltse	1-0	0	6	Philadelphia
April 15, 1909	Red Ames	0-3 (lost)	2	9	Brooklyn
Sept. 6, 1912	Jeff Tesreau	3-0	2	2	Philadelphia
April 15, 1915	Rube Marquard	2-0	2	2	Brooklyn
May 7, 1922	Jesse Barnes	6-0	1	5	Philadelphia
May 8, 1929	Carl Hubbell	11-0	1	4	Pittsburgh
June 15, 1963	Juan Marichal	1-0	2	5	Houston
Sept. 17, 1968	Gaylord Perry	1-0	2	9	St. Louis
August 24, 1975	Ed Halicki	6-0	2	10	New York
Sept. 29, 1976	John Montefusco	9-0	1	4	Atlanta

LEADING GIANT SHUTOUT PITCHERS

1883-1987

Pitcher	Giant Shutouts	Career Shutouts
Christy Mathewson	83	83
Juan Marichal	52	52
Carl Hubbell	36	36
Hal Schumacher	29	29
Mickey Welch	28	40
Hooks Wiltse	27	27
Joe McGinnity	26	32
Tim Keefe	22	40
John Antonelli	22	26
Gaylord Perry	21	52
Rube Marquard	21	30
Freddy Fitzsimmons	20	29
Jim Barr	20	20
Mike McCormick	19	23
Red Ames	15	27
Art Nehf	14	30
Ed Halicki	13	13
Ray Sadecki	12	19
Bob Knepper	11	18
John Montefusco	11	11
Bob Bolin	10	10

MOST CONSECUTIVE PITCHING WINS

1883–1987

Pitcher	Year	Consecutive Wins
Tim Keefe	1888	19
Rube Marquard	1912	19*
Mickey Welch	1885	17
Carl Hubbell	1936**	16
Jack Sanford	1962	16
Joe McGinnity	1904	14
Christy Mathewson	1909	13
Burleigh Grimes	1927	13
Hooks Wiltse	1904	12
Christy Mathewson	1905	11
Hal Schumacher	1935	11
Sal Maglie	1950	11
Johnny Antonelli	1954	11
Slim Sallee	1917	10
Jesse Barnes	1919	10
Clarence Mitchell	1930	10
Juan Marichal	1978	10
Juan Marichal	1966	10
Vida Blue	1978	10

*Under present scoring rules, Marquard would have been credited with twenty consecutive wins (see Day-by-Day entry for July 3, 1912).

**Hubbell won his last sixteen decisions in 1936 and his first eight decisions in 1937 for a two-season consecutive-game winning streak of twenty-four.

GIANT CAREER RECORDS OF TOP SAN FRANCISCO GIANT WINNERS

1958–1987

Pitcher	Games	W	L	Pct	Innings	Hits	Strikeouts	ERA	Shutouts	Saves
J. Marichal	458	238	140	.630	3,443	3,081	2,281	2.84	52	2
G. Perry	367	134	109	.551	2,295	2,061	1,606	2.96	21	10
M. McCormick	357	104	94	.525	1,741	1,651	976	3.68	19	9
J. Barr	394	90	96	.484	1,800	1,863	650	3.41	20	11
J. Sanford	233	89	67	.571	1,404	1,289	781	3.62	9	4
B. Bolin	345	73	56	.566	1,282	1,088	977	3.26	10	21
G. Lavelle	647	73	60	.521	981	910	696	2.82	0	127
V. Blue	179	72	58	.554	1,132	1,030	704	3.51	7	0
J. Montefusco	185	59	62	.488	1,182	1,143	869	3.47	11	0
R. Bryant	195	57	55	.509	909	870	502	3.90	6	1
B. O'Dell	204	56	49	.533	921	912	620	3.55	7	7
M. Krukow	158	55	49	.529	986	985	709	3.88	5	1
E. Halicki	182	52	65	.444	1,028	968	691	3.58	13	1
F. Linzy	308	48	39	.552	532	510	268	2.71	0	79
S. Jones	126	47	37	.560	633	566	504	3.30	7	5
B. Knepper	136	47	50	.485	873	878	484	3.63	11	0
G. Minton	552	45	52	.464	871	857	352	3.22	0	125
B. Laskey	131	41	48	.461	687	697	290	3.84	1	1
J. Antonelli	122	41	30	.577	636	569	365	3.28	5	15
S. Miller	269	40	35	.533	681	626	446	3.07	1	46
A. Hammaker	118	39	39	.500	719	688	460	3.37	5	0
S. Garrelts	218	37	27	.578	466	371	410	3.18	1	35
R. Moffitt	459	35	46	.432	683	678	393	3.68	0	83
R. Herbel	240	33	29	.532	719	756	364	3.59	3	4
R. Sadecki	128	32	39	.451	685	652	517	3.52	12	0

*Pitchers with 32 or more Giants wins

Most Giants Wins in
a season

Year	W	L	Pct	Pos
1904	106	47	.693	First
1905	105	48	.686	First
1912	103	48	.682	First
1962	103	62	.624	First
1913	101	51	.664	First

Most Consecutive Giants Wins

Year	Won	Home	Away
1916	26	26	0
1904	18	13	5
1907	17	14	3
1916	17	0	17
1912	16	11	5
1951	16	13	3
1936	15	7	8
1913	14	6	8
1965	14	6	8
1905	13	8	5

Most Consecutive Giants Losses

Year	Lost	Home	Away
1902	13	5	8
1944	13	0	13

Most Lopsided Decisions

	Date	Opponent	Score
Giant Win	April 30, 1944	Brooklyn	26-8
Giant Loss	June 7, 1906	Chicago	19-0

WHERE THE GIANTS FINISHED

1883-1987

Year	Pos	W	L	Pct	Manager
1883	6	46	50	.479	Clapp
1884	5	62	50	.554	Price
					Ward
1885	2	85	27	.759	Mutrie
1886	3	75	44	.630	Mutrie
1887	4	68	55	.553	Mutrie
1888	1	84	47	.641	Mutrie
1889	1	83	43	.659	Mutrie
1890	6	63	68	.481	Mutrie
1891	3	71	61	.538	Mutrie
1892	8	71	80	.470	Powers
1893	5	68	64	.515	Ward
1894	2	88	44	.667	Ward
1895	9	66	65	.504	Davis
					Doyle
					Watkins
1896	7	64	67	.489	Irwin
					Joyce
1897	3	83	48	.634	Joyce
1898	7	77	73	.513	Joyce
					Anson
					Joyce
1899	5	60	90	.400	Day
					Hoey
1900	8	60	78	.435	Ewing
					Davis
1901	7	52	85	.380	Davis
1902	8	48	88	.353	Fogel
					Smith
					McGraw
1903	2	84	55	.604	McGraw
1904	1	106	47	.693	McGraw
1905	1*	105	48	.686	McGraw
1906	2	96	56	.632	McGraw
1907	4	82	71	.536	McGraw
1908	2	98	56	.636	McGraw
1909	3	92	61	.601	McGraw
1910	2	91	63	.591	McGraw
1911	1	99	54	.647	McGraw
1912	1	103	48	.682	McGraw
1913	1	101	51	.664	McGraw
1914	2	84	70	.545	McGraw
1915	8	69	83	.454	McGraw
1916	4	86	66	.566	McGraw
1917	1	98	56	.636	McGraw
1918	2	71	53	.573	McGraw
1919	2	87	53	.621	McGraw
1920	2	86	68	.558	McGraw
1921	1*	94	59	.614	McGraw

Year	Pos	W	L	Pct	Manager
1922	1*	93	61	.604	McGraw
1923	1	95	58	.621	McGraw
1924	1	93	60	.608	McGraw
1925	2	86	66	.566	McGraw
1926	5	74	77	.490	McGraw
1927	3	92	62	.597	McGraw
1928	2	93	61	.604	McGraw
1929	3	84	67	.556	McGraw
1930	3	87	67	.565	McGraw
1931	2	87	65	.572	McGraw
1932	6	72	82	.468	McGraw
					Terry
1933	1*	91	61	.599	Terry
1934	2	93	60	.608	Terry
1935	3	91	62	.595	Terry
1936	1	92	62	.597	Terry
1937	1	95	57	.625	Terry
1938	3	83	67	.553	Terry
1939	5	77	74	.510	Terry
1940	6	72	80	.474	Terry
1941	5	74	79	.484	Terry
1942	3	85	67	.559	Ott
1943	8	55	98	.359	Ott
1944	5	67	87	.435	Ott
1945	5	78	74	.513	Ott
1946	8	61	93	.396	Ott
1947	4	81	73	.526	Ott
1948	5	78	76	.506	Ott
					Durocher
1949	5	73	81	.474	Durocher
1950	3	86	68	.558	Durocher
1951	1	98	59	.624	Durocher
1952	2	92	62	.597	Durocher
1953	5	70	84	.455	Durocher
1954	1*	97	57	.630	Durocher
1955	3	80	74	.519	Durocher
1956	6	67	87	.435	Rigney
1957	6	69	85	.448	Rigney
1958	3	80	74	.519	Rigney
1959	3	83	71	.539	Rigney
1960	5	79	75	.513	Rigney
					Sheehan
1961	3	85	69	.552	Dark
1962	1	103	62	.624	Dark
1963	3	88	74	.543	Dark
1964	4	90	72	.556	Dark
1965	2	95	67	.586	Franks
1966	2	93	68	.578	Franks
1967	2	91	71	.562	Franks
1968	2	88	74	.543	Franks
1969	2	90	72	.556	King
1970	3	86	76	.531	King
					Fox

Year	Pos	W	L	Pct	Manager
1971	1	90	72	.556	Fox
1972	5	69	86	.445	Fox
1973	3	88	74	.543	Fox
1974	5	72	90	.444	Fox
					Westrum
1975	3	80	81	.497	Westrum
1976	4	74	88	.457	Rigney
1977	4	75	8/	.463	Altobelli
1978	3	89	73	.549	Altobelli
1979	4	71	91	.438	Altobelli
					Bristol
1980	5	75	86	.466	Bristol
1981	4	56	55	.505	Robinson
1982	3	87	75	.537	Robinson
1983	5	79	83	.488	Robinson
1984	6	66	96	.407	Robinson
					Ozark
1985	6	62	100	.383	Davenport
					Craig
1986	3	83	79	.512	Craig
1987	1	90	72	.556	Craig

*World Champions

GIANTS MANAGERS' RECORDS

1883-1987

Manager	Years	W	L	Pct
John Clapp	1883	46	50	.479
James Price	1884	56	42	.571
Monte Ward	1884 93-94	162	116	.583
James Mutrie	1885-91	529	345	.605
Pat Powers	1892	71	80	.470
George Davis	1895 1900-01	108	139	.437
Jack Doyle	1895	31	31	.500
Harvey Watkins	1895	18	17	.514
Arthur Irwin	1896	38	53	.418
Bill Joyce	1896-98	177	122	.592
Cap Anson	1898	9	13	.409
John B. Day	1899	30	40	.429
Fred Hoey	1899	30	50	.375
Buck Ewing	1900	21	41	.339
Horace Fogel	1902	18	23	.439
George Smith	1902	5	27	.156
John McGraw	1902-32	2,658	1,823	.593
Bill Terry	1932-41	823	661	.555
Mel Ott	1942-48	464	530	.467
Leo Durocher	1948-55	637	523	.549
Bill Rigney	1956-60 1976	406	430	.486
Tom Sheehan	1960	46	50	.479
Alvin Dark	1961-64	366	277	.569
Herman Franks	1965-68	367	280	.567
Clyde King	1969-70	109	97	.529
Charlie Fox	1970-74	348	325	.517
Wes Westrum	1974-75	118	129	.478
Joe Altobelli	1977-79	225	239	.485
Dave Bristol	1979-1980	85	98	.464
Frank Robinson	1981-84	264	277	.488
Danny Ozark	1984	24	32	.429
Jim Davenport	1985	56	88	.389
Roger Craig	1985-87	179	163	.523

GIANTS CLUB PRESIDENTS

President	Years
(New York)	
John B. Day	1883-92
C. C. Van Cott	1893-94
Andrew Freedman	1895-02
John T. Brush	1903-12
Harry N. Hempstead	1912-18
Charles A. Stoneham	1919-35
Horace C. Stoneham	1936-57
(San Francisco)	
Horace C. Stoneham	1958-75
Robert A. Lurie	1976-present

MISCELLANEOUS TEAM RECORDS

1883-1987

Overall Wins and Losses

Years	Games	Won	Lost	Pct
1883-1957	11,141	6,243	4,898	.560
1958-1987	4,770	2,457	2,313	.515
Total	15,911	8,700	7,211	.547

GIANTS RECORD VS. OPPONENTS 1958-87

Opponent	Won	Lost	PCTG.
Mets	193	155	.555
Padres	180	153	.541
Pirates	236	204	.536
Cubs	235	205	.534
Expos	118	105	.529
Phillies	226	211	.517
Astros	237	228	.510
Cardinals	218	217	.501
Reds	274	274	.500
Braves	271	277	.495
Dodgers	269	284	.486
TOTALS	2457	2313	.515

1971 CHAMPIONSHIP SERIES

The Giants were confident heading into their first divisional playoff, meeting a Pirates' team they had beaten 9 times in 12 regular-season games. Their optimism crested when Gaylord Perry's complete game and Willie McCovey's two-run homer paced a 5–4 S.F. victory in Game 1. But it was Pittsburgh all the way thereafter, the Pirates winning three in a row to enter the World Series. In hindsight, the Giants bemoaned the fact Juan Marichal had to be used in the division clincher on the final day of the season, throwing the rotation out of sync for the NLCS.

1971 NLCS STATISTICS

1971 NLCS STATISTICS
PIRATES BATTING

Name	POS	AVG	G	AB	R	H	2B	3B	HR	RBI
Cash	2B	421	4	19	5	8	2	0	0	1
Clemente	OF	.333	4	18	2	6	0	0	0	4
Hebner	3B	.294	4	17	3	5	1	0	2	4
Robertson	1B	.438	4	16	5	7	1	0	4	6
Sanguillen	C	.267	4	15	1	4	0	0	0	1
Stargell	OF	.000	4	14	1	0	0	0	0	0
Hernandez	SS	.231	4	13	2	3	0	0	0	1
Oliver	OF	.250	4	12	2	3	0	0	1	5
Clines	OF	.333	1	31	1	0	0	1	1	
Alley	SS	.500	1	2	1	1	0	0	0	0
Davalillo	PH	.000	2	2	0	0	0	0	0	0
Pittsburgh Totals		.271	4	144	24	39	4	0	8	23

GIANTS BATTING

Name	POS	AVG	G	AB	R	H	2B	3B	HR	RBI
Fuentes	2B	.313	4	16	4	5	1	0	1	2
Henderson	OF	.313	4	16	3	5	1	0	0	2
Mays	OF	.267	4	15	2	4	2	0	1	3
Dietz	C	.067	4	15	0	1	0	0	0	0
McCovey	1B	.429	4	14	2	6	0	0	2	6
Speier	SS	.357	4	14	4	5	1	0	1	1
Gallagher	3B	.100	4	10	0	1	0	0	0	0
Kingman	OF	.111	4	9	0	1	0	0	0	0
Bonds	OF	.250	3	8	0	2	0	0	0	0
San Francisco Totals		.235	4	132	15	31	5	0	5	14

PITTSBURGH PITCHING

Name	W	L	ERA	G	IP	H	BB	SO
B. Johnson	1	0	0.00	1	8	5	3	7
Blass	0	1	11.57	2	7	14	2	11
Giusti	0	0	0.00	4	5.1	1	2	3
Ellis	1	0	3.60	1	5	6	4	1
Kison	1	0	0.00	1	4.2	2	2	3
Miller	0	0	6.0	1	3	3	3	3
Moose	0	0	0.00	1	2	0	0	0
Pittsburgh Totals	3	1	3.34	4	35	31	16	28

GIANTS PITCHING

Name	W	L	ERA	G	IP	H	BB	SO
Perry	1	1	6.14	2	14.2	19	3	11
Marichal	0	1	2.25	1	8	4	0	6
McMahon	0	0	0.00	2	3	0	0	3
Cumberland	0	1	9.00	1	3	7	0	4
Bryant	0	0	4.50	1	2	1	1	2
J. Johnson	0	0	13.50	1	1.1	1	1	2
Barr	0	0	9.0	1	1	3	0	2
Hamilton	0	0	9.00	1	1	1	0	3
Carrithers	0	0	--	1	0	3	0	0
San Francisco Totals	1	3	2.50	4	34	39	5	33

1971 PLAYOFF BOXES

GAME 1 — Oct. 2 at Candlestick Park

PITTSBURGH	AB	R	H	RBI	SAN FRANCISCO	AB	R	H	RBI
Cash, 2b	5	2	2	1	Henderson, lf	4	0	2	0
Hebner, 3b	5	0	1	0	Fuentes, 2b	4	1	1	2
Clemente, rf	4	0	0	0	Mays, cf	2	1	1	0
Stargell, lf	4	0	0	0	McCovey, 1b	3	1	1	2
Oliver, cf	4	0	1	2	Kingman, rf	3	0	0	0
Robertson, 1b	4	0	2	0	Bonds, rf	1	0	0	0
Sanguillen, c	4	0	1	0	Dietz, c	4	0	0	0
Hernandez, ss	2	1	1	0	Gallagher, 3b	2	0	0	0
Davalillo, ph	1	0	0	0	Lanier, 3b	1	0	0	0
Moose, p	0	0	0	0	Speier, ss	3	2	2	0
May, ph	1	0	0	0	Perry, p	1	0	0	0
Giusti, p	0	0	0	0					
Blass, p	1	0	0	0					
Alley, ss	2	1	1	0					
TOTALS	37	4	9	3	**TOTALS**	28	5	7	5

												R	H	E
Pittsburgh	.....	0	0	2	0	0	0	2	0	0	—	4	9	0
San Francisco	..	0	0	1	0	4	0	0	0	x	—	5	7	2

E—McCovey, Speier. DP—Pittsburgh 1. LOB—Pittsburgh 9, San Francisco 4. 2B—Cash, Henderson, Mays. HR—Fuentes, McCovey. Sac—Perry, Blass 2.

PITCHING SUMMARY

Pittsburgh	IP	H	R	ER	BB	SO
Blass (L)	5	6	5	5	2	9
Moose	2	0	0	0	0	0
Giusti	1	1	0	0	1	1
San Francisco						
Perry (W)	9	9	4	3	1	5

HB—Stargell (Perry). Umpires—Gorman, Crawford, Weyer, Olsen, Stello and Davidson. Time—2:44. Attendance—40,977.

GAME 2 — Oct. 3 at Candlestick Park

PITTSBURGH	AB	R	H	RBI	SAN FRANCISCO	AB	R	H	RBI
Cash, 2b	5	1	3	0	Henderson, lf	3	0	1	1
Clines, cf	3	1	1	1	Fuentes, 2b	5	2	2	0
Oliver, ph–cf	1	1	0	0	Mays, cf	5	1	2	3
Clemente, rf	5	1	3	1	McCovey, 1b	3	0	1	0
Stargell, lf	5	0	0	0	Rosario, pr	0	0	0	0
Robertson, 1b	5	4	4	5	Kingman, rf	4	0	1	0
Sanguillen, c	5	1	2	1	Dietz, c	4	0	0	0
Pagan, 3b	1	0	0	0	Gallagher, 3b	4	0	0	0
Hebner, ph–3b	3	0	0	0	Speier, ss	3	1	2	0
Hernandez, ss	4	0	1	1	Cumberland, p	0	0	0	0
Ellis, p	3	0	0	0	Barr, p	1	0	0	0
Miller, p	1	0	0	0	McMahon, p	0	0	0	0
Giusti, p	0	0	0	0	Duffy, ph	1	0	0	0
					Carrithers, p	0	0	0	0
					Bryant, p	0	0	0	0
					Hart, ph	1	0	0	0
					Hamilton, p	0	0	0	0
TOTALS	41	9	15	9	**TOTALS**	34	4	9	4

												R	H	E
Pittsburgh	.....	0	1	0	2	1	0	4	0	1	—	9	15	0
San Francisco	..	1	1	0	0	0	0	0	0	2	—	4	9	0

E—none. DP—Pittsburgh 1, San Francisco 1. LOB—Pittsburgh 7, San Francisco 12. 2B—Mays, Robertson, Speier, Cash, Fuentes. HR—Robertson 3, Clines, Mays. SB—Henderson, Sanguillen. Sac—Cumberland.

PITCHING SUMMARY

Pittsburgh	IP	H	R	ER	BB	SO
Ellis (W)	5	6	2	2	4	1
Miller	3	3	2	2	3	3
Giusti (save)	1	0	0	0	0	0
San Francisco						
Cumberland (L)	3	7	3	3	0	4
Barr	1	3	1	1	0	2
McMahon	2	0	0	0	0	2
Carrithers	0	3	3	3	0	0
Bryant	2	1	1	1	1	2
Hamilton	1	1	1	1	0	3

HB—Gallagher (Ellis), Hebner (Bryant). PB—Sanguillen. Umpires—Crawford, Weyer, Olsen, Stello, Davidson and Gorman. Time—3:25. Attendance—42,562.

GAME 3 — Oct. 5 at Three Rivers Stadium

SAN FRANCISCO	AB	R	H	RBI	PITTSBURGH	AB	R	H	RBI
Henderson, lf	4	1	1	0	Cash, 2b	4	0	0	0
Fuentes, 2b	3	0	0	0	Hebner, 3b	4	1	2	1
Mays, cf	4	0	1	0	Clemente, rf	4	0	1	0
McCovey, 1b	3	0	1	0	Stargell, lf	3	0	0	0
Bonds, rf	3	0	1	0	Oliver, cf	3	0	0	0
Dietz, c	3	0	0	0	Robertson, 1b	3	1	1	1
Gallagher, 3b	3	0	1	0	Sanguillen, c	3	0	0	0
Hart, ph	1	0	0	0	Hernandez, ss	3	0	0	0
Speier, ss	4	0	0	0	Johnson, p	2	0	0	0
Marichal, p	3	0	0	0	Davalillo, ph	1	0	0	0
Kingman, ph	1	0	0	0	Giusti, p	0	0	0	0
TOTALS	32	1	5	0	**TOTALS**	30	2	4	2

											R	H	E
San Francisco	..	0	0	0	0	0	1	0	0	0	—	1	5	2
Pittsburgh	.....	0	1	0	0	0	0	0	1	x	—	2	4	1

E—Bonds, Hebner, Fuentes. DP—none. LOB—San Francisco 8, Pittsburgh 4. HR—Robertson, Hebner. SB—Mays. Sac—Fuentes.

PITCHING SUMMARY

San Francisco	IP	H	R	ER	BB	SO
Marichal (L)	8	4	2	2	0	6
Pittsburgh						
Johnson (W)	8	5	1	0	3	7
Giusti (save)	1	0	0	0	0	0

WP—Marichal 2. Umpires—Weyer, Olsen, Stello, Davidson, Gorman and Crawford. Time—2:26. Attendance—38,322.

GAME 4 — Oct. 6 at Three Rivers Stadium

SAN FRANCISCO	AB	R	H	RBI	PITTSBURGH	AB	R	H	RBI
Henderson, lf	5	2	1	0	Cash, 2b	5	2	3	0
Fuentes, 2b	4	1	2	0	Hebner, 3b	5	2	2	3
Mays, cf	4	0	0	0	Clemente, rf	5	1	2	3
McCovey, 1b	5	1	3	4	Stargell, lf	2	1	0	0
Bonds, rf	4	0	1	0	Oliver, cf	4	1	1	3
Dietz, c	4	0	1	0	Robertson, 1b	4	0	0	0
Hart, 3b	3	0	0	0	Sanguillen, c	3	0	1	0
Gallagher, 3b	1	0	0	0	Hernandez, ss	4	1	1	0
Speier, ss	4	1	1	1	Blass, p	0	0	0	0
Perry, p	3	0	1	0	Mazeroski, ph	1	1	1	0
Johnson, p	0	0	0	0	Kison, p	2	0	0	0
Kingman, ph	1	0	0	0	Giusti, p	1	0	0	0
McMahon, p	0	0	0	0					
TOTALS	38	5	10	5	**TOTALS**	36	9	11	9

											R	H	E
San Francisco	..	1	4	0	0	0	0	0	0	—	5	10	0
Pittsburgh	.....	2	3	0	0	4	0	0	x	—	9	11	2

E—Cash, Hernandez. DP—Pittsburgh 1. LOB—San Francisco 9, Pittsburgh 6. 2B—Hebner. HR—Speier, McCovey, Hebner, Oliver. SB—Cash.

PITCHING SUMMARY

San Francisco	IP	H	R	ER	BB	SO
Perry (L)	5.7	10	7	7	2	6
Johnson	1.3	1	2	2	1	2
McMahon	1	0	0	0	0	1
Pittsburgh						
Blass	2	8	5	4	0	2
Kison (W)	4.7	2	0	0	2	3
Giusti (save)	2.3	0	0	0	1	2

WP—Perry, Kison. PB—Dietz. Umpires—Olsen, Stello, Davidson, Gorman, Crawford and Weyer. Time—3:00. Attendance—35,487.

ABOUT THE AUTHOR

Nick Peters has witnessed most of the San Francisco Giants' home games and many of their road games ever since they moved to the West Coast. As a San Jose State journalism major, he watched the historic first game at Seals Stadium, April 15, 1958, and began professionally chronicling the team for the *Berkeley Daily Gazette* in 1961. He was the California Collegiate Sportswriter of the Year as an undergraduate and was voted Alaska Sportswriter of the Year in 1962 and 1963 while stationed with the U.S. Army at Fort Richardson. He served as sports editor of the *Berkeley Daily Gazette* and the *Richmond Independent* prior to joining *East Bay Today* and the *Oakland Tribune* in 1979. Peters now covers the Giants for the *Sacramento Bee* and for *The Sporting News.* The San Francisco native resides in Reno, Nevada, with his wife Lise. He has authored *100 Years of Blue and Gold,* a history of University of California football, and is the co-author of *Giants Diary,* a 100-year history of the baseball team. Peters is an avid collector of memorabilia and enjoys researching and writing about the history of sport and its many interesting athletes.